# About the Author

After studying drama and becoming a founding member of Greenwich Community Theatre, William Wray taught and ran the community theatre department at Goldsmiths College. He then went on to teach at a newly founded school devoted to developing a new approach to education, which included meditation and philosophy. The success of this education initiative led to the establishment of seven other schools around the world run on similar lines.

He has written a number of plays for the professional theatre and worked as an actor. He is presently a senior member of the School of Economic Science, a long-established school of 'practical philosophy' with a particular interest in Advaita, the philosophy of non-duality. The School has branches and affiliated schools not only in England but also throughout the world. He is in charge of the Foundation Year of Philosophy and has written teaching material used in philosophy groups in these centres.

He started *Symposium*, a regular series of lectures and seminars on philosophical themes and is working on an outreach programme which is designed to take philosophical ideas into a variety of different contexts. *Philosophy Works* is intended to play a part in this programme.

By the same author

*Book of Reflections*
*Book of Decision*
*Book of Spirit*
*Venus*
*New Life*
*The Sayings of the Buddha*
*Through the Eyes of Leonardo*

# PHILOSOPHY WORKS

## ACCESSING THE POWER OF GREAT IDEAS FOR A HAPPIER LIFE

WILLIAM WRAY

WATKINS PUBLISHING
LONDON

This edition published in the UK in 2005 by
Watkins Publishing, Sixth Floor, Castle House,
75–76 Wells Street, London W1T 3QH



Designed and typeset by Paul Saunders

Printed and bound in Great Britain

British Library Cataloguing in Publication data available

Library of Congress Cataloguing in Publication data available

ISBN 1 84293 113 X

www.watkinspublishing.com

*To Patti*

## Wisdom Works

If you are interested in further developing a practical approach to philosophy in your own life and would like to be associated with the initiatives that are being created to promote the ideas found in *Philosophy Works* register at www.wisdomworks@yahoo.co.uk

# Contents

# *Introduction*

THERE MUST ALWAYS BE a good reason for the writing of a book, particularly a book of this nature in which philosophical ideas are seen to have an immediate relevance to our immediate experience of life. The need is an obvious one. Wisdom is always required. In this, our own time is no different.

I had a conversation recently. In a group I was taking we were discussing Platonic ideas. They were not the central point of what was being explored. They were referred to in passing. A member of the group asked if we could go back and consider them further. I said that maybe it was better that we should stick to the topic in hand, but that I would be more than happy to talk to him in the break. When the break came we were joined by the man's friend. Both of them were not only interested but also informed. After a while I asked them where they came from. They glanced at each other before telling me they were from Iraq. Inevitably the conversation turned to Iraq's recent past. They said with some sadness that the richness of Iraq's culture had been all but destroyed over the last sixty-five years, and that what the country needed more than anything else was wisdom. They thought it was crucial for the long-term development of the country that the principles that we had been discussing should be sounded out once more, but they also recognised that this was almost impossible, when all that people were concerned with was how to survive the following day. One of them ended the conversation with these words: 'There is really only one place to begin,' and he put his hand on his heart.

This conversation reminded me of a similar conversation I had two years ago. It was with a young Colombian lawyer who wanted to run courses in practical philosophy under the auspices of an organisation devoted to conflict management. 'My country has been at war ever since it was founded. It is dominated by armed groups who hold the country to ransom. We are desperate for peace but have forgotten what the word means. What your course is doing is teaching the principle of peace.'

Both conversations vividly illustrate the need for practical methods that explore philosophic principles to be developed. The issues we personally are facing may not seem so pressing, but without doubt the need for self-discovery, the need to unlock those fundamental powers we all possess, is a concern of supreme importance wherever we might look, and nothing is more immediately to hand in what we are facing now than our own lives. It's here that wisdom is required. What this book, and the courses associated with it, are doing is to explore the fundamental principles which wisdom has always turned to. Those principles allow us to develop as human beings and set us on the path of self-discovery and fulfilment. They allow us to become more conscious of who we are and how we might fulfil ourselves as human beings.

Consciousness is an essential power that we all possess. Awakening to the world in all its vitality and intelligence as it manifests now, is a conscious act. By acting consciously we both move out to meet the immediate need and return to who we really are.

And with that comes greater understanding.

And freedom from destructive states of mind.

From it arises the creative response.

And through it arises a deeper and more immediate contact with life, and in that is our only source of happiness.

Each of the twelve stages of the book has its own particular theme. They consist of a series of reflections and practices, things to remember and apply in the midst of life. These reflections are designed to draw you into the present and there to discover life's true vitality. They are designed to help you to break out of self-imposed limitations and connect with the unity of life. Many of them contain personal stories which should assist you to reconsider your own experience.

It's for you to discover how to use the book in a way that is most effective for you personally. Everything that is discussed is immediately relevant, but there may be certain areas which are of particular importance to you, and you may wish to return to them in order to reread the reflections and reapply the practices; but however you do decide to use the book, remember this is not theory that is being discussed. This is a practical book and something that is practical requires a constant exploration in the midst of life.

# *Self Remembering*

PHILOSOPHY IS ABOUT the love of wisdom, and if we are to develop a love of wisdom we need to become more reflective in our approach to life. At the heart of this book is a reflective exercise. It's called *Self Remembering*. Time has its own inevitability, forever pressing on, and the immediate moment can so easily be lost because of this pressure. By losing touch with this we lose touch with ourselves and with how best we might meet what life is asking of us. By connecting ourselves with the immediate present we become alive to life. It is to help us with this that *Self Remembering* is offered. Therefore, before we go any further let us consider what reflection is and in particular what is the nature of *Self Remembering*. It is essential to go through this process slowly and calmly, consciously resting at each step in turn.

1 Come to stillness.

2 Let go of the concerns that are at present possessing your mind.

3 Come into the present.

4 Bring your body into view and allow physical tension to dissolve.

5 Simply look. Look at colour, form, light, and the space that penetrates it all.

6 Now listen. Listen to sounds, and the silence out of which these sounds arise.

7 Rest in the awareness of all that is around you.

8 Become conscious of the power of the present in all its harmony and peace.

Now let us look at this once more, considering each step more fully.

**First step** – ***Come to stillness.***

Why stillness? What has that to recommend it? Besides, stillness can never be achieved. As long as we are living, something is in motion.

The body moves in order to sustain and regenerate, as indeed does the mind. But so much of our activity, both physical and mental, is unnecessary and stress-laden. There are those of us who seem to be unable to find stillness in any form. And even the most lethargic may very well be in a state of exhaustion because of unnecessary mental activity. What is certainly true is that, for those whose life is a continual whirl, peace is a blessed gift. Perhaps what is even more important is that the only way we can respond intelligently and creatively to life is by freeing ourselves from surface agitation, in order to touch a quieter and more potent place in ourselves.

**Second step** – ***Let go of the concerns that are at present possessing your mind.***

The source of all this unnecessary agitation is often concern of one kind or another. Many of these concerns are only too obvious, but some others are hardly recognised, manifesting as a background interference of stressful agitation. As the body starts to become still so the physical tensions start to dissolve. These physical tensions are maintained by this constant mental and emotional agitation. The first step in stilling them is achieved by stilling the body. As the agitations arise they have their effect on the body. Conversely, by stilling the body, heart and mind are encouraged to come to stillness.

**Third step** – ***Come into the present.***

The present is all important. The only time life lives is now. It doesn't live in the past and the future never comes. As living creatures our most essential ingredient is life itself, and we must learn to live when life lives. Therefore, constantly come back to the present.

**Fourth step** – ***Bring your body into view, and allow physical tension to dissolve.***

Remain grounded. Bring your attention back to your body, limb by limb: feet on the floor, weight of the body on the chair. Release tension in the stomach muscles. Be aware of the evenness of breath. And in all this, rest ever deeper in stillness. As the agitating thoughts begin to arise, bring the body back into view. Release tension. Grow in stillness.

Then turn your attention completely outward.

**Step five** – ***Simply look. Look at colour, form, light, and the space that penetrates it all.***

Connect your mind with the senses. There is a world out there, and it is so easy to pass through life without ever being truly in touch. NOW is your chance to connect. There is no other time. Be aware of the vast variety contained in the colour and the form of things. Notice their shape and texture. Be aware of light and shade and, above all, the space that surrounds and interpenetrates everything.

**Step six** – ***Now listen. Listen to sounds, and the silence out of which these sounds arise.***

Hearing is the finest of the senses. Traditional wisdom states that the five senses are each related to one of the five elements. Hearing is related to the finest – ether. When full connection with this sense is achieved, silence is discovered at the heart of sound. Try it. The sounds arise out of this silence. They hold for a while and then disappear back into the silence.

What you are doing in the process is to simply move to:

**Step seven** – ***Rest in the awareness of all that is around you.***

Your mind will inevitably be caught by the things that arise before it, but returning to open awareness brings depth to your thoughts and feelings. Space and silence are to be found just as much within as without. Beneath all the agitations of thought and emotion, unaffected by any of it, are space and silence.

With this appreciation there will come the awareness that everywhere there is intelligence to be discovered, in so many different ways – intelligence and beauty – and it's manifesting now.

In fact only in the awareness of this present moment can we act beautifully and intelligently in a way that is entirely appropriate to the present need.

**Stage eight** – ***Become conscious of the power of the present in all its harmony and peace.***

With greater awareness of this power comes the acknowledgement that this power has peace as one of its major attributes. This power by its very nature harmonises a discordant mind and brings peace. It also brings us back to the present where things are really lit. The current situation arises precisely in the present, and if we are to fully meet the situations we are presented with, it's to the present we must continually return.

Retaining the stillness and presence that is to be discovered in this practice, turn outward to meet the current need, spontaneously and creatively.

To prove all this to yourself, practise now. Quietly go through the stages before reading on.

## The Alternative

So what is the alternative? We all know what the alternative is. It's what we normally experience as 'my life'. We know we are alive and are certain of our existence, but are we always the same person when we seem to be changing all the time? We are often under the sway of passing moods, caught by confining ideas, possessed by the situations we meet. No one would be false to themselves willingly, but life has a way of drawing us in and encouraging us in the habit of forgetting. And the more we forget the less energy we seem to have, and the less freedom.

Self-forgetting would of course be far less of a possibility if *Self Remembering* became part of our life. *Self Remembering* allows us to become alive to life. It offers us a way of reconnecting with our essential energy and discovering our own individual purpose.

## STAGE ONE

# Essential Energy

So what is this power we possess, the energy to take on life, the consciousness that powers our perceptions, the force that makes us what we are? It is greater access to consciousness which will allow us to see things more clearly and to act more wisely.

We all have our devotions, those myriad things that occupy our minds. Some of them cause us great happiness, some are the source of despondency. There are those that give us energy, and there are others that take it away. But regardless of whether we are nourished by them or not, when we think about ourselves we are quite certain that we discover our identity in the sum total of these devotions. Regardless of their relative merits, are these concerns the essential thing, or are we, in seeking our identity in them, missing out on something more truly ourselves? Is there something else that we might remember that will enable us to tackle our responsibilities more effectively, tackle our tasks more creatively, live life to the full and finally discover the complete satisfaction we all long for?

One thing's certain. There is something about us that's beyond all the captivating involvements, and that is the energy that gives them power, gives us power.

We are conscious beings, and it's the empowering force of consciousness, the very life of our life, which activates and sustains us through this journey of life. What can be more central than that? By being constantly captivated, is there a danger that in our captivations we overlook the power of consciousness? And, as with everything else we ignore, is there a possibility that consciousness becomes less effective through neglect? Should we develop modes of living which put us in touch with our own essential energy, and then, rather than being on the receiving end of life, make of life a conscious act?

There is a problem, however. Where are we to look for this consciousness in order to gain greater access and control? The answer is that it's impossible to look for consciousness because it's consciousness we are employing in the search.

## Conscious Connection through *Self Remembering*

Although we can't grasp consciousness, we can learn to rest ever more deeply in it and creatively employ the energy that is found in that rest to benefit both ourselves and others. The practice of *Self Remembering* is designed to do just that.

Those times of so-called greater consciousness are times of greater meaning, insight and happiness. It's greater consciousness that reanimates all of life's activities and concerns, that brings to them freshness and vitality. When we think of those times of greater awareness, when dullness of heart and mind is for a time shed and we experience life as a vivid reality, it's then that we speak of being more conscious, and it is then that we believe ourselves to be more truly alive and more truly ourselves.

All of us would in some way love to live more fully, more wisely, to dissolve the barriers that pen us in; and there are ways and means of achieving this, techniques to connect fully with our own essential self. You have already been introduced to one of great importance, and practices found throughout the book will give you further assistance. They are all there for you to employ in the midst of your daily life. Although we may discuss these things, it's practice that really counts, and it is practice that this book is seeking to encourage. Keep practising even in the midst of the usual turmoil, in fact then more than at any other time. These are not theoretical matters under discussion but matters severely practical.

To illustrate all this let me give you the words of somebody who underwent this process to great effect.

> Whilst driving my car in Washington DC, I spotted an art museum, and I thought it would be nice to spend some time there. Since moving to London I had become fond of museums and galleries. On returning home to the States I thought I'd start visiting some over there.
>
> I walked around and admired the many sculptures and paintings. I found for the first time a set of works by Thomas Cole entitled 'The Voyage of Life'. There were four in the set: 'Youth', 'Manhood', 'Old Age' and 'Death'. I found them fascinating, and spent nearly half an hour standing there admiring them.
>
> Eventually I came to an atrium where I decided to just sit down and be still for a moment. It was the colours that I noticed first. The columns were grey beige. Sunlight streamed down them. There were palm trees of various kinds. All had beautiful leaves of many shades of green. I noticed how their colour beautifully complemented the colour of the columns.
>
> I then became aware of the distinct sound you hear in museums, a quiet murmur, then the sound of a fountain, that beautiful sound of falling water.
>
> It was then that I realised that I had unconsciously been practising *Self Remembering* I didn't want to lose the moment, and in my mind I heard, 'Look for the perfection of the present moment.' Without hesitation I obeyed. I became aware of the emotions that I was feeling: contentment, happiness, hope, peace. I didn't question the reason I was feeling these emotions, though I knew on some instinctual level.
>
> Eventually I became very still, not physically still, for I had been that for some time, but inwardly still. I didn't think so much as know and feel.
>
> What became evident, seemingly all at once, was where I was located with respect to every other place I had ever been, how

every moment I had experienced in life led up to this moment, that this moment like each and every moment we all experience is indeed significant.

In that moment I had the most amazing experience. I remember feeling, not thinking, 'I get it. I finally get it.' It was like becoming quietly aware that I was in possession of new knowledge without knowing or even caring about the type, shape or quality of the knowledge. I don't know how long I sat there but then the analytical mind cut in. 'What is this? Is this happiness? Is this bliss? Where is this coming from?' And so on and so on, and, just as quietly as the feeling had come, it left.

I don't feel disappointed by this, for I know that I carry that knowledge with me, something that remains as a constant beneath the shifting experience of life.

## To Find Your Vitality, Give It

In the story you've just read, the man was being given the gift of himself, the gift of his own vitality. When we seem to offer our own vitality, it's not so much a personal gift, although it can appear like an act of supreme generosity. It's more a matter of joining in that great flow of energy that sustains the whole universe. By refusing to enter that flow we are not acting in the spirit of things. When we find that we exist in some dull corner, we can be sure we have turned away from the flow of life and, inevitably therefore, turned off that flow within ourselves. Regardless of how much we blame outer circumstances, there is only one person who can turn on the flow. It may appear that in some way or other the world has turned its back on us, but after quiet examination it will become evident it is we who have turned our back on the world. We may feel utterly justified in doing that, but the result can only be personally damaging. It's our essential energy we must embrace, and the best way to do that is to simply turn back. Meet the need, whatever it might be, with generosity of spirit. Enter the flow of life with enthusiasm, and by so doing let others find their enthusiasm too.

It is undoubtedly true that if we find that we lack vitality we should give it. If we give what we lack in ourselves, suddenly we will find that what appears to be a lack has become a fullness. Does it matter that a certain effort is required, if, by so doing, we become emotionally nourished, and nourish others too? And have you noticed that even physical tiredness is overcome if the need that lies before you is fully met without any self-regard?

The energy is given. In fact the energy is there all the time. It's merely a matter of accessing it.

What we must also remember, however, is that there is another aspect to this – *Self Remembering.*

The man's story is a beautiful example of just that. And here's another beautiful observation. It describes perfectly generosity of spirit being tempered by *Self Remembering*. It was given by a nurse who looks after old people.

> Today, at one stage, all of us were bodily exhausted by the continuing needs of the patients. I just said to them all, staff and patients, 'I need to pause.' I sat down in the middle of all the agitation and commotion, closed my eyes and practised *Self Remembering*. All the fuss died away as everyone stopped to look at this still person. On opening my eyes and arising from the seat, there was ample energy and precise knowledge of what was needed next.

What is evident is that generosity of spirit allows the nurse to give fully of herself, but if in the process physical exhaustion begins, then the inner resource is always available even in the midst of action. Precise knowledge of what is needed allows for the precise expenditure of energy, nothing in excess.

## PRACTICE

In order to find your vitality
you must first offer yourself with enthusiasm.
Turn on the flow,
measuring it to perfection
through the power of *Self Remembering*.

## Work For Inner Contentment

The only problem with enthusiasm is that you can easily get carried away. Enthusiasm provides its own pleasure and we might, in our desire for that pleasure, seek it in its own right rather than recognising real pleasure for what it is, a spin-off from generosity of spirit. When this happens the desire for pleasure can so easily take over and the measure is lost. Inner stability goes and strangely enough so does true contentment. When we lose the measure, our pleasure will inevitably be taken from us. When this happens we might be tempted to seek yet more pleasure in whatever way we can find it.

Alternatively, when we find the energy is depleted and our happiness is gone, we might consider some other strategy than desperately seeking some new form of excitement. We might come to the realisation that the good and the pleasant are two different things, for in truth, although the good may appear to disappear, the good is an eternal constant and never comes to pass. Only pleasure passes away. So when you discover that you've got carried away with it, check to see how far you've gone. Then return to the real you as quickly as you can.

It's only when you make this return to the centre of things that you discover true contentment. You carry your inner resource with you all the time. Return to it whenever you remember, and even if you don't know who the real you is, this is where to begin. It's called *Self Remembering*.

The other time we get carried away is not through pleasure, quite the opposite. We get carried away by negative emotion. It may take the form of the pressure of the day which can easily turn into a constant irritation and eventually burst into outright anger. However it manifests, it creates stress, and it must debilitate. The stronger it is, the more energy it consumes, a background hum of pressure, stress and anxiety can often become a constant in people's lives, and all the time it's there it's imperceptibly draining us of energy. If you are determined on a full and energetic life, don't entertain negative emotion in any way, no matter how justified you feel. The great thing about perceived wrongs is that you can always find a justification for feeling negative about them regardless of how big or small they are. Criticism is like a cancer, self-criticism the worst of all. When you are carried away by any of this, return home.

> I had this anger in me. I don't know where it came from originally. It was as if it had always been there. This was part of life. It was part of me. I couldn't imagine an alternative. There was so much to set it off. It was all around me. It was the sound in which I lived. I never realised until recently that it wasn't necessary, that I could turn it off, or come to recognise it when it returned. What a relief, what a new source of energy. It's like being given a new life.

The trouble with negative emotion is that we make it our own, and once we have taken it on we have a vested interest in maintaining it. After all, it may not be much, but it is ours, or so we believe, and as we all very well know, there's something about our own possessions that can easily turn round and possess us. By claiming them we end up living our life askew, never in line with who we really are and not even having the energy to find out; but, as with everything else, there is a choice, even if you have to keep renewing that choice. The observation above was given by somebody who is doing just that, practising *Self Remembering*.

## PRACTICE

Keep coming back.
Whatever it is you're carried away with,
constantly return.
Find inner stillness and contentment.
Make that the beginning and end of any action.

## Humanity is Bound by a Common Bond

One of the most obvious forms of irritation in life is that caused by other people: him or her or them. They're always out there causing a problem. There's always a difference, and you know what difference can lead to: division, conflict and even outright warfare. How much energy is thrown into this, to what a destructive end. What poverty of all kinds inevitably arises from it, over and above the sorrow and loss, but despite this constant aggression we do share a common bond. We are all part of the fabric of humanity and, after all the division and destruction is over, the remarkable thing is that the common bond constantly reasserts itself. It's called peace. Peace may begin with you and the apparent other finding between you a bond. Where this bond is recognised we as human beings live up to our name. We become humane. Where the bond is broken, where we draw a line and believe that people live beyond the limit that we have created to separate them off, then we become less humane.

And there is that other division, the one within. The difficulties encountered whilst living in a world of division become multiplied when you are divided from yourself, when all those fragmented elements of your personality are separated from their common source. If life is experienced as so many jostling parts, in which your own desires are tearing you apart, the uniting factor must be missing. It's not so much that 'the centre will not hold', more that the centre has been lost and forgotten. It's understandable that the most renowned of all philosophical instructions consists of two simple words: 'Know yourself'.

By recognising the common bond in those you meet, you are in fact making contact with the uniting factor within yourself. Likewise, when any act of *Self Remembering* takes place, the common bond is recognised, both within and automatically with those around you. The common bond is also the common source of energy. By finding that source for yourself, inevitably you must find it for others.

**PRACTICE**

We share a common bond.
Find it in yourself in order to share it with others.
We also have a common source of energy.
Find that so that others might find it too.

## Look to the Light

> I remember the occasion vividly. It was one of those times that have a lasting impact. It seemed like some real information was being given. I was looking after the children for the afternoon. My wife was out shopping. Suddenly for no apparent reason this depression descended. Maybe it had been lurking unnoticed for some time, but suddenly it was there in full force. Even visually everything went dark. I noticed my little child crawling across the front room like a dark shape. My first response was to try to find something to blot this darkness out, turn on the radio, anything. My mind was desperately searching when I heard this voice saying, 'Don't turn away. Stay there and look.' The voice was so clear that I didn't think of doing anything else. I became very still, and every time the depression seemed to be creeping over me, rather than giving it my attention, I turned out and looked. How long this continued I don't know, but suddenly the darkness dissolved. Not so much that it dissolved, more that it turned over and revealed its reverse side. Before, everything seemed to be cast in darkness. Now it seemed to be full of light.

This is a dramatic example of transformation. It does not tell us how long the shadow of depression had been carried in the man's mind, but it does tell us that on this occasion the depression became so evident that it cast a shadow over everything. Even his own child was *cast in darkness.*

But then a method was suggested to him. Notice the technique that he adopted. *I became very still, and every time the depression seemed to be creeping over me, rather than giving it my attention, I turned out and looked.* He didn't try to blot the depression out. He didn't become immersed. He let it go by turning outward.

In that ancient work of wisdom, the Isha Upanishad, are to be found these words: *Not this, not this. Thou art that.* In his own way it was the direction offered by these words that this man was following. Every time the depression threatened to creep over him he refused to give it his attention. He refused to identify himself with it. By turning outward, he simply let it go. He could so easily have given way to its demands. Even trying to blot it out is a way of giving it his attention.

We normally identify with what we experience, and when something as powerful as this takes us over it's difficult to treat it as anything else but ourselves. By giving it our attention, we give it our energy. The more energy we give to something, the more powerful it grows and the stronger is the identification. By turning his attention out in stillness, there arose both inner connection and outer connection, and suddenly the energy that is empowering the shadow of depression establishes itself in its own right, the source of brightness and light. In that moment of realisation it flooded through him and illuminated everything.

Mind you, he was fortunate. He had that bright little creature crawling across the floor. Have you ever seen a child giving off its brightness? If not, have another look. In fact look again, whatever the circumstances, whoever is in front of you, and you will find that everything has its own concentration of light and energy. When you recognise that, you recognise yourself.

## PRACTICE

Find your centre of energy and brightness
in looking out for the essential brightness in everything.
Remember that even the
darkest shadow is cast by light.
Look to the light.

## The Mood of the Times

We all live in time and there is no doubt that times change. There are constructive times and destructive times. We often refer back to good times and bad times as if they are personal, but to what degree are these good and bad times affected by the general state of mind? Times can get so bad that people who are normally capable of living a rational existence suddenly lose their minds and start acting in the most atrocious way. Mob rule is often referred to, and it certainly exists. A whole nation can be infected by it. We don't have to look far. Open the papers almost any day, and you'll find examples of this sort of infection. The cynics might shrug their shoulders and say, 'This is humanity for you,' but the word human suggests something more than savage. Humanity in its ignorance acts atrociously, but humanity in its wisdom does not.

'Ignorance' is an interesting word. It means 'the state of ignoring something', turning our back. The question is on what are we, in moments of ignorance, turning our back. Ignorance of this kind involves us in turning our backs on our real self, that source of energy and light which is entirely constructive, the light of reason, the source of wisdom. This energy is a high-powered fuel and must be used in a way that is true to its origins. This is why it is so important to consider how much you are being affected by the mood of the times. You may not see it in a general way. Just consider your immediate circumstances, how they are affecting you, or indeed how much are you fuelling that mood. Our thoughts and feelings do have their influence.

> We went off to teach in Johannesburg in our gap year. It's supposed to be one of the most violent of cities, and that was certainly the experience of many of the people we spoke to. It has led to a lot of fear. It has also led to the opposite, a sense of purpose, of determination and new possibility. Where we were teaching it was full of it. That's what made it so great to be there. We wanted to do our very best, and there was so much energy available to help us to do just that.

The two young men who made this observation went on to say how they were determined to do something useful. They've become involved in a charity to raise money to plant trees in Soweto, the huge black township outside Johannesburg. They think that planting trees and grass will change the state of the place, give new life to a town which is now almost entirely arid. Whatever influence they have on Soweto, they will certainly have an influence on their friends.

**PRACTICE**

When you feel affected by something in the air,
avoid being blown away by it.
Hold the firmer to your own centre of stability.

## Meeting the Same Old Situation in the Same Old Way

One of the best ways to take the life out of anything is to import into the present things best left in the past: the same old habitual ways of dealing with things, the same set views, the same oft repeated habits of heart and mind. And if it was misconceived in the first place, what hope has it now? Repeated patterns of negative emotion are the most deadening thing of all. And even if the original idea wasn't negative – indeed it was just the right thing at the time – it doesn't mean to say that it is perfect now. For better or worse things have moved on. Check where you are coming from and from what script you're reading, and how many times you have read the words before. To meet the current situation free from preconception is a great gift. It is the best possible way of reformulating the eternal qualities that never grow old, never lose their vitality, of allowing them to perfectly meet the present need.

The thing that makes these old habits of thought so adhesive is the fact that we've written our name on them and, having laid claim, we go on repeating them, and with each repetition the habit gets stronger, making attitudes of heart and mind harder to shift.

In the following extract from 'Mending Wall', Robert Frost

speaks of those habitual attitudes that can so easily confine our thinking.

*I see him there,*
*Bringing a stone grasped firmly by the top*
*In each hand like an old stone savage armed.*
*He moves in darkness as it seems to me,*
*Not of woods only and the shade of trees.*
*He will not go behind his father's saying,*
*And he likes having thought of it so well*
*He says again, 'Good fences make good neighbours'.*[1]

As you might have suspected it's his neighbour that Frost is describing. For this man the long-established ideas are all important – *He will not go behind his father's saying.* With each repetition of an idea it becomes more his own. *He likes having thought of it so well.* It is this identification, claiming ideas as one's own that makes them so hard to shift.

Notice that the poem is all about building walls, dividing ourselves off from each other. *He moves in darkness.* The worst wall we can build is the wall in our own hearts that blocks out the light of our own vitality and prevents it from springing up in all its freshness and spontaneity to meet with wisdom the present need.

**PRACTICE**

If you find that the force of personal identification
is building obstacles in your heart,
take them down,
stone by stone.

## True Wealth Lies Within

There's nobody who doesn't want to improve the quality of their lives. The only question is how. The first inclination is to address our outer circumstances. This may have its validity. Our outer circumstances do have their effect, but our outer circumstances directly reflect the inner, and to ignore the inner by being focussed too desperately on the outer is a grave mistake.

Our state of heart and mind directly influences how we greet events. If our inner world is dull and dreary, lacking light and air, we can live in the most elegant of mansions and still have a life that is listless and devoid of purpose. Beauty is all around us but may lie there unrecognised. It would appear to us that life has left, but the truth is that we fail to recognise the beauty because we in some way have left life.

The source of rest and refreshment is always available. It is the most essential thing that we possess. Access to this is a great gift. The Platonic philosopher, Plotinus, makes this point very simply and very clearly.

> You must close the eyes and waken in yourself that other vision, the birthright of all, but which few turn to use.[2]

Turn to this inner resource as often as you remember. It is the inner wealth we all possess. Once having discovered this, everything changes, and without it everything must run down. You can surround yourself with material possessions but, lacking the means to enjoy them, remain impoverished. You end up desiring even more of the same in the vain hope that it will provide what is being experienced as lacking. This lack we experience is not caused by what nature provides. Her riches surround us everywhere. It is more the frame of heart and mind which prevents these riches from being enjoyed. Regardless of apparent wealth or lack of it, the source of lasting wealth lies within, and, by mistaken thinking, poverty does too.

> I was coming into Victoria Station. It was a dull overcast day. I sat on the train lost in thought. Suddenly something made me look up. I was crossing the river. My view suddenly opened up. The sky was black towards the east, but the low sun was shining brilliantly, turning all the buildings gold. The well-known London landmarks stood out brilliantly against the black sky. It was

> stunningly beautiful. I wanted to hold it, but it couldn't be possessed. It was a fleeting experience of profound beauty, startling and unexpected, a complete expression of this present moment – the only time when such riches can be enjoyed.

They can only be enjoyed now because this is when life lives. It is only in the present that the eternal principles, the source of true riches, can be possessed, if they can be possessed at all.

**PRACTICE**

Don't be entirely ruled by the desire for material possessions.
Possess yourself first of that which is truly your own.
True wealth lies within.
Discover that and you'll find riches everywhere.

## The Consciousness that Grants Us that Experience

How much more conscious are we when vividly alert to the beauty of this world. How much less conscious when lost in thought. In this lost state what are we lost to? No doubt that train going into Victoria Station had among its passengers a fair number of people who were mulling over the concerns of the day, totally unaware of the beauty that surrounded them everywhere. There are times when we wake up and times when we lose consciousness, and this is not just at night. Our levels of awareness vary greatly during the course of the day. We may even be startled into greater awareness by being propelled into the present by the beauty that manifests there. In these more conscious states we become more alert to the need and more creative.

Although it would appear that consciousness varies, the truth of the matter is that consciousness is constantly conscious. What changes is our access to it. What this book is providing is a series of creative keys to unlock that great store of conscious energy we all possess.

What we are also lost to when we are lost in thought – random thought with no thread – is, strangely enough, ourselves and our own innate energy. That is why the deeper we plunge into these imaginings the more exhausted we become. One train of thought leads onto another. Although loosely connected, the only thing they truly hold in common is that they denude us of our energy, because the energy that is required to sustain them is sucked in. This is a dull state, and the more this dullness prevails, the less energy we have to meet the present need intelligently.

There are of course brilliant ideas, which possess, as the word brilliant suggests, freshness and vitality. When they arise, energy seems to flow from them. They are like this because they act as vehicles for consciousness. When these hold the mind, the joy of life is rediscovered. We learn to wonder and see things as if for the first time. This book is full of ideas and insights. Dwell on them and reflect on their implications.

The man telling the story of travelling by train into Victoria continued in this way:

> After getting off the train I had to push my way through the crowd that was thronging the platform, everyone there intent on one thing, going in the opposite direction from the way I was going. The force of their joint desire to get on the train and go home seemed to close everything down. That was until I caught a glimpse of a face in the crowd. It was a child in a buggy, her eyes wide open, taking in everything – so alert, so perceptive, so full of wonder.

How do we come to recognise the wonder and the beauty? Because the wonder and the beauty that is within us rises in response to what is seen. Beauty and wonder are part of ourselves. These things don't stand by themselves. Beauty and wonder cannot be recognised in the exterior world if they aren't within waiting to be summoned. All these things – wonder, beauty, love – form the first emanations of consciousness. In recognising their presence – better still, in celebrating their presence – we are enjoying that consciousness and thereby automatically becoming more conscious.

**PRACTICE**

Be aware of the forms of consciousness everywhere.
Rejoice in their presence, and by so doing,
become more conscious yourself.

## Acknowledge the Consciousness Within

Just as you acknowledge this vital world bathed in consciousness through the presence of its beauty, so acknowledge your own inner vitality and, through it, the consciousness that grants that vitality. This is an observation made by a dancer:

> There's a pain involved in dancing, certainly, also something beyond that pain. Sometimes I become one with the music and, when dancing with partners, with them too. I become aware of observing myself become aware. That awareness grows. It is a stillness at the heart of movement, and it's this acute awareness that allows for all the limitations to drop away. I'm not saying that what arises is perfect, but it's as good as it gets. This is the reason I do it, to taste the supreme pleasure of the thing.

The knowledge of stillness in the midst of movement, provides a sense of the unaffected observer, both objectively looking on and intimately concerned. In moments like this we are lifted into something greater, a presence that informs everything that we do, giving it its own particular magic. And when we are the audience to this magic – watching the beauty of dance for instance – we experience something of the same: growing awareness, stillness in action, the dropping away of limitations and, in the great moments, a sense of unity. It's not as though all the differences disappear, just that they are all contained in an overriding presence, a presence into which we are all warmly welcomed, welcomed for the simple reason that in essence this is who we really are.

Even when we feel somewhat isolated, as we can so easily do in one way or another, this is the time to be especially observant. Give what you lack. Be aware of the signs of consciousness everywhere. See it being reflected back at you, however it manifests.

Why are we so glad at such things? Because, like the dancer, when moments like this arise we unite with the music of life performed in the presence of a consciousness which both performer and audience share. What could be more revitalising than that?

What of when we fail to feel our vitality, but only feel our exhaustion? There's not much consciousness then.

Remember the nurse. When you feel exhausted, withdraw the energy back into itself. Allow your body to come to complete stillness. With attention wide, restore yourself through inner stillness and *Self Remembering*. Don't let your energy flood out, let it feed within instead, by flowing freely through your body without the hindrance that tension brings. Come to stillness and, without making any effort, let your inner energy with its own unobtrusive power unravel the knots.

Come to complete rest, and in that rest unite with the power that is everywhere: sustaining, maintaining. Let that give you strength and courage and power to go on.

> Teaching can be an exhausting business. The demands are constant. The one thing that's certain about teaching is that you can never do enough. It's so easy to be caught up in these demands and end up exhausted, incapable of giving anything. I've found that a solution to this is to take a moment or two to reflect between lessons. *Self Remembering,* no matter how briefly it's done, has proved so effective that I encourage my classes to practise too. Just drawing these vital teenage boys to stillness has its effect: they have another reference. It also brings a sense of measure, a proper starting and finishing point – a full stop before moving on. I asked for their response the other day. Here are one or two things they said: 'It calms me down and allows me to concentrate.' 'It refreshes me and gives me a clear mind ready for the next lesson.' 'When I'm angry and frustrated I do it. It helps.'

This sense of your own stillness is also a sense of your own energy, the source of true vitality freed from the noise that usually occupies the mind. This noise is the sound of scattered energy, unfocussed and unmeasured. Out of the stillness arises another possibility – energy that is bright, intelligent and utterly focussed. When that's put to good use, without all the usual influences that prevent its employment, then an altogether more creative approach becomes possible, creative in that it meets the need beautifully.

**PRACTICE**

Find your own energy;
sense your own stillness.
Acknowledge the consciousness within.

## What are You Doing with this Huge Power You've been Given?

Meeting the need beautifully implies responsibility, an ability to respond. This requires not only the knowledge of what to do but also the willingness to take on the role, whatever it might be, and to fulfil it effectively. This is wise use of the power we possess, and without wise use it must be lost. *Even that which you have will be taken from you.* It's inevitable. We all have our talents, and there isn't one of us who doesn't want to seek fulfilment in some way. The truth is that fulfilment doesn't take place sometime in the future when the situation is ideal or we have in some mysterious way perfected ourselves. Self-fulfilment can only take place now. What is needed for the future is given to us in the present.

The result of vision, insight, wisdom may take many years to reach complete fruition, but looking at it differently, the only way that any of these can be accessed is NOW. This is our only opportunity, no matter how imperfect we believe ourselves to be. This moment NOW provides us with our opportunity and our point of responsibility. This responsibility is very personal. It's no one else's function; it's ours alone to fulfil, and the present is the only possible time for it to happen. This is when our energy is released; this is the only time when effective action can take place.

Act NOW rather than letting the moment pass and smothering all moments thereafter with personal regret. Opportunities multiply when this is no longer the case. The greater the awareness of the need, the greater the energy there is to meet that need. From the greater fullness with which we meet the moment arises greater fulfilment. This must be so, for the simple reason that the power we have been given at conception, which has been seen as something personal, has been given to allow us to flow out beyond personal containment in the service of the wider whole. In this we are being true to our own essential energy.

**PRACTICE**

Self-fulfilment happens now.
Let your essential energy
flow out in service to the wider whole.

STAGE TWO

# Finding Freedom

All of us are confined by our circumstances in life, some dramatically so, and yet we can always avail ourselves of freedom. This freedom is brought about not so much by changing our outer circumstances, as by discovering freedom of mind.

There is the outer world and all the events we meet, and there is the inner world by means of which we connect with the outer.

Much more than our outer circumstances, it is our confining thoughts and feelings which create our experience of life. The reflections in this chapter provide us with a key to unlock those confines which habitually hem us in. They allow us to meet events in an entirely new way: creatively and responsively, with spontaneity and freedom.

## Withdraw Your Belief

There's every reason to attend to our outer circumstances. Fully addressing the issues that constantly arise is of obvious importance. If we don't attend here where do we attend? The current event is our immediate concern. This is the place where we apply our consciousness. If we're not there we're nowhere. Keenness of attention, single focus of thought, allows for the bright light of the mind to fall cleanly on the present need. The present moment is only lit when the bright light of the mind shines unimpeded on that moment.

There is the outer world with all its riches, and there is the inner world which grants us access. We cherish our freedoms and rightly so. Tyranny is not something we readily welcome. Who would want to be forced into a narrow and restricted view of life because of somebody else's will? And yet why are we so willing to defend our outer freedoms whilst at the same time cultivating inner restriction, confining ourselves through patterns of thought and emotion?

It is these patterns that create our experience of life. Everything that occurs to us is filtered through these confines, and they rule our reaction to them.

Because of their continual presence it's so easy to grant these patterns credibility. We come to believe that this is the way life is, and if it's true for us it must be true for everybody else.

All this creates a confined view of the world and, what is worse, a confined view of ourselves. The thing that holds it rigidly in place is personal identification: ME. This is who we believe we really are, and the less perception there is of a wider world, the stronger becomes the identification with the confines we have created for ourselves.

But you don't need to invest your personal power in any of this. Observe the confining walls dropping into place and, before you give yourself the opportunity of spraying your name on them, step free by refusing to grant them credibility.

You are something much greater than any of this.

## PRACTICE

When you find that you've boxed yourself in:
thinking about the same old things,
ruled by familiar desires,
sucked in by the usual states of mind,
simply withdraw your belief.

## Seek the Simple Solution

Because they are fundamentally untrue and unnatural, it does of course require considerable energy to sustain these limitations. Our response to life under their influence is inevitably convoluted, unclear and complex. Our decisions and actions must be affected by this. There is that in us that wants to be straightforward, to discover a more simple way of living. The only problem is that life often appears to be far from simple. This may have a lot to do with events, but it has even more to do with how we meet those events.

> My problems seemed unresolvable. People had tried to help, but nothing seemed to work. Maybe I wasn't committed to what they had to say. I needed to find some kind of release within myself.
>
> I was on holiday, and I went into a cathedral. What I automatically did was to lift my eyes over the heads of the tourists who were filling the place, and instead of crowds I found space. It was so pure and unaffected. It dissolved those inner confusions that seemed to afflict me, and I knew that supportive space was in me too. I needed only to look above the confusions that beset me to find it.

Traditional wisdom speaks of five physical elements: earth, air, fire, water and ether. Ether is considered to be the finest. The space that is often experienced in these great buildings is more than the confinement of space. It is the amplification of space. Space is not just an emptiness between solid objects. Space is everywhere, possessing its own quiet vibrancy. It is energy in potential. This is the space we all move in but never notice because our minds are so full. We get tied into the toils of our private world.

Although the central point of reference, ME, can so easily predominate to the exclusion of everything else, there is also simplicity and space. When we discover that simplicity and space, life takes on a beauty it wouldn't otherwise possess. We should look for it, both in ourselves and in the world around us. And, when the space is lost, look up, see the beauty and seek the simple solution.

This is available to us always but only when we look beyond the individual perspective and connect with the universal principles which, although beyond this individual life, allow it to reach its full stature and particular beauty.

**PRACTICE**

Lift your mind above confining thought.
Look up.
See the beauty
and seek the simple solution.

## Are You Really Awake at Present?

When we clear the clutter of the mind and look out and begin to appreciate how everything finds its place within the wider whole, when we begin to appreciate that there is not only the jostling multitude of sights and sounds but also underlying space, silence and stillness, then we begin to connect with the unifying factor. When that occurs we appreciate a rise in consciousness. We feel much more aware, and the beauty in things can be appreciated.

When life becomes crowded by the constant demands, then the space is lost and with it our appreciation of beauty. But even in the most crowded of conditions it is possible to connect with the stillness and space that exists everywhere.

Discover rest in action by moving away from the tensions of constrained living. Connect instead with that vast space that flows through everything. In particular connect with the space that flows through heart and mind.

Come into the present, the only time that this can be appreciated, and allow physical tension and mental agitation to dissolve.

The present is lit by consciousness. Why life often appears dull and uninspired is because we leave the present and indulge instead in idle dreams of the past and future. Although consciousness empowers our idle meanderings, indulging in them can hardly be called conscious living. Focus and precision are lost in this dream of life, and in addition past and future can often be filled with regret and fear. Life is not like this, but it can often seem so if we exhaust our energy sustaining this dream.

**PRACTICE**

Ask yourself if you are really awake at present.
Ask yourself how keenly you appreciate things.
Ask yourself what you can do to make a step towards
greater awareness, at present,
in this moment now.

## The Quality of the Decisions We Make

We believe we possess free will. We are free to choose what we want. Freedom is much valued in a free society and rightly so. But how can we be free when confined by our own thinking and feeling? How can we be free to make sound judgements when our judgements are subject to all those inner constraints we are subject to? To step free of these constraints we must somehow find the means of going beyond their influence. One way is to simply clear the desks. This is an observation made by an advertising art director:

> We'd been struggling to find the right thing. It was a major account, one of the world's leading airlines. In the two weeks we'd been working on it we'd come up with all sorts of ideas but had dismissed them all. We were racking our brains trying to find some creative spark. In the end I said, 'Stop. Let's start again. Clear the table.' All the ideas we'd been mulling over, all the paper covered in drawings, all the ideas we'd jotted down, we scrapped the lot and that included all those things we thought had promise. It all went in the bin. Then, having cleared the table, I attempted to clear my mind. I sat in stillness. Every time ideas began to formulate, I kept letting them go. I don't know how long I waited, but in that time I became very still.
>
> After half an hour or so it came, the whole thing in one. I sat down with a pad of paper and drew out the storyboard. Afterwards we didn't alter a thing. That's creative freedom.

Clearing away the mental clutter opens up the world. In this example, the impulse arose out of an obvious need. In the usual run of things we are more than content to live with the clutter. It's such a common factor in our lives we don't even notice its presence. When we come to making decisions we try to act out of all this clutter.

The well-informed mind doesn't operate from that, but from something far clearer and stiller, open and receptive. Such receptivity requires not only a full appreciation of the demand but also a still and creative mind in which to allow the problem to rest.

Depth of mind does exist, and height as well as depth. Think of an open sky on a summer night – how still and bright it is, how calm and free. It's our task, even in the midst of action, even when the pressure's on, to discover the calm freedom of an open mind. Regardless of our perceived limitations, all of us have that possibility. We are all conscious beings and are capable of informed choices, but only if we cut the clutter and connect with the clear light of consciousness, the source of perfect freedom.

**PRACTICE**

Regardless of our limitations,
remember that within us all
through the use of *Self Remembering*
is the source of perfect freedom.
Consciously turn to the source
before making decisions.

## *Self Remembering*

What has just been outlined is a creative response. Without access of this nature art directors do not find themselves in much demand. A creative response it was certainly but, as I'm sure you're aware, this is not only a creative response but also a rational one. It is above all a personal one, of the essential person. It's through the process of *Self Remembering* that calmness can be brought to an agitated mind, for it's not the essential person that's in a state of agitation, not at all. The things that fill the mind, the things upon which we lay all personal claim come and go. Lying behind these complex and often contradictory factors is something still and simple. It's been there from the beginning and will be there to the very end. It has looked out of your eyes and listened through your ears. It has studied your thoughts and been a cool onlooker of all your emotional involvements.

There have been many factors that have accounted for your development as an individual. Out of your stock of experience much wisdom may have arisen, but the thing that grants any real understanding of what life is presenting arises out of an acknowledgement of the *Conscious Witness* in the background. This is the central and unchanging factor. It was there at the beginning and will be there at the end. In the final analysis we are not so much characters in the play of life as the audience of that play. It's this that remains constant whilst the play takes place, and constancy is a mark of *Self Remembering*.

Some people claim to be too passionate about life to be detached, and *Self Remembering* suggests some kind of ultimate detachment. The problem with this way of thinking is that in cultivating our passions there is every danger of us becoming subject to the ultimate detachment, detachment from the rational light of consciousness which empowers everything, including our passions.

There is that kind of passion which consists of nothing more than thrashing around in the dark, utterly committed, totally dedicated but without the clarity of mind to bring to our plans any brightness or wisdom and, strangely enough, any purity of emotion either. The more entangled we are in our passions, the more muddied they become, muddied and involved. They are involved because we are involved. Upon them have we laid a personal claim. Under these circumstances, the passions are in reality not the most important thing. Rather it is we, the passionate, who are central. This kind of passion is not part of a free and vital commitment to the play of life. Somebody has intruded, ME.

Your light, however, is there always, the light of consciousness.

This is the constant factor, the unchanging. Into that you must step whenever you remember. Allow it to brighten your mind by acknowledging its presence.

The truth is that the more we detach ourselves from all our personal involvements, the more possibility there is of conscious assessment of what life is really asking of us. The more conscious we become of life's demands, the more energy we have to meet them. With this greater vitality, the greater chance there is of carrying them through to their ultimate fulfilment. There are no half measures in any of this. This is passion without possession.

When you feel the bonds tightening remember the words of the Upanishads: *Not this, not this. Thou art that.* Not all these entanglements, not all this egotistical confusion. The alternative, according to Plato, is wisdom.

> When the soul contemplates in herself and by herself, then she passes into another world, the region of purity and eternity, and immortality and unchangeableness which are her kindred, and with them she ever lives, when she is by herself and is not let or hindered; then she ceases from her erring ways, and being in communion with the unchanging is unchanging. And this state of the soul is called wisdom.[1]

**PRACTICE**

Use the exercise of *Self Remembering*;
use it in the here and now;
use it to step back from the immediate emotional involvement;
use it to see the matter clearly.
Allow your own light to brighten your mind.

## Go Beyond

'Understanding' is an interesting word. Originally it meant 'to stand under'. A cursory look at the word indicates as much. This is certainly different to the meaning of the word 'comprehension' which is the synonym we normally associate with understanding. Comprehension implies a mental embracing, whereas understanding indicates some kind of acceptance of authority and, because we accept the authority of this thing, we are willing to go to the trouble of discovering its true significance. After some initial exploration we may very quickly dismiss the authority of whatever it is we are trying to grasp. Alternatively our understanding may grow, and with it comes a growing trust in the truth the subject offers. For certain, those things that carry the marks of the good and the true are worthy of a full and proper understanding, and with that understanding there must inevitably arise a deeper appreciation of how that subject may enrich our lives and grant us the freedom to live life to the full. This does of course presuppose that we can recognise the good and the true. If we stand under things of limited wisdom, become enthralled by things that have little to offer, then our search for freedom will be limited. If we go even further and live by ideas that are destructive there will be an inevitable result.

Real understanding is of a different nature. At the heart of it is an understanding of ourselves.

> I must first know myself, as the Delphian inscription says; to be curious of that which is not my concern, while I am in ignorance of my own self would be ridiculous.
>
> PLATO *Phaedrus*[2]

> Our general instinct to seek and learn, our longing to possess ourselves of whatsoever is lovely in the vision, will set us inquiring into the nature of the instrument with which we search.
>
> PLOTINUS *Enneads*[3]

To properly understand the significance of such statements, not only must we accept the authority of the wise but, even more importantly, we must put ourselves under that inner authority of which they speak. This as far as our life is concerned is not only the source of life but its final authority. This is the calm still light of consciousness, and to this authority we must constantly refer.

By consciously turning to that light, the self-adopted limitations dissolve: confining ideas, habitual responses, patterns of negative emotion. Likewise when we recognise these constraints and consciously put them to one side, so the habits of heart and mind are weakened and we are far more capable of seeing ourselves with understanding, meeting others with the same understanding, claiming nothing for ourselves, but simply allowing the light of consciousness to work unimpeded.

**PRACTICE**

Allow the calm still light of consciousness
to be the final authority in the way we meet life.
Rather than working from the usual confines,
consciously turn to the still source.
Recognise this as the source of understanding,
both of yourself and others.

## The Only Time for Opportunity

We are so busy preparing for some other time that what the present offers is often left unrecognised, ignored. This is of course an obvious form of ignoring. It is, however, much practised. Logic tells us that the future never comes. You can't reach out into the future and somehow pull it to you. There's only one time for living, and life is never achieved without meeting life where it manifests.

> There's something free about spontaneity, something entirely of the moment. Of course preparation is all important, but no preparation can be done in a mechanical way. Practice of that sort might make the music accurate, but it slowly kills the spirit of the thing. Practice with attention is entirely different. It becomes a meditation. Without being overly concerned with error, the accuracy comes. The whole thing is a matter of atten-

> tion. That's when you hear the music arising out of the composer's mind. You go to that place with him. But as soon as your mind moves a fraction of a second away from that moment another world takes its place. The notes are a means not an end. The source of real satisfaction comes from the space beyond. It's there you taste freedom. The two worlds touch in that moment and unite the whole thing. That can't happen at any other time than the present moment.

This is a real musician speaking. The word 'music' is derived from 'muse'. The muses are the poet's creative force. They seem to speak from the world beyond. They are in fact immediately at hand when we shake off the dream of life and meet the immediate present.

We talk about the opportune time, usually in respect of something we have long planned for, and it's true that if we can connect with the full force of consciousness there are potent moments that will have their effect, sometimes far reaching, but in truth every moment is opportune if we awaken to its particular beauty and possibility.

Seize the moment by centring your attention on all that the moment offers, a fraction of a second away and another world takes its place, an imposed dream of life centred on a private identity. It is about this person that personal concerns for the past and future revolve. It is this individual we spend so much time promoting and protecting. His fears can be all consuming. Apart from our essential energy, what is being consumed? A proper understanding of who we are and a delight in life being lived now. Seize the moment by being there when it happens, and serve it by offering yourself to what the moment is asking of you.

So much stress is caused by trying to force events to some preconceived end. If we find that sitting within us is an obsessive who wants to take complete control and then force things only in the way his desire dictates, beware. In getting his own way, he has a way of making us miss out on what life is actually presenting in the present moment.

> I walk to work every morning through Russell Square. My head is down, my thoughts involved in all the things coming up during the day and things that might have gone better the day before. Now that I've adopted this practice, I've discovered a world out there in which the birds sing and the trees catch the sunlight.

The practice referred to in this observation is the practice of *Self Remembering.*

**PRACTICE**
There is only one time for opportunity.
Find freedom of action in what the present offers.

## Control Over My Small Corner

> Every morning I plan my day, and every day I see those plans unravel no matter how hard I try to force things the way I want them to go. There's always someone who wants something from me. It's a continual source of stress.
>
> Of late I've adopted a new approach. The energy I expend on feeling stressed I'm lending to the work in hand, however it might manifest.

This desire to control, regardless of what the flow of life demands, is a fruitless business, and, as the observation indicates, an exhausting one too. Partiality can only be partial and the partial view can never accommodate the whole. We might think it's the whole because it's the only thing that's important to us. It fits into our scheme of things and, like all schemes, it has at its heart a schemer who is never free enough to accept what the play is offering, not freethinking enough to use and enjoy without trying to force a result, and stamp on it some kind of personal claim.

There is in this way of thinking an inherent rejection of life. What is accepted can only be that part that fits in with our controlling influence. This is not an expansive approach. We can only take what we think is best, as if we, in this confined state of mind, have any idea of what is in reality best. There we remain stressed and strained and forced into a corner, a corner which might not at the end of the day amount to very much but at least it conforms to our will, or so we would believe.

As the observation makes clear, there is an alternative. Accept what is given rather than expending your energy in all the stress which arises trying to repel it.

> I am responsible amongst other things for the school plays. This can be an exhausting business, so much to concern yourself with, so much to contend with. I've discovered that if these plays are to be a success there is one thing of supreme importance – trust. Plan certainly, come with some general ideas, but also trust in the children. Be alive to their offering. They are brimming full of their own natural qualities. The task is to recognise this fact and allow them to make their offering as fully as possible.
>
> My father-in-law had a wonderful way of making pastry. He hardly touched it at all, but he did seem to breath air into it. It was so light. It may have been a little ragged at the edges, but his was pastry of genius. This is how I try to produce the plays: teach the general principles, create an overall structure, give clear direction when required. After that it's a matter of allowing the qualities my cast already possesses to shine through, allowing their vitality, which is the beauty of life itself, to create the magic. When you open up to this freedom all kinds of unexpected possibilities arise. They arise but only at one time – the spontaneous present.

All this speaks of enthusiastically joining in the play of life rather than creating some kind of wooden sub-plot that requires considerable tension to sustain; personal it certainly is, but a poor reflection of the real thing, and after all our efforts to control this corner, life has a wonderful way of breaking in.

**PRACTICE**

Don't be so keen to entertain your partialities.
Be all embracing instead.
Don't be so keen to control your life
according to the dictates of your partialities.
Look for something within yourself that is more expansive.

## What is the Moment Asking

What is the moment asking? This is an interesting question to pose. Without doubt the moment is asking something of us. It may be a gentle enquiry or an outright demand, but regardless of how it manifests we are being asked to interact with life. For that we must be grateful. Without that continual request, there's every danger that we would retire completely into our private world with the same old set of thoughts rotating round our heads. This is never new. It's never free. It is energy-wasting, and the more the same old patterns rotate, the deeper is ground the groove.

Met in the right way however, the demands of life can be life-enhancing, for they come with their own energy. If we are prepared to connect with that energy, all kinds of possibilities open up. Even though these demands may appear unpromising at the time, after committing ourselves to meeting them, the outcome is often a source of genuine pleasure.

Those people who embrace life to the full have a light-heartedness about them. They are looking for opportunity, not trying to escape the demands of life, separated out and self-regarding. Every time you find yourself adopting such attitudes to life, shake off these restrictive patterns of heart and mind, and ask yourself what the moment is asking of you.

> I suspect that in common with a lot of daughters I have a relationship with my mother that's littered with 'habitual responses', 'well-worn triggers' and 'emotional baggage'. Each time I meet her I see these emotional responses arising. In the past I would

> leave feeling guilty about how unsympathetic and irritable I had been, especially as she is frail and elderly, and I am not.
>
> I have of late, however, been better able to observe my reactions and, rather than judge my mother or react in a way that's based on habit and history, I have been able to simply listen and act out of reason in the moment. I'm beginning to find pleasure in her company rather than being filled with dissatisfaction and guilt.

This is a wonderful example of freedom in action. Out of it arises something to replace the negative emotion that characterised the previous relationship of this mother and daughter, and the possibility before death intervenes, of a true relationship being reestablished.

When the understanding of which we have been speaking arises, the differences disappear, and the unity which underlies 'history and habit' has a chance of expressing itself in the potent present.

In the final analysis the present is only asking one thing. It is asking you to join it fully in the very moment when you and the moment exist, and it's in that moment that unity is experienced, and it's out of unity that happiness and true satisfaction arise.

**PRACTICE**

Rather than getting stuck with the same old set of thoughts
that go round and round your mind,
connect with what the moment is asking of you.
Take pleasure in responding to that.

## Build on Your Insights

For observation to take place two things must be present: the observer and the object of observation. This goes without saying. The problem is that we are so often totally identified with what we see and hear and think about, that we lose complete touch with the *Observer* in the background. The *Observer* is the silent witness that looks on unaffected at all the events of life. Remembering the *Observer* is not so much a matter of remembering a concept, more a matter of bringing yourself back to yourself. Everything that is to be found in this book is dedicated to this end, for it is only in coming to yourself that true freedom becomes a possibility. Any move towards the conscious core of our being has that effect. It opens up everything because, in the process, we are disengaging from all those things we too readily identify with, to rest in that which observes, that which has the power to bring to all the diversity of experience a sense of harmony and unity, that which has the power to go beyond our confined modes of thinking and feeling.

What such an approach must by necessity offer is the capacity to see things afresh, to discover new and appropriate ways of meeting the need. When real observation takes place there is genuine insight, an insight which not only involves a deeper understanding of the subject under consideration but also of ourselves. It provides a means of stepping free of the 'optical delusion of consciousness', as Einstein describes it, in order to gain a sense of what Max Plank, a scientist of equal genius, calls 'the ultimate mystery of being'. He states that in all his research this understanding is of ultimate importance, his great discoveries about the nature of quantum physics being of secondary value.

These two men were genuine freethinkers who challenged the limitations of accepted thought and were capable of coming to an entirely new way of understanding. From their writing it is obvious that they did this because they were capable of stepping free of the self-centred consciousness we normally experience into a wider and unconstrained world out of which arose brilliant new concepts. We know that these men thought like this because they left a record of their thinking.

Records of how great people thought are, quite obviously, of considerable importance. These are just two examples, but when you think of all the great works, what are they but a record of human insight. These works are of great importance to us and they were, of course, of great importance to those who formulated them. It allowed them to bring into sharp focus all those things they needed to know and to remember.

It may not be our role to discover the sorts of things that these people discovered, but there are things we do need to know and to remember. It's so easy to forget, so easy to believe in the thoughts and feelings that are ruling us at present, regardless of their wisdom. It's so easy to revert back to habitual modes rather than treading the path of evolution indicated by our insights. We may even forget that we ever had these insights in the first place. By formulating our understanding it becomes something coherent, not a vague impression. This is particularly useful when all the usual confines are about to lock into place.

A word of warning however: the formulation of insight is one thing, the deep understanding out of which that insight arose is quite another. Value formulation certainly, but only as a means of returning to the place of insight. Being content with 'my understanding' turns understanding into claim. As such, what is intended to be of benefit becomes an impediment to knowledge. To find freedom return to the essential thing that lies at the heart of all human experience, our inner core of consciousness.

## PRACTICE

Observation – Formulation – Application
Build on your insights
rather than allowing them to be forgotten
amidst the usual habits of mind.

## STAGE THREE

# Truly In Touch

Everybody wants to be in touch or to keep in touch. When we are out of touch we can never quite get it together, and when we lose touch we lose something of profound importance, our friends and those we love. We may even feel at times that we have lost touch with life itself, and in doing that the alienation begins and nothing has much meaning any more.

Yet, despite all this, lying at the heart of our perception of life is the consciousness that allows for connection of every kind. Without consciousness nothing could be seen or understood. To be truly in touch we must first come to an ever deeper recognition of our all empowering energy, that very thing that gives vitality to life. When we acknowledge that, the divisions disappear.

With awareness of the abiding presence of our inner power, we become more in tune with all that is around us. What arises is the harmonisation of the inner and the outer and the recognition that our fragmented lives,which can easily be experienced as so much separation, division and conflict, may be made whole and complete.

Through the use of the reflections in this chapter and the practice of *Self Remembering* keep continually in touch with your own centre of strength and calm, the integrating power we all possess.

## Making Connection

There are some people who have the power of touch. They are naturally in touch with the demands of the situation. They have a subtle touch and, because their senses are so finely tuned, it seems they have a kind of magic, particularly to those who don't have the touch. Here's a story of one such person. It was told to me by the man himself. He's one who certainly has the power of being in touch. He has the responsibility for the maintenance of the harbour cranes in Port of Spain in Trinidad.

> A crane was delivered to the port authorities. It was a German crane – state of the art. The whole thing was controlled by a central computer which controlled a complex block of hydraulic valves. It was really sophisticated. But it wasn't long after the crane had been installed that it had broken down. I knew very little about this crane, but I do know something about machinery. I go round regularly listening to how the crane engines are running. You can really get in touch with an engine if you give it your full attention. You can discover so much without having to strip it down. I thought I knew what was wrong with this hydraulic block. I put my hand on top and knew for certain. I tried to explain, but nobody would listen. They thought that I couldn't possibly understand such a sophisticated piece of machinery. They knew exactly what to do: get on the phone to the Germans.
>
> The Germans made a number of suggestions, but no matter what adjustments were carried out the same thing happened every time. In the end they sent out their top engineer.
>
> He came with his book of 'schematics', and he worked through the possibilities one by one, all to no effect. After three days I again offered my assistance. The others met me with the usual response, but the German engineer was prepared to listen. I asked him to put his hand on top of the block, and then I asked somebody to start the engine. I asked him if he could feel anything. He said not. I told him to trust me and to give his complete attention to what he felt through his hands. The motor was

> turned on and off a few further times, until at last he agreed that he had felt an almost imperceptible knock. I explained that I thought that a ball bearing was being forced out of its valve seating when the hydraulic pressure increased. This was undetectable because the motor was turned off when an inspection was carried out. By that time the bearing had fallen back into its seating, and everything seemed fine.
>
> The German engineer looked at me in amazement. 'How did you know that?'
>
> 'I've been told that when you're really in the present, and really in touch, the knowledge is given. In addition I love machines.'
>
> He laughed, but I don't know if the manufacturers laughed when they had to recall all the hydraulic valve systems from all the cranes of this design.

This is a wonderful story, and the principle it illustrates is true for all of us. We may not be natural engineers, but all of us have our talents, and we all have our loves, and as we'll discover in the coming chapters there is only one time for love and one time for inspired knowledge, and both require complete connection.

When you love something such connection is a relatively easy matter, but not so easy when you feel closed down, alone and separated off from even those things which in better times you find it easy to embrace. When this is your experience, consciously reach out. Give what you lack in yourself, and in giving what you think you lack you'll realise that in truth there is no lack at all.

**PRACTICE**

Make total connection with what's before you
regardless of how you feel about them or it.

## Discover the Beauty in What You Do

With care and attention there naturally arises beauty. By practising care and attention in very simple things you are training your mind to take care of the larger things, things like living life beautifully. A beautiful life is one full of care and attention.

There's so much to dismiss in life. We all have our partialities. The trouble with partialities is that they are partial. They are not the whole, and the more we are partial to, the more we dismiss, and the more we dismiss the more separated we become from the beauty of it all. Pursue those things which interest and aptitude draw you to, but only as a means of exploring ever wider horizons, horizons which appear to live outside your immediate interest. Learn to live in an ever expanding world, not one that slowly closes down.

Start this process by getting totally in touch with the thing in front of you. It's there your attention should rest. Don't be distracted. Don't dismiss. By resting your attention connection is made. That contact is a switch that releases energy. Regardless of how seemingly humdrum the activity, when contact is made energy flows, transforming a seemingly insignificant action into something which possesses its own particular beauty.

> I work as a part-time waiter. Serving eighteen tables, all with their separate demands, can sometimes be very stressful. One night last week I was feeling particularly like the ultimate harassed waiter.
>
> Later, when we'd closed up, I was left mopping the floor. Regardless of how I felt, I remembered to drop everything and simply give my complete attention to the task. There was a transformation. One moment I was just mopping the floor, and the next moment I was *just* mopping the floor. There were no other concerns. My whole attention came to rest in that simple action.

In this instance it's the mop that creates the contact which releases the energy. Can you imagine what it's like mopping floors after spending an exhausting evening serving at tables. Surely the tendency would be simply to get the thing over and done with. This frame of mind would certainly shut you off from this manifest moment. It would certainly confirm your tired state, certainly when *just mopping the floor*, a task of no particular importance or interest, but by resting the attention where the mop meets the floor, connection is made and the energy flows. By giving your consciousness you are automatically given consciousness. It's this that creates transformation. Every action possesses its own fulfilment. In this case there was ***just*** *mopping the floor*. Nothing else was needed. In that was experienced a sense of satisfaction and completion.

There is a Chinese poem written by one of the ancient sages, P'ang Yun. These are the words of a man of wisdom who lived in utter simplicity and great contentment.

*My daily affairs are quite ordinary;*
*but I'm in total harmony with them.*
*I don't hold onto anything, don't reject anything*
*nowhere an obstacle or conflict.*
*Who cares about wealth or honour?*
*Even the poorest things shine.*
*My miraculous power and spiritual activity:*
*drawing water and carrying wood.*[1]

*Even the poorest things shine* because of the consciousness invested in them. He is describing the energy switches that can be discovered in everything.

**PRACTICE**
Regardless of how important or inconsequential you think it is, find the beauty in all you do.

## Coming Together as One

'Communion' and 'communication' are, evidently enough, words that are closely related. When proper communication takes place people can't help but come together. When the bond is strong there is an intuitive awareness and support. It can also release an energy that finds its expression in so many beneficial ways.

A journalist once attended a class I was taking where these kinds of ideas were being discussed. Naturally enough he was determined to stand back and retain a professional objectivity, but as the conversation developed he couldn't help himself. He was desperate to make a contribution. It took a considerable force of will to disentangle himself and return to a state of cool observation. Afterwards he asked some pointed questions about what had happened. 'What's your secret?' he demanded to know.

'What secret?'

'There are people here from all walks of life, of all races and ages. How is it that after such a short space of time they are capable of communicating so profoundly?'

'Willingness.'

Not much of a secret. The truth is that all of us have important things to explore. We would hardly be human if that were not the case. After the outer defences have been breached, a common ground is often discovered. When we discover this common ground real meeting can take place. Meetings of this nature are of great significance to us, for in meeting others we meet ourselves, and through meetings of this nature not only is it possible to nourish others, it's possible to nourish ourselves. In fact it's impossible to nourish others without nourishing ourselves. This is the joy of real teaching, regardless of the circumstances, especially when what is being taught is of fundamental importance.

Whilst writing this I have just finished a ten-week course. During the last session people spoke with enthusiasm of what they had gained from the course. One thing they constantly returned to was the sense of unity they experienced, unity arising out of the sharing of experience, of being able to speak freely of matters they considered of real importance in their lives, of central importance. In speaking to people, it became evident that what they had received was of vital importance.

With so many people present, so many different lives, so many different experiences of life, one couldn't but enquire into the nature of this unity of which people were speaking. At the heart of it all, at the heart of all our experiences, below the obvious promptings of me and mine, there is a place where personal experience may be placed within a larger context, and it was of this, each in their own way, that people were talking.

The interesting paradox in situations like this is that the more we are able to give up the personal, the more we are able to experience what is personally dear to all of us, the experience of real knowledge, love and lasting happiness. Inner communion of this kind encourages connection of all kinds.

**PRACTICE**

Create connection.
Open up channels of communication,
both outwardly and inwardly.
Return to your central self
to create connection of every kind.

## The Common Ground

I'd like to return to my Trinidadian friend for a moment. There is a little more to relate to complete the story. After telling me of the circumstances behind his meeting with the German engineer – the man with the 'schematics' – I asked him if he ever got in touch. 'Oh yes. He phones once a month.' When I asked what they talk about, he replied with some amazement, 'Motors of course!'

Two men from opposite ends of the world, possessing an opposite approach, are able to share things because of a common regard for mechanics. A shared love of things mechanical is possible because of something far from mechanical. It's called the common ground. The common ground may manifest in a multitude of different ways. We normally think of it as a shared interest, but there's something more important than the things to be discovered in this ground, and that is the nature of the ground itself. When you have a love for something you naturally want to share your love with others. Everything has its own inherent truth, and it is natural for the enthusiast to want to share that truth with others. In sharing this he conveys his passion. This kind of enthusiasm is emotionally sustaining for all concerned. Think back to your school days. Think of those teachers you found of most benefit. Did they love their subject or not?

By entering the common ground all kinds of possibilities are opened up. Let me give you another example of just this. This time a little closer to home. I had just sat down to continue writing this book, when it occurred to me that I couldn't go on. I was in the process of recommending something that I wasn't practising myself. I had been meaning to phone a friend for about a month, but with life, appearing to be so full, the opportunity hadn't arisen. Now I wanted to press on with the book, and I was about to put it off again. I stopped typing and went to the phone.

Let me tell you a little about my friend. After pursuing a successful career as a pop musician, he decided at the height of his success to leave the group he was the leader of, not to pursue a solo career, but to abandon the whole thing. Being a man of considerable ability, he found plenty to occupy himself with. His great loves are music of course but apart from this he loves mathematics and Platonic philosophy. In all this there is plenty to occupy his mind, and to these areas he has brought considerable insight. He has chosen his pursuits with care and there is no doubt that they have been most rewarding.

At the beginning of the year, however, he decided to abandon his usual way of thinking and to accept whatever was offered, to simply say yes. No sooner had he made this decision, than he received a phone call from the owner of a record company that had just bought his entire back catalogue of music. It transpired that he wanted to re-release it all, everything that had ever been recorded. More than that, he was very keen for my friend to record new music. In their conversation it became apparent that this man knew more about my friend's music than he did himself. He was a real fan. There was a point in the conversation when my friend admitted that he had lost whole sections of the music.

'Never mind, we'll look it up on the web site.'

'What web site?' was my friend's reply.

'Don't you know that you've got a dedicated web site?'

It transpired that there was a worldwide network of fans sharing their enthusiasm for his music. All this was going on whilst he was living an unobtrusive life pursuing his studies.

In our phone conversation he told me that he'd agreed for the recordings to be released and what was more – and this is the real point of the story – he had asked the company to send copies of the re-released recordings to the rest of the members of the band. They, as you could well imagine, were deeply distressed when he had originally called a halt and walked away all those years before.

By him sending out these recordings, the band inevitably got together and in those meetings things were discussed and issues put to rest. As a result of this rediscovery of a talent turned away from and a friendship re-established, they agreed to get together once more. The common ground had slipped back into place. In fact this story is full of common ground. The common ground of the band, the common ground of his enthusiastic fans and the common ground of our friendship. If I hadn't allowed a sense of the common ground to encourage me to phone, he wouldn't have told me the story, a story which so perfectly illustrated the reflection I was considering. In addition I told him about the ideas I had about the development of my book, *Philosophy Works* and associated projects. He enthusiastically agreed to make his own creative contribution. There is no end to the common ground, but efforts have to be made to speak about it, to make contact. This book is one such effort.

## PRACTICE

Keep in touch with your friends.
Let your own passions rekindle their enthusiasm.
Constantly return to the common ground,
The place where friendship is shared.

## Lasting Satisfaction

Reaching out in this way can only take place if at the same time there has been a reaching within. We all have our desires. In the story you have just read it was desire that made my friend turn his back on a whole way of life, maybe rightly so. And more recently it was desire to open himself to whatever life offered that allowed him to discover that a whole new generation had found pleasure in his music. These desires may or may not be important. What is undoubtedly of importance is the desire to look within and discover there your own centre of stillness and certainty.

When we discover and start working from the common ground, we discover that there is more than common interest that links us. What we might also discover is that the fundamental element in a true and lasting relationship is that in it we enter the common ground together.

To communicate knowledge of that place has always been at the heart of important cultural developments. Kandinsky, one of the founders of abstract art, talks about the 'inner need'. The more profoundly in touch the artist is with the common ground, the more strongly is felt an imperative to express what is known. This is the true creative urge. It's like a coiled spring generating its energy, an energy that can create so many beautiful expressions. I don't know how it will come to express itself through my friend. Maybe by turning back to something he had turned his back on, he can bring to it something of the insight and understanding the years of study and reflection have granted him. One thing's certain: he will bring understanding and creative energy to the *Philosophy Works* project.

Recently, in one of the groups, we had been discussing the nature of desire, particularly in respect of how desire draws you away from the present where things actually happen. A response came from a woman in the group. 'What if you've got a really burning desire?' When I asked her what her burning desire was, she went on to explain how she was a counsellor in one of the big London hospitals, but that in addition she had a number of people who came to her privately for counselling. 'And that's a great problem.'

'How is this a great problem?'

'I see them in my kitchen.'

'Well?'

'There's 250 of them, and I can't fit them in. I've got this burning desire to set up some kind of organisation to help these people.'

She got in touch last month. With financial assistance from her local council she had started running courses in 'Positive Awareness'. Now she has just obtained a government grant in order to widen her activities, in particular to support her in providing motivation to the long-term unemployed. She had become subject to the creative spring and, in pressing down on it, creative energy had been released, energy that had found its form in courses dedicated to the release of energy in others.

The passionate desire she was talking of is an expression of the 'creative imperative'. Resist this at your peril. This kind of desire has nothing to do with the promptings of sensory appetite, but everything to do with the promptings of the human spirit. To these directives we must respond, or the energy we have will never find its proper expression.

A response of this kind has nothing to do with all the plans about which we might talk and dream. It does have everything to do with being completely in touch, using all the given energy to fully meet the needs that will continually present themselves. To have any hope of doing this you have to constantly return to the source of the original inspiration and then, regardless of success or failure, find not only a source of creative renewal but also a steadiness of heart and mind, the source of true endeavour and enduring satisfaction.

## PRACTICE

Rather than being ruled by desire,
enter ever more deeply

into that which grants true satisfaction,
your own centre of stillness and certainty.
Keep in touch with that at all cost.

## Life is Shaped by Our Minds

Just think about the state of your mind and how that state affects everything. Life is full of possibility. Possibility surrounds us everywhere. How much we are aware of this fact is entirely dependent on our state of mind.

When we are awake to possibility, opportunities present themselves freely. We are then faced with a choice: do we respond or not, and if we do respond what will that response entail. 'Will I have to go beyond these narrow boundaries within which I operate?'

If your thinking is dominated by negative thoughts, it's inevitable that negative situations will be attracted by those thoughts. In turn it's inevitable that those situations will encourage the growth of yet more negativity until it becomes impossible to experience things differently. It all becomes part of a self-inflicted downward spiral called 'my life'.

> I go up to work in the train in the rush hour. Because of the packed carriages it's very easy to connect with a general sense of irritation, but all that's required is a little connection with someone, a little smile and the attachments associated with the situation drop away and you're content.

This is a common experience, so common that the significance of it can be easily overlooked. So much of what can influence our whole life is contained here. It's so easy to blame outer events for all the irritations and minor discouragements. It's so easy to pass them on. We become an agent of irritation, and because we believe that: 'I'm experiencing this, and therefore it must be part of me,' we become identified with it, and as soon as that has happened, we have a personal interest in maintaining that set of thoughts and emotions. After all this is what we are supposed to do with all our personal possessions.

This is how we shape our lives, all those situations we meet and events we create. If you have any doubt about this read the papers in the morning. They are full of people doing just this, usually to disastrous effect. What is recorded there may be extreme cases, but all of us are easily subject to something of the same nature. But notice what was said in the observation: *...all that's needed is a little connection.* Such a simple thing, so easy to achieve. When this occurs we no longer feel pressed in, deprived of our personal space. Instead we turn outward, step out and recognise common humanity, people in the same boat, or in this case the same crowded commuter carriage.

To be able to smile at adversity has always been considered a philosophic virtue; *Attachments drop away, and you are content.* This is another important principle being referred to, for these attachments are the little hooks of self-identity that allow things to cling to us, regardless of their worth, so closely that they completely shape our lives, or more often misshape them. By being dropped, contentment is discovered: *You are content.* Let go attachment and identification. Create connection of another kind – the common bond, the common ground, both outer and inner, and happiness is bound to be discovered.

**PRACTICE**

Every time you see the present
being shaped by the past,
abandon the past,
and embrace the present.

## The Underlying Factor

The senses turn outward, and naturally enough we follow them, which encourages us to find lasting satisfaction in the outer life. What is undoubtedly true about the outer life is that it is subject to constant change. To seek lasting satisfaction in the midst of all this change is impossible, especially if that which is seeking satisfaction is also subject to constant change. The meeting of two inconstants doesn't make the foundation for a steady relationship.

Another element has to be brought into play: the underlying factor that balances our nature. The ancients believed in what they called 'the mirror of the mind'. In this mirror are reflected all the events that occur in life, all the sensory impressions that rise before the mind and, in addition, all our thoughts and feelings. All this is there to be seen and experienced because also reflecting in this mirror is the light of consciousness. Take that light away and nothing is experienced. What do you see when you look into a mirror in a darkened room? Nothing. Things become visible only when you turn on the light. This is fine, but when we look in the mirror it's not the light we are interested in, it's what is reflected. The ancients believed that so fascinated do we become with all the forms, fascinated and utterly identified, that we neglect the light that allows all this to be seen and understood.

To turn away for a time from the welter of thought and feeling, to enter ever more deeply into that clear light, allows for a steady appreciation of the constant flow of events. It also allows us access to the divine qualities which are the mark of the truly humane. Only by being humane may a person's humanity be properly realised, and only by that can a sense of the unity that creates harmony in life be discovered.

> We were in the desert near Ayers Rock. The desert is vast. In the face of it you feel insignificant. I began to feel more and more alone until that sense gave way to a feeling of unity and vastness. It wasn't as if I was being driven into a state of insignificance and isolation, but rather this vastness was speaking of myself.

Plotinus, the greatest of the Neoplatonic philosophers, made the claim that in his life he was making the journey from the alone to the Alone. What is described in the observation above is the same journey. It is the journey which is made from a sense of smallness and isolation to one of vastness and unity. 'Alone' and 'all one' are closely related terms. This all-oneness is an empowering experience, for all-oneness is the true source of creativity and freedom.

Here is another desert story. It contains the same elements: desert, aloneness, communion, freedom.

> I was on holiday in Jordan. I went into the desert to stay the night with a Bedouin family. I was travelling on my own. I had no idea what to expect. I was dropped off at about 8 p.m. The desert felt vast and so quiet. I was welcomed by this man who spoke good English and was most well informed. I don't know if it was because of the desert or the welcome I received – both I suspect – but I felt full of the most amazing energy. The mood was wonderful, and the evening was spent talking about the man's family and about life in general. I felt free and open to communicate. I had no preconceptions. It was utterly liberating.

**PRACTICE**

Make the journey from the alone to the all one
by finding the underlying factor which unites and connects.
Seek that connection everywhere.

## Inner Seclusion

These desert observations present us with one of those paradoxes of which life is full: isolation as a source of unity, lifelessness as a source of nourishment. The desert for the people involved became a gateway to the inner world, but the kind of connection being described here occurs only in exceptional circumstances. For the most part we are not desert dwellers, but we do have the desire to escape the turmoil of life and discover the peace to be found in such places, especially if we live our lives in crowded cities. Why else do many of us head for the mountains, or the peace of the countryside, or the vastness of the ocean?

This has always been so. Take for instance this Chinese poem written about thirteen hundred years ago:

*From the vault of the light*
*at the going down of the sun,*
*The voices of the birds*
*mingle with the voice of the torrent.*
*The path beside the stream*
*Winds into the distance;*
*Joy of solitude,*
*Will you ever come to an end?*[2]

Such peace and happiness are not discovered in isolation. This is a song of unity. A friend recently put on a beautiful exhibition in his gallery. He took four of his artists to Ireland in order to paint the Lake Isle of Innisfree. The paintings were exhibited with Yeats's poem of the same title, printed so large that it went from ceiling to floor. The exhibition was an undoubted success, partly because of the quality of the paintings, partly because the poem created the right setting to appreciate the paintings.

*I will arise and go now, and go to Innisfree,*
*And a small cabin build there, of clay and wattles made:*
*Nine bean rows will I have there, a hive for the honey bee,*
*And live alone in the bee-loud glade.*

*And I shall have some peace there, for peace comes dropping*
*slow,*
*Dropping from the veils of the morning to where the cricket*
*sings;*
*There the midnight's all a-glimmer, and noon a purple glow,*
*And evening full of the linnet's wings.*

*I will arise and go now, for always night and day*
*I hear lake water lapping with low sounds by the shore;*
*While I stand on the roadway, or on the pavements grey,*
*I hear it in the deep heart's core.*[3]

The poem is so evocative, speaking of something that we all recognise and appreciate. The desire to escape is something that we all have, but escapist philosophies have little merit, and yet they speak of a need that must be met, and in meeting that need we not only nourish ourselves, we also find the vitality to meet the multitude of immediate demands we all of us face. This is how Marcus Aurelius dealt with such promptings:

> Men seek seclusion in the wilderness, by the seashore, or in the mountains – a dream you have cherished only too fondly yourself.

As ruler of the Roman Empire he lived a life where an almost constant response was required of him. As a practising Stoic his philosophy indicated exactly how he should meet these demands. In addition, by recording his reflections, he passed on a book that has provided a source of practical wisdom for centuries.

He continues with his meditation by dismissing any thought of the kind of escapism that requires you to bury yourself in some rural retreat: *such fancies are wholly unworthy of a philosopher.* He does, however, speak of the inner retreat that we all carry with us always, regular visits to which nourish and revitalise:

> Nowhere can a man find a quieter or more untroubled retreat than in his own soul. He who possesses resources within himself, which he need only contemplate, will secure immediate ease of mind. Avail yourself often then, of this retirement, and so continually renew yourself.[4]

## PRACTICE

Seek inner seclusion,
The source of rest and renewal.
You carry it with you everywhere.

## Conscious Connection

We speak of such things as 'shallow thinking' and 'deep experience'. There are undoubtedly different levels of mind, and when we talk about 'thinking deeply' we are certainly not worrying away on the surface in an agitated fashion. We are, instead, reflecting upon things seriously and with a still mind. When we feel things deeply it may mean that we are subject to strong emotions, sometimes of a negative kind. It may alternatively mean that a person who experiences things in this way touches something profound about life.

When Cézanne's son asked his father why he painted the same scene over and over again, Cézanne replied that it was in order to enter ever more deeply into it, into the realm of 'light and love' as he once called it. At another time he claimed that the paintings, which in the course of time became so valued, were merely the residue. What was important was what he knew at the time of painting. When reading Yeats's poem one might consider whether the memory of the Lake Isle of Innisfree is a key to the 'deep heart's core' or a nostalgic indulgence which merely generates a melancholic desire for something once experienced but now no longer attainable. To dwell on imaginative recreation has its dangers, all the more so if what is dwelt on is of itself a powerful insight into the true nature of things.

One of Wordsworth's most famous poems, 'Intimations of Immortality', starts in exactly this way.

*There was a time when meadow, grove, and stream,*
*The earth and every common sight,*
*To me did seem*
*Apparelled in celestial light,*
*The glory and the freshness of a dream.*
*It is not now as it hath been of yore; –*
*Turn wheresoe'er I may,*
*By night or day,*
*The things which I have seen I now can see no more.*[5]

Regardless of these lines' significance and poetic beauty, there is the danger that by following the poet into a nostalgic view of the past we are infected by his regret. To live consciously, the task is to be truly in touch with the here and now, regardless of our present state and the present situation. It's only here that we are effective. This is where we meet the particular need which is ours alone to meet. It is here that we can find fulfilment and discover the energy which is required to meet that need. When we live a kind of dream life unrelated to the present, what energy we do have is taken from us, and the more denuded of energy we become, the greater is the temptation to dream. Our task, like Cézanne's, is to enter ever more deeply into things. Regardless of the seeming difficulties and evident obstacles, it is for us to turn from what was once known in order to return to what is known. Now is the point of knowledge, the working surface where self-development takes place. It is also the place where the divine qualities described in the poems are discovered. Looking back with regret won't allow that.

**PRACTICE**

Enter the present.
Constantly return,
and there make deliberate and conscious connection.

## Underlying Perfection

The reason most frequently given for living a disconnected life is that the present is far from perfect.

> Who would want to experience the dreary reality that constitutes my life? Far better to use my imagination to discover something more encouraging.

Of course there is much to be said for discovering an encouraging life and abandoning a discouraging one. This book is designed to do just this. The question is where and when are we to discover this new life, and what's to be discovered at that time and place. If we can never relive the past except as an exercise in nostalgia, which can so easily turn into nagging discontent, we must train ourselves to constantly return to the only time in which reality is to be discovered, the present.

Regardless of what the present is apparently offering, the present is our time of opportunity, and how we meet the present creates our life. What is more, the depth at which we meet this point of interaction governs the qualities which manifest in the here and now, regardless of how encouraging or discouraging our circumstances might appear.

The outer nature of things may seem to be far from perfect, but the ideal is not to be discovered at any time other than the present. The perfection which would grant our lives true happiness can only be discovered now, and then only when the now is penetrated, when we have gone beyond the surface impression.

'Theory' is derived from the Greek word *theoria*. It means 'seeing in depth'. The task is to go beyond the limits we have trained our minds to work within, to see beyond the surface view we hold of life. Perfection is only to be discovered by allowing the mind to look deeply, and this can only happen when the mind falls still and those involving agitations that usually dominate our view are put to rest.

We can only discover the underlying perfection by being reflective in our thought. To be reflective we have to turn back to that still unperturbed light of consciousness which is there in constant attendance. This requires us to step back from our involvements and to connect with the still point of certainty and illumination. The Isha Upanishad starts with a prayer. W. B. Yeats, the same poet who wrote 'The Lake Isle of Innisfree', translated it like this:

*That is Perfect.*
*This is Perfect.*
*Perfect comes from Perfect.*
*Take Perfect from Perfect*
*And the remainder is perfect.*
*May peace and peace and peace*
*be everywhere.*[6]

Even a few steps towards this underlying perfection bring tranquillity to the mind. When we are disturbed by those sources of anguish that none of us are entirely free from, turn to the source of contentment which is ever close at hand. Shakespeare, like many Platonists before him, called this power 'the light of reason'. By living in conscious contact with the source of consciousness, we cannot help but live a philosophic life.

At the beginning of this book is the key exercise to which constant reference is made. The practice of *Self Remembering* is a method to still the mind and make contact with the essential, and, through contact with that, find the perfect response to the present need. Thus perfection arises from perfection and, when the action is complete, returns to the underlying perfection which remains pure, perfect and complete throughout. The more fully we teach our minds to do this, the less likelihood there is of passing through life in a self-imposed and utterly personalised isolation, out of touch with others, out of touch with ourselves, out of touch with life itself.

## PRACTICE

Despite the power of life's many involvements,
constantly return to the underlying perfection
in order to connect with what is right for right now.

STAGE FOUR

# The Time of Your Life

THE GREAT THING ABOUT the present moment is that it is the only time that we are truly alive. But so busy are we preparing to live at some other time we miss this obvious fact.

The experience of what is currently on offer is so often overlaid with preoccupations, distractions, fear and expectation, and yet it is only in the present that genuine concerns can be met with any understanding. It is only in the present that things can be timed to perfection, tackled with a touch of true artistry.

Every other way of working must be dull by comparison. This is self-evident. Yet emotional involvement has its way of possessing heart and mind, and methods have to be consciously adopted to realign our perception and connect with the present.

The reflections contained in this chapter are designed to bring the mind back from the concerns for the past and future. They allow you to become aware of what NOW might offer and to discover the time of your life in all its fullness and power.

## Knowledge is in the Moment

You may have command of all the relevant information, and this information may have utter validity, but the effective application of that information, the creating of a perfect fit, is only possible at one time.

> I had all the information at my fingertips. I was so well informed. There wasn't anybody at the meeting who could possibly have what was available to me. I was certain that I could dictate events.
>
> What I didn't have was an understanding of the dynamic that existed at that particular time. To have that I had to embrace the whole situation as it manifested then, and that included all those things that were not in my way of thinking. This became evident as the meeting progressed. I had to look again and think again. It was only when I abandoned my script and gave my attention fully to what was happening that the knowledge of what was really required become evident. By making that connection all the information I had marshalled became the servant of the moment, and things that were right for that time naturally arose.
>
> The interesting thing was that not only was there a precise and creative application of that information, there was also a deeper understanding of myself. It was as if I had somehow touched a deeper resource.

This observation is not so much about facts and figures, regardless of the importance of those facts and figures; it's more about the context in which those facts and figures found their precise application. When awareness of this order arises, conflicting interests and divisive arguments, no matter how compelling, are subsumed into the brightness of this present moment, and precisely what is being demanded by the present becomes clear. It's here that knowledge really arises, and that's why it's important to look again and think again, and maybe even abandon cherished approaches.

What is evident in this observation is that rather than using information to force a result, the speaker offered it in service of the present, and in the process what arose was 'a deeper understanding of myself', the ability to touch 'a deeper resource'. By honouring the present he came to a deeper understanding of himself which in turn allowed for a more creative response.

**PRACTICE**

Gather the knowledge needed in the only time possible.
Make sure you haven't overlooked the obvious.
Look again. Think again.

## Now

Now is a potent time. It's where everything lives. We think about past, present and future as being the same sort of thing. The truth is that our perception of the present is quite different from that of past and future. The past is a recreation of what once existed, the future a speculative assessment of what might be. Unlike these two, the present is not an imaginative exercise. It's what actually is. If we could but free ourselves from the other two and make contact with the present and all that it offers, we would make contact with a reality that the other two couldn't hope to possess.

Now is where the act of creation takes place. For us to act creatively we should make every effort to live in the present.

We look back at the past often with regret, time past. We may often try to recreate the past in a more favourable way, indulging ourselves in an 'if only' exercise, which is bound to be full of regrets and recriminations. Likewise we may endeavour to look into the future in an attempt to divine what it holds in store. Driven by desire, we often fill our minds full of fearful expectations. Cool reassessment of the facts and the creation of well-laid plans do have their validity as long as it is appreciated that the longer we live in the past and future the longer we are missing out on real time: the only time when reality occurs. Even when we believe ourselves to be living now we are only partially present, for the present is constantly coloured by thoughts and feelings about the past and future. This is an imaginary world governed by hosts of unrecognised assumptions, ruled over by that one presiding power central to all our preoccupations: ME.

Give up the idea that ME, in my past and future, searching for some personal benefit, has any relevance to what the present is actually offering. Insight doesn't require us to search through a heap of personal claims. It's my past and my future that so often draws us away from the present.

> The academics I work for are funny people, not all of them but many. They claim to be in pursuit of the truth, but so much of their energy is devoted not so much to doing this but rather to disproving the theories of their rivals in order to prove themselves superior. One can't help but wonder what they're missing out on because of this kind of distraction?

This observation suggests why a little humility isn't such a bad thing. When the ego enters, the present must be coloured by ideas we have about ourselves, which by necessity are carried from the past to be projected onto the future where we might gain something of what we desire or avoid something of what we fear. Under these circumstances there is every danger of us discovering only what we want to know not what we are really being told by the circumstances we are actually facing. If this is true for academics, it's also true for us all.

**PRACTICE**

Discover this present time – the only time –
in all its originality and particular power.

## There When it Happens

To possess the present we must first ask of ourselves what our world is at present. To pose this question indicates the possibility of observation. There is that in us that stands back and looks at the situation. Usually, however, we are so deeply engaged in all our involvements that this silent observer in the background disappears beneath them all. By disengaging from the involvement there is the possibility of true objectivity taking place. Under these circumstances observer and object of observation fulfil a proper relationship.

This is what is meant by 'stepping back'. When we step back we step back from all those things we are agitated by. We step back into the calm clear presence of the *Silent Witness* in the background. This has an automatic effect on the state of the mind. All the agitations naturally begin to settle and a proper connection with the present becomes possible. On that taking place, what the present holds becomes increasingly clear and bright. When the present is lit, our role, that which is ours alone to fulfil, becomes increasingly evident. Only under these circumstances are we free to act. Every other form of action is necessarily affected by the agitations of mind. We are not really free, as our actions are dictated by our mental state. We do not so much decide; rather we are driven.

Nor, under these circumstances, are we really conscious of the present. Our state of consciousness has a direct impact on what we know of the present. When our minds are filled with movement, a screen is formed between ourselves and the present, and that agitation has the effect of colouring everything. We are green with envy and see red with anger, ending up with having the blues, and none of this is to do with the present. The present is not coloured in any way.

To move into the present we must first move towards ourselves. Equally by coming closer to ourselves we move into the present. By accepting the authority of the present we stand under the *Silent Witness*, allowing the clear unwavering light of this observation to inform everything the present presents. This is why true understanding meets you moment by moment, and why it is important that we should be there when it happens. It may even be argued that there can be no understanding except under these circumstances; what takes place otherwise is only an imaginary impression we have of ourselves interacting with a highly coloured version of reality.

**PRACTICE**

Step back from involvement.
Step back into conscious awareness.
Step into the present
to meet what the moment is asking.

## Give Yourself Time

Time ticks by with the even pulse of a metronome.

> We went to Greenwich to the observatory on the top of the hill. We went in particular to see the Harrison clocks. They are so beautiful. The mechanics are exquisite, and although made hundreds of years ago they keep time to perfection. The interesting thing is that, although they are in perpetual movement, they have a sense of stillness about them. They don't make time stand still, but they do give to the moment an immediacy, a presence. They seem to both measure time and continually draw the mind back to this moment now. When standing in front of them time seems to expand.

We talk about a given time, the time allotted for a specific task, or allotted for a life, but this time as it passes is not as even as the clock seems to indicate. Our impression of time changes. Think of how time passed when you were a child, how the summer holidays seemed a lifetime. Think of how time passes now. Then there are circumstances which seem to force us into an altogether different sense of time.

> I was at one time in my life a fighter pilot. I had just taken off in this jet when I felt it go. One of the engines had dropped off. Ahead of me was a wood. The rule book states that under the circumstances I had to fly into the trees, put the thing down, but, as you could well imagine, the sense of self-preservation forces you to consider your options. My first instinct was to turn the plane round and land it on the runway from which I had just taken off. But I remembered how another pilot had recently attempted the same thing. The G-force had killed him. It was then that out of the corner of my eye I saw a little blob about the size of my thumbnail on the horizon. I remembered what it was, another airstrip. I adjusted the aircraft as best I could and headed off. I managed to get there and put the plane down. I destroyed the plane, but I did save my life.

> The interesting thing about the whole incident was how much time I had, time to reject what I had been trained to do, time to reflect on my current situation, time to consider my options, time to adjust the aircraft as best I could. How long was all that? Ten to fifteen seconds. Under the kind of circumstances I was facing time expands, and the present is a vivid and immediate reality.

We imagine time travelling at an even pace, but the very fact that we experience time so differently at different times indicates that this mind-created thing, time, is subject to our states of mind. Events as indicated by this observation may propel us into an entirely different perception of time.

This may be forced on us. Alternatively we may train our minds to appreciate what each moment offers – taste it, give ourselves time to enjoy, savour the present.

By giving ourselves time to appreciate what the present is offering we may live longer by living life more fully, both in the fullness of time and in the fullness of experience. Rushing on is a sure way of remaining disconnected from the space and time of now.

**PRACTICE**

Give yourself time
by becoming vividly aware
of this present moment.

## Let It Go

> *He who bends to himself a Joy*
> *Doth the wingèd life destroy.*
>
> WILLIAM BLAKE[1]

Savouring the present doesn't involve clinging on, grasping after something which has already passed by. By doing this you are allowing the present to slip into your imagination where this centre of identity called ME is so desperate to retain a fleeting pleasure.

No, rather than clinging on, make a full and complete connection with NOW in this very instant, and then, rather than trying to prevent this instant from running through your fingers by seeking to transfix it in your imagination, abandon all personal identifications in order to meet what the real NOW is offering. The real NOW is the one that is actually happening. Everything else is coloured by past and future. In the real now there's no fear or regret, only a full and total connection with what is.

There is a wonderful piece of advice in the Isha Upanishad: E*njoy. Do not covet.* By being covetous we cling on, often try to possess things which are not ours to possess, and when we try to cling on to the thing that has passed, we are certainly trying to cling onto something which is no longer ours. Enjoyment under these circumstances is not a possibility, but frustration certainly is.

Enjoyment without claim is of the present. Enjoyment with claim requires us to abandon the present in order to plunge into the past in the vain attempt to recreate something which no longer has reality. It also requires us to create an enjoyer of that imagined pleasure. This double fantasy takes us away from the present, away from ourselves and away from the pleasure that is actually on offer at the only time true pleasure is to be experienced.

Reason indicates that trying to attain lasting satisfaction by grasping after something that is not only by nature fleeting, but in truth has already gone, is an impossibility. The same is also true of perpetually loving in expectation, another effective way of missing out on the present.

By constantly running into the future, the true satisfaction to be derived from coming completely to rest in the present is lost. The music of life manifests now, not when the music ends. There's only one thing that lies at the end of life. This is so evidently true, but so often we spend our time trying to get things done and finished with, and how we deal with all the passing bits of life will be true of how we deal with life in its totality.

The desire to discover the rest we so naturally wish for on the completion of something has nothing of rest about it. Such desire creates agitation, frustration and stress. What is discovered by coming completely into the present is rest in action. This seeming contradiction is no contradiction at all. The present moment now is ever at rest. The material world may be full of activity, and the subtle world of mind definitely is, but by resting in the present what is discovered in that poised moment of attention is stillness and depth. Try it.

**PRACTICE**

Open out completely
and discover the underlying stillness
out of which all activity arises.
Act from that,
and at the same time enjoy it to the full, without claim,
now.

## Cutting Off

The pulse of life pulses now. The vitality is here now. The joy of life which we all quest after can only be discovered when life takes place. If we lose something, we would never think to look for it where it can't possibly be found. It is utterly unreasonable to seek life and all the joys that may be discovered in life at a time when life doesn't exist. It's utterly unreasonable. This is self-evident, and yet there is something about us that demands that we should do just this: that something is the ego and all its vested interests.

Consider the time when the ego was formed. This is the past we are talking about, when all those things we struggled so hard to attain, all those things we are fearful of losing were formed. When we use this as the basis of life, we constantly try to recreate the present in terms of the past, and not even the past as a summation of human understanding, just our own past. The whole thing is based on personal claim and personal claim is rooted in desire and aversion. It arises in a multitude of forms, each with its justification intact, ready to defend its position against any perceived threat. Under these circumstances where do you think the attention rests? Certainly not on what the moment is offering. Or if there appears to be a connection with the present, that connection is coloured by claim, the claimants being concerned that this present enjoyment will be taken from them. The irony is that in thinking like this the very thing that we are concerned about has already happened, and we ourselves are the ones who have done the depriving.

This continual practice of self-deprivation is a habit that is hard to shift, and, as with all habits, it's an activity inherited from the past. The first thing to recognise is that this is taking place, and when that's happened use it to trigger the opening of the senses. Disconnect the mind from past and future in order to come to your senses in the present, and there discover what the senses are telling you about the present. When you need to look, simply look; when you need to listen, simply listen. There is so much information to be gathered in this present moment, gathered by abandoning likes and dislikes, and personal predilection of any kind.

Recently I was talking to a wine taster. She had just won a national competition and was talking about the pleasure of wine tasting.

> It's a wonderful exercise to simply rest in the present and concentrate on one thing. It's only by doing that that you can possibly connect with all the subtle flavours that a wine possesses. A useful exercise is to taste unidentified wines. You carry with you so many preconceptions, and this is one way of tasting it for what it is, not what others have claimed, or the wine's reputation.
>
> The interesting thing is that, regardless of what you carry in mind about the wine, when you are fully focussed such prejudice doesn't interfere. The other interesting thing is that when you give your awareness to something like wine tasting, your palate improves in general. I remember the same thing happening when I took up life drawing some years ago. By being utterly awake to the present you're tuned up and your sensory perception becomes so much more sensitive. With wine tasting there has to be single-pointed attention: this wine at this moment and nothing else.

As is evident from this observation what is true of sight and hearing is true of taste and touch. Being in touch was explored in the last stage. What needs to be emphasised here is that there is only one time to be in touch, the present.

Sportsmen talk about getting their eye in. They undoubtedly need to study their opponents and decide on their tactics. They must study their own game to learn from their past mistakes, but at the time of play there is only that time. Immediacy is all.

**PRACTICE**

Observe what it is that cuts you off
from the present,
and in the process
what are you hanging onto
and missing out on.

## What is the World for Me Now?

> The world is wider and more still and more at peace. I know it is because that's what I'm experiencing now. All those internal agitations which ruled my experience of life just a few minutes ago have dissolved into a sense of this still presence. What is present now that wasn't present previously? Something seems to have slotted in.

This was an observation given by someone after practising *Self Remembering*. It speaks of a transformation of consciousness. This transformation is not so much due to something 'slotting in' more 'slotting out'. Just as when you run different images through a projector what is seen on the screen completely changes, so does what we perceive completely change when the state of heart and mind changes.

The truth of the matter is that often we see more of the past than we do of the present. All those things that colour our perception are imports. What is described as something 'slotting in' is in fact the dropping away of mental agitations which circulate around these ideas we carry about ourselves. Only then do we meet the present in all its purity.

> To get home I have to drive through South London. The buildings on either side naturally confine the road, but it's not just the buildings, it's the whole intensity of the city. But shortly before arriving home I climb Blackheath Hill and out onto the wide expanse of Blackheath itself, an area of open land that lies alongside Greenwich Park. This has the same effect every time: the vision opens, the sky is seen, the whole perspective changes. This opening is not just a visual thing. The mind opens too.

Heart as well. The intensity of life has a way of closing us down. Life in a big city can be very intense, so much to do, deadlines to meet. This intensity can have the effect of compressing us, and if it's not the demands of the job, it's the demands of others. Our effectiveness as a human being is dependent on our power to respond. That ability is entirely governed by where we are coming from. If where we are coming from is small and narrow, for whatever reason, then the thoughts we think, the emotions we feel, the actions we take are conditioned by that place. This is why we need to continually assess the current situation and ask ourselves, 'What is the world for me now, what does the world look like, how is it coloured by my state of heart and mind?' These very questions create a distance between ourselves and the involvements that are compressing our view of life.

If it proves upon inspection that your life has been closed down in some way, step out into the open by stepping into the present. Come to stillness and connect. The question: *What is the world for me now?* reminds us of the present, that place which is ever lit, expansive and free. Put the question to the mind and see what happens.

**PRACTICE**

'What is the world for me now?'
Use this question to assess the present,
a place which in truth is ever lit, expansive and free.

## The Perfect Present

If in attempting to come back to the present, the sense of the present is one of dullness and dissatisfaction, be certain of one thing, the present hasn't yet arrived. The present fully discovered has its own perfection.

> I'd been struggling all day. Nothing seemed to go well. All that was evident to me was imperfection. 'Why couldn't it go right?' The sense of frustration coloured everything. Whether it was the intensity of the emotion that alerted me to my state I don't know. Whatever it was it enabled me to examine what exactly my world did consist of at that particular time. Normally I'm so sucked in I don't notice, but then I was able to stand back.
>
> The first thing that became clear was that my present didn't exist. The past certainly existed. What had I been doing but going over and over events that were gone, that certainly wouldn't provide what I wanted from them? I opened my mind to the present by simply accepting its presence. By so doing I was automatically accepting the value of the present. It took on its own beauty. None of this had anything to do with my so important concerns, or appeared not to.

In coming into the present like this you are changing your values. You are moving out of what is important for 'me' in the past and future in order to honour the immediate present. In honouring a thing we must give it our attention, recognise its importance. When doing so, whatever it is to which we are giving our attention begins to reveal its secrets. Very often the first thing that is recognised when we are doing this is that the present is a far brighter place than past and future, and in addition it possesses its own particular perfection.

> We were driving back to where we were staying. It had been a full day, so much to be considered and remembered. It was getting on for dusk. As we passed by, I noticed up on a hill, silhouetted against the sky, this clump of trees. It was perfect. Even at the time I thought: 'What makes these trees so perfect? You couldn't change anything about them. This is a random group, not artistically placed, just simply there in all its perfection.' What makes something perfect?

A thing is perfect because it simply is. It has its own presence, its own being. Is there anything more to add to it or take away from it? Is it complete unto itself in its own perfect way? Being a real perfectionist doesn't require you to tinker away on the surface in order to arrive at some preconceived idea of the ideal state. The ideal can only exist at one time. Perfection arises in the present because the present is perfect. When you allow the business of life to drop away in order to rest in the underlying 'isness', the first thing that is recognised is the sense of simple presence. Rest in that presence, the presence of this present moment.

Remember that beautiful Sanskrit prayer:

> *That is perfect. This is perfect. Perfect comes from perfect.*
> *Take perfect from perfect, the remainder is perfect.*
> *May peace and peace and peace be everywhere.*[2]

Peace is found in perfection. Both arise from the underlying being which is at the heart of constant becoming. The perpetual movement of life in which we must play our part can easily become no source of freedom, caught up as we can easily become by perpetually trying to push the past into the future in our own peculiar and utterly imperfect fashion. By finding the present we find perfection. We must also discover an utterly right and satisfying way of playing our part with a kind of careless excellence.

The man who made the observation about coming back to the present after struggling all day concluded by saying that only by abandoning *his so important concerns* to meet the present did there arise out of the stillness of the present an insight into a possible solution of the problems that had been besetting him all day.

**PRACTICE**

Find rest in the presence
Of this present moment,
offering up your concerns
to that moment.

## Be Wise Now

Be wise now not after the event. Wisdom is not for the past. There's only one time for wisdom, and it can only possibly be now. Here there's plenty of opportunity. What isn't opportune or wise is acting wisely after the event. It may be worth considering the wrongs we have committed, utterly determined to learn from our mistakes, but the irony is that so often are we caught in the effects of our past mistakes that we fail to notice falling foul of the same sort of thing here in the present. This is particularly so when our level of consciousness has been reduced by the effects of self-criticism.

One way of avoiding repetitive error is to consciously keep the company of the wise, constantly returning to the gift the wise have given humanity. It is far easier to meet people and events as if for the first time when the mind is refreshed by the company of those whose thoughts and deeds are full of reason and love.

It is of course far easier to be wise in those conditions that encourage wisdom, far less so when circumstances seem to work against us. It is those times, however, that not only test our resolve to be open and aware, but also provide us with the strength to face our difficulties, the strength to let go and attend to the immediate circumstances. It's pointless to be wise about things that are not our concern, or to be wise in theory only. Philosophy – the love of wisdom, as opposed to theoretical speculation – is in reality an entirely practical matter. The test of true philosophy is to remain true to philosophical principles at the time of test, and that time can only be in the present, meeting the situations that are ours alone to face, meeting them with insight and understanding. The present is lit. It is also unified. If we can meet the moment free from agitation – and agitation must be our experience when meeting the present with our minds full of what we are trying to force from the present – then we'll meet the unity that's found in the moment. Doing this will help bring the pain and concern which is the hallmark of difficult situations to a rational resolution.

> I was having a row with my husband. Suddenly I saw myself becoming trapped by my anger and vitriol. In that moment I decided to step out of it and centre my attention instead. When that happened it was as if I had actually stepped out of myself and was able to observe the whole discussion taking place. I was amazed at how positive the outcome was.

We will later discover more about those principles that are to be discovered in the present. Needless to say, wisdom and unity are two of them. Think of what this woman discovered when she tapped into the power of the present and decided to be wise in the event.

Evident in this observation are many of the features we have been discussing. By stepping into the present she was stepping out of the negative emotion that was possessing heart and mind. By centring the attention in the empowering consciousness she prevented that consciousness from empowering the vitriol that was about to erode her relationship. By stepping out of herself, which at that moment was nothing but all those negative feelings which she was about to lend her identity to, she discovered *a positive outcome,* the outcome being the principle of unity arising to dissolve division. In this she acted wisely.

## PRACTICE

There is no wisdom after the event.
Be wise at the only time wisdom is possible.

## No Time for Fear

Anger and fear, worry and concern are always out of step with the present. They may be very pressing, so demanding that they blot out everything. They certainly blot out the present. Sometimes, however, the sheer naked demands of the present have a way of laying to one side our captivating concerns. The attention goes outward, and when it does it leaves behind those concerns that are always personal. To free ourselves of worry, to free ourselves of anger, serve the moment.

> I was called out on an emergency. A man had climbed up some scaffolding which was cladding an office block and was threatening to jump off. I was called upon to go up and persuade him to come down. Now, I have this problem. I suffer from vertigo. I can't even look at a photograph taken from the top of a cliff or a tall building without feeling the effects. But suddenly, there I was, making my way, hand over hand, up this scaffolding. I knew exactly what to do. The whole thing was so vivid; each moment was utterly real, and I had all the time in the world. When I got to the top, again I knew exactly what to do, how to approach him, what words to say, and remarkably there was not one moment of fear throughout.

All sense of personal concern disappeared in the moment of life and death. That included a fear which had previously held complete sway. In this situation there was only one utterly dominating factor: the need of the moment.

When you suffer from vertigo it's no minor concern. It may become a dominating feature in your life, but notice what happens when there is no time for personal concern: whether those concerns be petty or of an all consuming nature, they disappear. The writer states: *Now, I have this problem.* The truth is that in the NOW the problem disappeared. *I knew exactly what to do. The whole thing was so vivid. Each moment was so utterly real, and I had all the time in the world.* What he is describing are clear indications of qualities found in the present: knowledge, reality and the expansion of time.

He added one other comment:

> What I discovered at that time was that fear doesn't exist in the present. Fear only exists when projecting the past into the future.

**PRACTICE**

Rather than projecting the past into the future,
overcome fear by stepping into the present.

## The Time for Opportunity

> At the age of 23 I had a massive stroke. I couldn't walk or talk. I could do hardly anything. In one sense it destroyed my life. Previously I had been totally career-orientated. I had been successful and was determined on success. My life was utterly focussed on my career to the exclusion of everything else.
>
> With the stroke all that changed. Previously anything that didn't fall within my limited focus didn't exist. Afterwards everything existed. People looked at me, at the state I was in, and saw nothing but limitation of the most severe kind. For me it was entirely different. Every moment was a blessing.
>
> When you don't know whether you'll survive till the end of the day, every second is precious. You can't help but live in the present. When the future may no longer be an option for you, the present becomes a profound experience. A simple conversation which previously would be dismissed as of little importance, hardly worth giving your attention to, becomes a glorious thing. You honour the present and you love life.
>
> It has taken five years of determined effort to relearn things the stroke wiped out. This process of re-education is not complete. What is complete is the reorientation of my life. Previously everything was entirely related to me and what I was determined to get out of life. Now I turn out to life in gratitude. This embraces far more than my other way of living could possibly

> have done, focussed as it was entirely on what I was determined to gain for myself at some time in the future. Now I live now.

Who can say what might happen to any of us. In the midst of life there is death. We can make our plans. We can devote ourselves to personal success, but fate has a way of intervening, and the wise tell us that it is not our fate to live a blinkered life of self-centred concern. It is not our true purpose to dismiss the beauty of this world, the glory of the present by being possessed by desire.

What, on the surface, can appear to be a terrible fate can also turn out to be a God-sent opportunity in which everything becomes a subject for reassessment. The whole purpose and nature of our lives is opened up for reconsideration. What is more, if we choose to open our hearts and minds, grace is given in order to experience life in a far more profound and perceptive way, loving each moment as a precious gift, embracing the beauty that is everywhere. It takes courage to do this, and I'm sure that the woman who spoke of her experience above is full of courage. There is also love and wisdom. These are divine principles that exist in the present. The other thing that you'll notice is that she's making her way to a recovery. Could this have happened without the presence of these divine powers? Could this have happened if she had, for the past five years, met the present with anger and frustration, fear and regret, which would have been understandable given her circumstances? Understandable though they may be, these qualities have nothing to do with the present, but everything to do with the past and future.

When faced with the circumstances described here, the choice is stark. It was her choice, but it's ours also. We can awaken to the joy of life, but there's only one time for this awakening to take place. The present offers opportunity, but we don't take it by seizing it. We take our opportunity by giving. We give ourselves body and soul, with the totality of our being. We throw off our guarded moments. We throw off all those clinging thoughts of things gained and sought for. The woman went on to speak about her gratitude. She was grateful for the terrible circumstances that fate had forced on her, grateful that in coming into the present she had encountered the totality of her being, a totality that contained courage, love and wisdom, a totality that granted her such assistance in her journey to recovery, and we should be grateful too. Such examples encourage us in our recovery, recovery of the present, a return to where in reality we have always been and will remain when all the dreams of life have passed.

## PRACTICE

Who knows what tomorrow might bring?
Take the opportunity that's on offer now.

STAGE FIVE

# Vital Mind, Vital Body

There are times when we feel vitally alive, ready and willing to cope with any demand life presents. At other times, however, accessing our energy seems an utter impossibility. This may not have much to do with our physical condition, but more with our state of mind. We can easily entertain thoughts and feelings which do nothing but drain us of our power.

Under these circumstances what is needed is a change of mind, a new way of meeting events. This way has everything to do with self-discovery, of developing something more than a surface response to life. It is to do with training our hearts and minds to make connection with our real selves, our own source of creative energy, and learning to act from that.

To re-energise mind and body we must re-educate our thinking. Turn to the constantly new rather than old habits of thought that do nothing but wear us down.

Use the reflections in this chapter to unlock your own creative core and tap the vitality to be found there.

## Life Enhancement

There is no doubt that there are levels of consciousness, or that is how it seems to us. We rise out of sleep to meet the day and immediately our level of consciousness has risen. As we go through the day we become more effective. Research indicates that people are most productive between ten and twelve in the morning. By that time they have thrown away the lethargy of the night and are as alert and energetic as they are likely to be. After twelve the energy begins to wane as does alertness. Think of those long afternoons in centrally heated office buildings. What's our state like then?

This is the mechanical run of things. It requires no special effort. It's automatic. The problem is that the more we practise living mechanically the less available the conscious core we all possess becomes. We may become effective but only in a mechanical way. We fly on automatic pilot. We work only in the way we have programmed ourselves to work. Our response to life becomes a matter of habit. This, of course, even in our areas of expertise, makes us less and less effective. We are only able to respond to life, to a lesser or greater extent, in accordance with those factors that were there when our personal paradigm was programmed in. We may learn more in areas of particular interest or use, but the wise application of that knowledge will be limited when habit rules.

There are of course other ways of working, and we are capable of developing as human beings right up to our last breath. This is a life well lived. The body may be old, but the inner life is consciously developing. I'm sure that for all of us there are times in our lives when we recognise conscious development and other times when we are merely treading water.

The choice that all of us face is whether to live mechanically or consciously. The problem is that by living ever more mechanically it becomes ever more difficult to envisage any other way of living. The exercises and reflections in this book are designed to develop a conscious approach to life. To do this involves replacing energy-destroying habits with life-enhancing ones. These are not really habits at all, for the more they are adopted the more free we become, free from the gradual rundown all of us are subject to without conscious input.

It is, therefore, important to assess the current state of play. We may judge how conscious we are by checking how much energy we possess and how effective that energy is in enhancing our own lives and the lives of others. It's a simple truth that the more conscious we are the more benefit we are, not only to ourselves but also to those we come in contact with, and indeed, in the final analysis, to life in general.

**PRACTICE**

In any situation quietly assess what's going on.
Ask yourself if, at this moment,
your way of thinking is more life-enhancing or energy-depleting.

## Your Power is a Quiet Presence

> I was at home the other day. I was feeling dull and heavy. I felt fed up and generally inert. I decided to go for a run. I didn't ask myself why. I just heaved myself out of the chair and went. When I came back I felt much better, so good indeed that I settled down and wrote, which is also something I like to do but only manage in my better moments.

What this observation describes very simply is a change of mental, emotional and physical qualities. It describes the movement from lethargy to activity. Out of this activity arose a more reflective state of mind. What it also describes is a rise in consciousness. To bring about a rise in consciousness, a conscious decision has to be made. Here the decision was simple: *go for a run.* This is straightforward enough, but when you're in the grip of lethargy going for a run is the last thing you want to do, especially if you are totally identified with your state. 'If this is how I feel, then this must be who I am.' This is our usual thinking. The truth is, however, as in most cases, not what it appears to be.

The power we really possess is a quiet underlying presence. When we seek out that presence rather than becoming identified with any of the qualities that at any time dominate the mind, then what we need at that particular time will become evident. It may require a movement out of inertia into action. It may require a movement out of an active state into a reflective one. From reflection there may be seen the need for action. One thing's certain: action under the direct influence of reflection is action which is informed and creative. It is also brighter and energy-enhanced. When lethargy holds sway then following in its train can come a whole string of negative emotions. In the observation these negative emotions were summed up with the words: *fed up.* This is a funny expression. It would seem to mean 'fully nourished', but when we feed ourselves on negativity, nourishment is the last thing we get. Feeding ourselves on frustration, anger and concern debilitates rather than enlivens. Negativity by its very nature draws consciousness into itself. Vitality, when given to negative emotion, creates the opposite of itself, debility.

The more debility holds sway, the more identified we become. The more identified we become, the less consciousness we appear to possess. To cut through all this requires a conscious decision. The start of conscious action may be provided by two potent words: *Not this.* This is an ancient but entirely effective formulation. In fact it is said twice: *Not this. Not this.* It's not repeated just in case you didn't hear it the first time. It means *Not this:* you are not all these physical involvements which can so easily come to dominate your thinking, in this case the sense of lethargy. *Not this:* you are not all the emotional toils that have come to colour your thinking: *I felt fed up.*

*Not this. Not this.* This cuts through everything. It prevents conscious energy from empowering these thoughts and feelings.

In the moment of disengagement, new possibility becomes available, but only if immediate action is taken. Don't ask questions. Simply respond. *I didn't ask myself why. I just heaved myself out of the chair and went.* At moments like this the quiet knowledge rises to the surface and presents the knowledge from which we must act. Failure to do this means that the habitual and the unconscious are inevitably being re-established and reinforced.

## PRACTICE

Don't trust the apparent thoughts and feelings
that are dominating the mind at present.
Constantly go back and connect with the essential.

Then act from the knowledge that is presented in the moment. Trust in that.

## Conscious Effort

The law of entropy states that everything in this material world by nature runs down. Buy a car and experience first-hand how the law works. Your car requires regular service which you neglect at your peril. We, like cars, are also subject to entropy. But we, unlike cars, are not merely mechanical; or rather we need not be merely mechanical. The truth is, however, that without regular service that is exactly what we become. Service, as far as we are concerned, apart from regular exercise, involves us in constantly remembering our true nature, which is anything but mechanical. This kind of service requires us to return to that which makes us conscious beings, the consciousness itself.

We sleep at night, and that in its way renews us. It refuels the body and restores the mind, makes it fit for another day, but adopting reflective practices allows for renewal of another kind. It allows us to reassess the direction of our lives, reconsider our own particular contribution, serve the need with generosity of spirit, be aware, creative and of immediate benefit. The following story is by a young teacher. She has a degree in philosophy, but she had forgotten certain principles which would allow the philosophy she had learnt to be of real benefit to the pupils she taught.

> I entered on a teaching career. I started enthusiastically enough but after a couple of years the work became less and less fulfilling. It seemed that the energy I had for my subject, for my pupils, for the job began to fade. As this continued I felt myself becoming more and more separate from my pupils. They irritated me, and the more irritated I became the more difficult they were to handle. This made the situation worse, and I used to go home exhausted and depressed.
>
> It was then that I rediscovered something, a positive way to live that I'd known earlier in life. Possibly because of the situation

> I faced, I returned to it with a new determination. It changed everything. Through it I discovered myself and an energy I didn't know I possessed. What I also discovered was how to use this energy effectively, certainly not to fuel my negative emotions, but for something far more creative.
>
> By turning from these layers of frustration and discontentment, I discovered something quite different about myself. I also discovered something remarkable about the children I taught. I began to look below the surface impression they showed the world. I discovered that they had their own particular qualities which were quite different from those which they projected and, although I had to continue dealing with the usual problems, I worked from an entirely different centre within myself. By so doing all kinds of possibilities suggested themselves in what I taught and the way I taught it. My whole approach was renewed. I rediscovered my enthusiasm.

The story beautifully illustrates everything this particular reflection is drawing our attention to: the need for conscious renewal and the effect that this has both on ourselves and all those around us. It demonstrates that by making connection with the essential energy not only do we become revitalised but, by transference, the energy is passed on for the benefit of others.

**PRACTICE**

Rather than allowing entropy to rule
seek conscious renewal constantly.
Benefit yourself. Benefit all.

## Where the Power is Found

There is a story by Rumi, the Persian mystic poet, about the lion, the wolf and the fox who go out hunting together. They catch an ox, a goat and a hare. The wolf and the fox hoped to gain equal amounts despite the lion doing the lion's share. The wolf in his foolishness offered the lion a deal.

'You take this, and I'll take that, and the fox can have what's left over.'

The lion in his rage instantly killed the wolf. When the lion asked the fox to divide the spoils the fox said, 'Let the ox be your breakfast, the goat your lunch. That leaves you the hare as a tit-bit for your supper.'

'Fox,' said the lion, 'who taught you such wisdom?'

'You, King of the World. I saw what happened to the wolf.'

We may be grateful that we can learn from the past and therefore avoid making the same old mistakes over and over again, but learning from the past is one thing, trying to live in it is another. As the fox was well aware, the past is only relevant to the extent that what's to be discovered there has an immediate application to the here and now.

*Now is the only time.* Although you may have heard this said before it's as relevant now as it ever was. The important thing about the world's great teaching stories is the same thing as the truths they embody. They are true for all time, and all time doesn't mean a long period of time. It means at every time, which means now. It's often said of Shakespeare that he is a great writer because his works are capable of contemporary reinterpretation. People say this, but the truth is that Shakespeare is great because no matter how his works are dressed up, his timeless genius will shine through. It cannot be helped. The author was vividly present when the works were composed. They, therefore, pulsate with energy, and that energy will be transferred regardless of the seemingly archaic language in which they were written. This is why people return to the works over and over again. They are always new. We know that we are in the presence of a vital mind and by the transference of that vitality we are conducted to a vast and vividly lit place where the plays were composed. By so doing we become vital too and vitally present.

I was recently given these reflections by a boy of fourteen. They are part of a much longer project about a school trip to Florence.

> I walked out of the centre of Florence into the new town. It was full of contemporary city life, all those things that make me who I think I am. It reminded me of what I had been expecting when I came on the trip. I expected Florence to be a dreary, dusty town with too many paintings that would bore me to tears. When I saw all the wondrous art, the architecture and all the beauty that Florence possesses, this expectation had died instantly. I was overwhelmed. For the first time I saw my world in a different light. The trivial things which play such a central role in most of our lives exposed themselves to me.
>
> I saw the irrelevance of much of our modern extravagancies, how inconsequential so much of it is. In short, when compared to the brilliance, beauty, talent and ingenuity found in Florence, the unnecessary parts of out lives pale into insignificance.
>
> The trip changed my view of the world I live in and changed me. The pride of the Florentines and all the wonders they left behind allowed me to see things from a different perspective. Far from being dead and dreary, what I saw was something really alive.

By visiting the past he became more vividly aware of the present, and, paradoxically enough, what was discovered in *contemporary city life* was for him somehow lacking in meaningful life. What was also evident from his essay was that given the right circumstances beauty and true vitality can be readily awakened in us and provide us with a vivid awareness of the present.

Check where the mind is going. Don't make of life a bunker for depleted energy. Life is not a habitual repetition, a long preconception. These things create an impression of life only. Be like Shakespeare and many of the more renowned figures of the Renaissance, people born again to their own vitality and vividly alive to the present.

## PRACTICE

Don't constantly return to the past,
the home of depleted energy.

Instead be vividly alive to the present
and become vividly aware of your eternal powers.

## Greet Life with Enthusiasm

The great thing about those who are alive to life, indeed the very thing that makes them great, is their boundless enthusiasm. To them nothing is impossible. You look at their legacy, and it seems hard to believe that they achieved what they did; the skill is unbelievable. One of the things the boy saw on his visit to Florence was Michelangelo's 'Prisoners'. These are half-finished sculptures clambering forth from the huge blocks from which they were being carved. It's an amazing sight. They are incomplete and yet perfect. It seems as though as soon as the chisel was laid on the rock the perfection of Michelangelo's conception was imparted, and even in their incomplete state we are conducted to the perfection of that vision. What is also amazing to discover is that he was carving his masterpieces right up until a few weeks prior to his death – a man in his eighties. Have you ever tried to carve anything out of stone? I'm not talking about a masterpiece. It's physically exhausting. This man had a vital mind and a vital body right up to the end.

This is 'the creative imperative' working through him. He had to do it. The breath of enthusiasm empowered him. The pietà he was carving at the time is a vivid recreation of life and death, a portrayal of that vital intersection which he himself would soon be facing. This carving of Christ being taken down from the cross embodies and calls from us many of the major human emotions, above all love and pity, but it doesn't stop there. This is no frozen moment. It takes you beyond the drama of the event and even, in a way, beyond all that the event represents. It takes you into the presence of that which lies beyond life and death. This is why people speak of the presence that such work possesses. This presence is our own presence. How could we recognise it if it were not the case?

I was at a wedding. At the reception an incident occurred that could have been a source of embarrassment, but was in reality more a source of celebration. This was natural enough because it was a speech in praise of someone. The best man had just spoken. He had spoken, as is usual in this kind of speech, humorously about the groom. Because of some of the things said the groom's brother felt impelled to make an impromptu speech of his own. He wanted to tell the real story. What he spoke of was his brother's virtues, of what made him a man: his generosity of spirit, his boundless energy, his vision, his enthusiasm and his entirely positive approach to life. 'This is a real man,' he said, and then turning to the best man, 'the best of men.' His was a true statement for the 'best of men' is the 'real man'. Anything else is something less. Meet life therefore as a human being, full of energy, vision and enthusiasm. Give these and discover what you receive in return. Your brother's devotion might well be guaranteed.

**PRACTICE**

Be the best of men or the best of women.
Meet life like a true human being,
full of energy, vision and enthusiasm.

## Draw Strength

This chapter is called 'Vital Mind, Vital Body', and inevitably everything being developed in this chapter is supporting the claim that the body follows the mind. If you don't develop the right frame of mind, the frame of the body will become distorted. By bringing harmony to mind you bring harmony to the body. The ancients understood this only too well. They had a name for it – 'nootherapia', mind healing. It wasn't for nothing that Apollo, the god of healing, was also the god of harmony and the god of poetry and music. In their healing methods the ancients fed their patients with fair sights and sounds by making full use of the arts. Then, having encouraged them to undergo a change of heart and mind, they used gymnastics to bring their bodies into tune. Harmonisation and revitalisation were at the heart of it all.

When life is young, energy seems abounding. Think of the energy a young child possesses and its capacity to make total contact with the here and now. Have you ever tried to walk down the road with a three-year-old? You have somewhere to go. You are projecting yourself ahead of yourself, and you are hurrying to meet yourself in this imaginary time and place. Whilst you haven't arrived, the child certainly has. This is what makes it so frustrating for you. Children discover a multitude of things which their curious minds have been aroused by in the here and now. This is their point of arrival. Future possibility may not be their concern, but present wonder certainly is. If you know a young child, make a list of the things that his interest is aroused by, what he wonders at. Then, instead of arriving at your destination exhausted by chivvying your child along, learn to wonder at their wonder, and by being full of wonder yourself become a source of inspiration for them. Unite in the wonder, and discover the vitality of life lived as if for the first time.

Here's a beautiful description of just that from Thomas Traherne's *Centuries:*

> The corn was orient and immortal wheat, which never should be reaped, nor ever was sown. I thought it had stood from everlasting to everlasting. The dust and stones of the street were as precious as gold; the gates were at the first end of the world. The green trees, when I saw them first through one of the gates, transported and ravished me: their sweetness and unusual beauty made my heart to leap, and almost mad with ecstasy, they were such strange and wonderful things. The Men! O what venerable and reverend creatures did the aged seem! Immortal cherubim! And young men glittering and sparkling angels, and maids strange and seraphic pieces of life and beauty! Boys and girls, tumbling in the street, and playing, were moving jewels. I knew not that they were born or should die, but all things abided eternally as they were in their proper places. Eternity was manifest in the Light of the Day, and something infinite behind everything appeared.[1]

This is what a child's wonder can be like. Sometimes if you're in a child's company you get a glimpse of it. A word of warning, however: don't start looking back to your own childhood with regret, thinking about how it once was. Instead, rediscover the wonder now by looking at things with a sense of wonder. This is one way of encouraging positive thought and emotion and drawing strength from it. And once you have rediscovered a sense of wonder, convey it. In this you have to make no effort. Transference will naturally occur. This of course provides another way of encouraging positive thought and emotion. From this all may draw strength.

A friend, Michael Mayne, has done just this. He has written a beautiful book called *The Sunrise of Wonder*. You may gain from the title an indication as to what it's all about: the sense of wonder as it manifests in art and literature, and one of the wonderful things about this book is that it is written in the form of a series of letters to the author's grandchildren. This is the kind of gift any grandfather would like to make if he had the energy and insight to do it. In Michael's case he couldn't avoid it. The energy was provided. You too could access this energy but only by positive thought and conduct. Lending your vitality to the negative can do nothing but debilitate.

**PRACTICE**

When you find yourself draining yourself of strength
by lending your consciousness to negative thinking,
draw strength from a positive approach to life.

## The Effect of Company

There's an Irish poem about a drunkard and a pig:

> It was an evening in November,
> As I very well remember,
> I was strolling down the street in a drunken pride,
> But my knees were all of a flutter,

And I landed in the gutter
And a pig came up and lay down by my side.

Yes, I lay there in the gutter
Thinking thoughts I couldn't utter
When a colleen passing by did softly say,
'You can tell a man that boozes
By the company he chooses' –
At that the pig got up and slowly walked away.

Like the discriminating pig we must seek the best company and avoid the worst, that is if we want to be enlightened and enlivened. This is particularly true when it comes to the thoughts and feelings we keep company with. What comes out of the mind is dependent on what goes into it, and what is true of the mind is also true of the heart.

> My father used to pay me to learn poems. I learnt them alright. I wanted the money, especially as after practising I could learn the poems with very little effort. Not that I told my father this. I didn't want to devalue the currency.
>
> By learning by heart I still have that stock of poetry in me to this day. It's a source of good company. Those poems continue to have their effect.

We need to develop ways of nourishing ourselves at all levels.

> I have a whole repertoire inside me. Sometimes when I'm feeling downhearted I play Mozart, sometimes on the piano, sometimes in my head.

What a wonderful gift music is. This is what the great musician, Pablo Casals, had to say on the matter:

> For the past 80 years I have started each day in the same manner. It is not a mechanical routine but something essential to my daily

> life. I go to the piano and play one or two preludes and fugues by Bach. I cannot think of doing otherwise. It is a sort of benediction on the house. But that is not its only meaning for me. It is a rediscovery of the world of which I have the joy of being a part. It fills me with a feeling of the incredible marvel of being a human being.[2]

He praises the composer: we praise the performer. In both we are praising ourselves, for what is evoked by the magic of art are those divine powers within us all. Although artists have often talked about serving them, there is nothing these powers need from us, but by connecting with them their powers are released within us for the benefit of all. This is how the ancients thought, but not just the ancients:

> Standing at his appointed place, the trunk of the tree, he does nothing other than gather and pass on what comes to him from the depths. He neither serves nor rules – he transmits.[3]

This is not some Greek poet speaking but Paul Klee, one of the founders of modern art. When what he describes takes place, we are granted a benediction, a blessing, and the more we are blessed by these powers, the more we are nourished, and the more that we are nourished, the less likelihood there is that all those intervening states that create tiredness of mind and bleakness of heart will rule our lives. We nourish ourselves by constantly turning to the very best about ourselves through the agency of the very best the human mind can create. This is good company. Alternatively, when we turn from discouraging thoughts and feelings to seek that within us which grants courage and enthusiasm, then we are discovering the very best of company. This is the vital way to live. Anything else is something less.

## PRACTICE

Constantly seek the best company in all circumstances.
Seek the very best in yourself, the finest company of all.

## Your Life

If your life seems to lack life look for life and give life. This a living planet we inhabit, and life therefore is everywhere. Serve it. Tend it. Nourish it. Grow things. But before you do that get in touch with life. Those who possess green fingers have a natural ability in growing plants because they are in touch with life. Say to yourself: 'All this is the product of life and is in turn life giving. Regardless of where I look, what I see is seething life. It's all obeying an urge to live. Look at these beautiful trees and this beautiful grass. They are being nourished and in turn they are nourishing others.'

One summer I was staying in an Italian hill village. Every morning the old people went down to tend their *ortos*. These are small plots of land, some terraced, on the steep slopes. Every evening they would return carrying their onions or their beans. Working with the nature they had been making the most of their poor soil. Even as an outsider you could see the satisfaction gained in the relationship. It's little wonder that the two young men I mentioned earlier in the book were enthused by the idea of nourishing Soweto by planting trees and grass.

I had mumps in my mid-twenties and was laid up for five weeks. When I fell ill it was winter. When I finally was able to go out of the house, spring had come. I walked along my back drive. There are trees and shrubs on both sides and they were in new leaf. Being separated from the force of nature for so long, the green was so vivid my senses felt shocked.

The Spanish poet, Frederico Garcia Lorca, starts a playful poem with these lines:

*Verde que te quiero verde.*
*Verde viento. Verdes ramas*
*El barco sobre la mar*
*Y el caballo en la montana*

[Green how much I want you green. Green wind, Green boughs. The ship on the sea and the horse on the mountain.][4]

Look for life, and in the seething midst of life recognise your own life. You are in no way separate. Taking pleasure in this living world of ours is a wonderful way of ridding ourselves of any sense of listlessness. And having discovered life, give life in all you do.

**PRACTICE**

Seek life; serve life; give life in all you do.

## The Fabric of Our Lives

> I went out for a walk one evening last week. And down my road I encountered this lovely sunset. 'Must buy it!' I said to myself. I felt amused. It was a lovely feeling.

You'd think such a thought would cause frustration from the sheer impossibility of it. How could you possibly buy a sunset? Implicit in the observation is the absurdity of the desire. The immediate amusement and subsequent happiness arose by recognising this fact and letting the desire go, and discovering that what was left was the beauty of the sunset enjoyed without any desire to possess in the only time it could possibly be enjoyed, the present.

> It was a poor wicket. I wanted something better than this. I deserved something better! 'No wonder my bowling is so poor!' I couldn't get the line. I couldn't get the length. All I got was frustrated. Then I gave it up, gave up the idea of wanting something else, gave up my intense dislike for that miserable patch of grass, and my bowling improved immediately, and moreover I felt utterly re-energised. I was amazed and amused.

The writer was amazed that the locked state of desire and dislike could be dropped so quickly and then amused at the plight he was previously in. When we're caught up in these situations we are run ragged. It's only after do we see the funny side. Comic events, for those caught up in the comedy, is anything but funny. It's a matter of desperate concern. Ever seen a French farce? They're all about desire and dislike. The desire for something, and the absurd situations that desire leads the characters into. They exhaust themselves trying to cover up their misdemeanours. and we exhaust ourselves in laughing at them.

Notice your desires and dislikes. Firstly don't trust them, and then learn to view them more with amusement than concern. Learn how to laugh at yourself. When you can laugh you can be sure that you have 'slipped the trap'. Conversely, when you feel ragged and worn out you can be sure that your desires and dislikes have caught you fast. This goes for the seemingly serious issues as well as the patently petty. Rational solutions are only possible when we can stand back and take the personal out of the equation.

**PRACTICE**

Find the funny side.
Take the personal out of the equation.

## Power With Purpose

When you've discovered your source of creative energy, there is the danger that you may expend it fruitlessly. It's as if you're unable to control that energy. Measure is needed in all things, for in the final analysis what we are measuring is our vital force. Most of us experience life as a movement from high animation to inertia. In this a third factor is missing, maybe not entirely missing, for it must always be there in some measure. When it's there in greater measure then all kinds of things become possible that were not available to us previously.

> I always feel invigorated after a class, both mentally and physically. There's always a change of state. For me it has been a good week, and this session has been the cherry on the cake. That does not mean that I'm on cloud nine. I'll just leave the class in a clear state of mind.

The words *clear state of mind* give an indication of what is available when this third factor begins to play a more central role in our experience of life. It brings clarity to confusion. It also opens the heart and creates harmony.

When we spend out time rushing in the crazy pursuit of life we distract ourselves in so many ways and by being distracted we lose the measure. We do things either incompletely – nothing gets done – or excessively – we say too much, do too much. The effectiveness of our actions becomes lost because they are confused, possessing more smoke than fire. The clarity that comes from a still mind is not available to us. We either expend our energy straining after something, but after having strained, we shrink back. The real art of living is discovered in just the right word at the right time, knowing when to take the initiative and when to hold back. This is the way to conduct any business; this is power with purpose.

Connections must be made, firstly within ourselves in order to tap 'the wellspring of the good' as Marcus Aurelius expresses it. The task then is to connect with those around us. Our task is to meet the need, sensitively, appropriately, doing and saying nothing more than the situation demands, allowing the need to create the measure.

We may not rule an empire but we do have our responsibilities, and in meeting our responsibilities we do need to act effectively from a still and settled standpoint. This is power with purpose. Acting in this way is the wise thing to do, and in acting in this way you might even have more than *a good week*, you might discover a whole new vitality of body, heart and mind. Everything to be found in this book is encouraging the development of the third factor, that quiet vibrancy which is the source of the truly rational, power with purpose.

## PRACTICE

By finding stillness discover power with purpose.

STAGE SIX

# Living Beyond the Limits

> Our limits are only too obvious. We are limited creatures possessing a limited life, in touch with a limited circle of friends which we haven't time for because time is short. Our limited intelligence limits our understanding. What understanding we do possess is penned in by all the limited thinking forced on us by society. We are confined by our circumstances and the demands of others, and after we have exhausted our limited vitality we die and dissolve into dust.

It's so easy to slip into this way of thinking. Even so, all of us have had some experience of something within us that lies beyond all these apparent limitations, something to which even limited access would allow us an altogether more unlimited approach to life, allow us to meet the moment free from the usual constraints, free to act spontaneously, in accord with the need of the situation. That would give to all our limited circumstances a touch of the limitless.

Use these reflections to go beyond the usual limits.

## This Also Will Come to Pass

This is a story told me by a young woman:

> I went for a new job this week. I was determined to do well. I spent considerable time in preparing myself. This included time spent in grooming myself to perfection.

> I got there in good time. I was determined to look cool, calm and beautifully poised. It had rained heavily overnight and, as I was about to turn into the building where the interview was due to take place, a car came speeding by, caught a puddle and soaked me from head to foot. You can imagine what this did for my beautifully groomed appearance, and my poise.
>
> I staggered into the building like a drowned rat. I was disconsolate, not knowing what I could do to sort myself out in the short time before the interview. I went to the reception desk and explained my situation and the concern I felt. There was a man standing alongside me. He looked and smiled.
>
> I managed to make some repairs and went up to the interview filled with despair and dread, but as I waited to go in I spent a few moments in bringing myself to myself. 'And this also will come to pass'. I was keen to have the job, but in that moment I let the whole desire go.
>
> As I stepped into the office I saw standing behind the desk the very man I had seen in reception. He smiled. The interview went perfectly. They offered me the job.

You can imagine how this situation could have been entirely met from a sense of *despair and dread,* and possibly frustrated anger too, from the total conviction that everything that could have gone wrong had gone wrong. Apart from any sympathy her plight might have elicited from the man at the desk, you notice what made the difference: *I took a few moments in bringing myself to myself.* By doing this there is an opportunity of stepping free from those things that appear at the time to be of ultimate importance and simply offering the whole thing up to our centre of stillness of certainty. *This also will come to pass.* What doesn't come to pass is the *Silent Witness* unaffected by all the buffeting of fate. This is the source of real poise, not something that is pasted on the surface. From this still point you are free to act in the way most appropriate to the situation. From this, freedom of mind is achieved, and from freedom of mind, freedom of action is achieved. It is also of the moment. And if she hadn't got the job? Further opportunity to practise the same thing.

When you feel yourself being locked in by any of the circumstances you encounter, you don't have to walk away from them, but you do have to let them go, and, by so doing, walk free.

**PRACTICE**

Rather than being locked in by the current disaster,
discriminate between what comes to pass and what doesn't,
the source of true poise.

## Claim Nothing. Enjoy

In the story just told you notice how the man smiled. He didn't fall about, but he did see the lighter side. That wasn't her experience of course. When you are bound up in the toils of life you're not free to enjoy anything very much. It's only after that you can laugh. 'It certainly wasn't funny at the time.' How many times have we heard that said?

At the wedding I described in the previous stage, a delightful incident happened at the service. We were all waiting for the bride to enter. From where we were sitting we could see beyond the church door. Outside the bride's mother was arranging the bride's train and the bridesmaids were being manoeuvered into position. Her father then stepped forward to take the bride's arm, and just before they were about to set out, his wife slipped in ahead of them. She was elegantly dressed in her new suit and beautiful hat. When she saw us looking at her, she did a little stagger on her new high heels, blew out her cheeks in an exaggerated way and fanned herself with the order of service. She did all this to comic perfection, and all those who saw her, knew exactly how she felt. There was a ripple of laughter. Then the organ played and the solemnities began. In the midst of the ceremonies the bride became overwhelmed with tears. The congregation was gulping too, laughter and tears so close together.

The bride's mother could bring a comic touch to the proceedings because, despite all her concern and involvements, all the crises that had been met and overcome, she could see the funny side and laugh at herself. Likewise, despite the happiness she felt and the fact that she was the centre of attention, the bride could cry unashamedly. Maybe she couldn't help it. Whatever, we were glad for her. We had all come to witness a wedding, and the two who were to act on our behalf stepped forward at the appropriate time to formally sign the marriage register.

They acted on our behalf, but we had all come to witness, and that included the bride and groom. Regardless of the emotions we were all caught up in, the witness in us all was free, and it's that simple fact that made it all so enjoyable.

The fact that the *Witness* is free is a great thing to discover. It helps us to lay down the claims, the attachments, the involvements that life seems to lay upon us and to step free of claim and simply enjoy. The precept: *Claim nothing. Enjoy.* has been mentioned before. It's worth continuously bringing to mind.

**PRACTICE**

Claim nothing, enjoy.

## Peace in Action

To remain on the marriage theme for just one moment more. I've seen the photographs. There's one that stays in mind. The bride was stunningly beautiful. She designed her own dress, and it was gracefully cut in classical style. She was our bride. Her poise was perfect – that is until she started weeping in the middle of the ceremony, but even that had its own perfection.

Then came the reception and the speeches and, after the speeches, the dancing began. The photograph I have in mind was taken then. In this photograph there is a mass of dancing bodies, and in the midst, seeming to rise above all the commotion around her, is the bride, the still point in the midst of turmoil, radiating peace and happiness. If only life were always like this, utterly involved but also utterly at rest and, of course, completely happy. For those who achieve this state on a regular basis, let me assure you that for most people this isn't the usual experience. They play their parts differently, often feeling completely bound up in the ruck of life.

There's a well-known story about two renowned actors, Laurence Olivier and Dustin Hoffman, who were appearing together. Being from the 'method school' of acting Dustin Hoffman spent his time behind the scenes 'emoting'. Before plunging into his performance he paused for a moment beside Olivier. At that moment Olivier rather unkindly whispered in his ear, 'Dear boy, have you ever thought of acting?'

Unkind, because in his own way Olivier did much the same thing, but unlike Hoffman, who claimed to work from the inside out, Olivier worked from the outside in, starting with his costume and props. In his famous performance in *Richard III* he first prepared his putty nose, then his hump and his club foot, all the outer elements of the character. Only after all this did the inner take shape. Finally the process was complete, and he was ready for his 'winter of discontent'. Whether working from the inside out or the outside in, any decent actor will end up at the same centre.

Beautifully described in a book called *The Art of the Actor*, written by the French romantic actor Benoît Constant Coquelin at the end of the nineteenth century, this centre is divided into two, what he called the 'One' and the 'Two'. The 'Two' is deeply involved in the part, utterly committed to every aspect of voice and movement and all the subtle nuance of characterisation, of thought and emotion. After having covered all these areas you'd imagine that there's little left for the 'One' to achieve.

Coquelin, like Olivier, had a penchant for putty noses, inevitably, as *Cyrano de Bergerac* was written for him. He had the nose, more importantly he had the passion to play the part, but not only that, he had what he called the 'One'. If the 'Two' was about being at one with the part in every detail, the 'One' was about being at one with himself, still in the midst of action, utterly uninvolved and utterly observant. Even when completely committed to the role, centre stage, he remained the *Silent Witness* in the wings, looking on, ever observant of every inflection, every nuance. In this, he believed, lay the secret of the truly artistic performance. He called his book *The Art of the Actor*, and the 'One' was the essence of that art.

We all have our roles and some of them may have to be played passionately, but the art is lost if we neglect the *Silent Witness*. We are speaking here of the art of loving life. When there's a rise in consciousness, and with it a sense of the limits disappearing, of being more able to do things beautifully, to perfection, then be sure that a sense of the ever observant *Silent Witness* has also been discovered. This is the still point to which you must continually return.

**PRACTICE**

To find the artistic dimension to life
hold in mind the *Silent Witness*,
the still light of consciousness.

## Fools Rush In

It's a great saying: *Fools rush in where angels fear to tread.* Is it not encouraging us to be sensitive to the situation and aware of the dangers? Is it not encouraging us not to dash in without due thought? The blunderers amongst us are oblivious to such matters, oblivious to any danger. They go on regardless, saying and doing what we wouldn't dare say or do. This can be utterly infuriating but is often part of their charm. Some seem to be able to pass through the minefields of life oblivious and unscathed. But the only ones who really get away with it are the ones with disarming charm and innocence. People who, as well as being somewhat oblivious, are always good-hearted.

Having made that comment, this reflection isn't really about fools, innocent or guilty. It's about us, although we can certainly become fools if we don't give ourselves time and space. The giving of time and space may take the form of careful and considered action. It certainly involves being present, at rest and centred. You can often see sportsmen being all of these things.

One example springs to mind. It's a famous occasion in sporting history, when Arthur Ashe beat Jimmy Connors at Wimbledon. Connors was the firm favourite to win the men's singles. He had beaten everybody out of sight. He was able to hit the ball at 100 miles an hour. This was the first time Ashe had got to the finals. He had come this far, but what hope had he of winning against Connors? Ashe took his time and remained calm throughout, stroking the ball, nothing in excess. His was a beautifully understated performance. Between every set Ashe sat still, eyes closed, resting in himself. During the match, regardless of what people had previously believed, there was a growing certainty that this man was going to win. Ashe himself was certain.

The pleasure people gain from watching sport, apart from seeing their team win, is the sheer skill of it all, the physical control, the split-seconding timing, the total commitment and the utter dedication sportsmen have to the present moment. Another pleasure is to be discovered in the space sportsmen create: the space that runners open up in the closing metres of the race, the space that batsmen find with their beautifully timed strokes, the space that footballers run into to receive a brilliant pass. Sportsmen and athletes are forever trying to find space, create space and give space. Many do this internally as well as externally. This was exactly what Arthur Ashe was doing between sets, but not only between sets. In finding space he fell still and was evidently able to retain that sense of stillness and space even in the midst of the most fierce rally. By so doing he perfected the measure.

Here's another story. The trainer of one of the leading English football clubs taught the players who took the penalties, free kicks and corners to spend a moment or two connecting with their still centres before taking the shots. The team went from the bottom of the Premier League to the top in one season. The other players, enthusiastic about the success they'd achieved, were keen to adopt these techniques themselves. A day's intensive course was arranged to teach them this. However, the directors of the club, pleased at their men's performance, offered them all a week in the South of France. Inevitably the two things clashed. You can imagine which of the two the team chose.

By the time they returned, the players had forgotten all about exercises in self-awareness. The moment had passed. The next season the club went from the top of the league to the bottom. Possibly a coincidence, but there's a saying, 'go within or go without', and one can't help thinking that this story is an effective illustration of what happens when there is a failure of inner connection. The players were certainly given a wonderful holiday, but they did lose their position in the league and all the bonuses that went with it. More importantly they lost the chance of discovering something of ultimate importance about themselves.

There's always the temptation to fill every available space with activity. The space discovered in self-discovery has nothing to do with the pursuit of immediate pleasure, but it does have a lot to do with a quiet understatement, a constant matter of fact that underlies all action. To gain lasting satisfaction, make constant reference to the fundamental fact of the matter, the consciousness which sustains it. This is life lived beyond the limits.

**PRACTICE**

Rather than rushing in, turn inward.
It's there you'll discover the true measure.

## Creative Space

My wife came into my study with a pile of files. 'You'll have to do something about these. We need the space.' Now I'll have to find some space for the files to go. That means that something else will have to be thrown out. This is always a useful exercise. We seem to gather much about us in the conviction that this material will have importance at some time. I had an artist friend who was forever collecting things that he thought might be of use. These he piled up in the roof space above his studio. He constantly complained that there was stuff up there that was just what he wanted, but he could never find it. The problem was resolved for him when one day the ceiling collapsed and the whole lot came crashing down. At that point he had something of a clear out. 'You know what, William,' he said, 'I feel somehow that a weight has been lifted, and I feel so much more creative.'

The weight of all the material things we gather around us does have its effect, but much greater is all the mental junk we collect, all the little ideas and odd ways of doing things, the attitudes of mind, the peculiar little personal systems we have developed and patented, the patterns of emotion which we continually repeat, the ideas we hang onto with great tenacity. Some part of all of this has been produced with considerable care and attention, but much of it has been picked up unconsciously. What's even more fascinating about this material is that there are elements in our stock of thought and emotion that utterly contradict other elements. We talk about people being a mass of contradiction. We are all contradictory, it's just that it is more noticeable in others than it is in ourselves. Sometimes these contradictions are the result of deliberate hypocrisy, but more often it's because we haven't the clarity of mind to appreciate how we have adopted this mass of stuff, especially if we have lent to it a name: ME.

It may be useful to assess some of these things we hold dear, to look for the contradictions and attempt to rid ourselves of the more glaring examples, certainly to be conscious of their presence when they leap up and try to take complete control of the situation. Above all be amused by them.

However, what we don't want to do through this process of self-examination is to become self-obsessed. We may avoid this by turning constantly to the central factor rather than all the accretions we have added to ourselves. By so doing we are turning to space and not clutter. This space has no vested interest in sustaining itself, no desire to become something better. It just is.

People love space. They love to escape from the crowded city and discover the space of the countryside. They love to have space in their homes. They love to have spacious views. Any estate agent will tell you that a view across a river or a park will increase the value of a property enormously. Pressure subsides when space is found. Stress and all those stress-related illnesses may be cured by space. This is what medical research is continually confirming. Even a picture of a spacious scene has the effect of calming the mind and releasing pressure.

But the space we long for is with us always. The exercise of *Self Remembering* confirms this fact. Even when it doesn't appear to be too successful, it does have its effect and, as with any practice, the more it becomes part of our lives the more effective it is.

The other great thing about discovering inner space is that it brightens the mind, makes it more effective, and creative, and in discovering it for yourself you automatically give it to others. Your connection must transfer. It can't be otherwise. In finding space you give space for the benefit of all.

**PRACTICE**

Find space and give space for the benefit of all.

## Move Towards Unity

Another of the great joys of watching sport is seeing the members of a team playing as a totally integrated unit, so on top of their game that everybody is aware of what everybody else is doing. They constantly find the space and create the space. What is true of sport is true of all areas of human experience: the family, the community, the nation, humanity. When unity is discovered at any of these levels, then not only is there a new strength discovered but also an entirely different kind of awareness.

Working from this awareness can totally transform the situation. Here's a dramatic example of just this.

> It was our first night in Africa. We had parked the van just off the road south of Tangiers to get some sleep, the three of us in sleeping bags squeezed tightly into the back. Suddenly in the middle of the night I heard voices on all sides, and the door was sprung open. Two men leapt in, nervous and ready to kill. One put his

> hand into the pocket of my jacket which was flung over the front seat and found my knife. It had a long, sharp and pointed blade, and he came at us with it.
>
> I at once became extremely calm and alert, and in my rather stilted French engaged him in conversation. I managed to draw him out and discovered he had quite a tale to tell. They were not Moroccans but Algerians. They had no papers and had been in and out of jail many times in different countries. They had no money, were hungry, needed transport and were being hunted by the police.
>
> Whilst this was going on, my companions, who couldn't understand a word of this, were getting more and more restless. I muttered urgently to them not to make a move. The atmosphere was full of violence. Anything could have happened. In the end I struck a deal with the bandits. In return for some food and loose change, my boots and some clothes, they spared our lives and left us the van, our passports and traveller's cheques.

To be leapt on by desperate bandits whilst hopelessly jammed into sleeping bags in the back of a van is not a situation we would willingly encounter. Would we be able to keep our heads? It's evident from this story that by making one false move all three may very well have died. The narrator of the story was only too keenly aware of this, but despite it he was able to keep *calm and alert*. The sense of the *Observer* is so evident in this story as is the sense of being utterly in the present. In situations like this it would be hard to avoid this happening. Having said that, fear is about what might happen next and not what is happening now. In this instance everything that is being described is of the present.

What it also speaks of is unity. This is strange to say when the story concerns an attack by bandits. A more divisive situation is hard to imagine, but you'll notice from the details of the story how the narrator was working. Firstly he remained calm. From calm arises balance. He did everything he could not to disturb that balance. He warned his restless friends against any kind of sudden movement, actions that would do nothing but generate reaction, and thus disturb the balance. Instead of doing that, he communicated. As we have considered before, communion arises from union, and out of the situation fraught with division and danger, he went beyond the limits of the situation and found the common ground. He expressed a genuine interest: *he had quite a tale to tell.* By doing this his role changed. He was no longer a victim but a human being, who through his conversation created contact with fellow human beings, and this contact saved the situation for all concerned, including the bandits. They avoided having another three victims to haunt their consciences. His calm intelligence and courageous presence of mind allowed him to be totally aware of the whole situation, and in this situation he said and did nothing unnecessary. He worked from unity to establish unity. The limits gave way and allowed the bandits to take a small step beyond the confines of their thinking. They for a time rediscovered some human values, and this changed everything.

The man who told the story, although no doubt immensely relieved that they had survived their ordeal, spoke of *a kind of recognition*. Part of the reason this story was told, was to illustrate why he started his own journey of self-knowledge. The *recognition* that is being referred to in this reflection has everything to do with unity and self-awareness, and times like the one being described here can change the whole direction of a life.

**PRACTICE**

In all of life's complexities and confusions
work from unity to establish unity.

## Make the First Step

The step the man made in the previous reflection was a step towards unity. So much of human relationship is based on action and reaction. This may be a matter of petty tit for tat, but bitter revenge is also part of this, as indeed is a vendetta that may go on for generations, or bitter racial hatred that can engulf a nation.

Reason states that there is a third factor to which the source of conflict has to be referred. Within the family it is the unity of the family. Within the community it is the unity of the community. Within the nation it is the unity of the nation. Beyond that it is humanity itself, and it was in that context the man worked. The peacemakers are the ones who have within themselves a sense of this unity at every level and are free of personal interest.

> I was in those days, some years ago now, one of the last district commissioners in Malawi. I was one of the remnants of British Empire. Even now I look back at the whole situation with amusement. It was exactly as the cartoonists portrayed it, the white man with his baggy khaki shorts coming into the village, spreading out his Union Jack on the table and dispensing justice. There I was, the symbol of foreign oppression, but I never felt in danger. I was welcomed. I was considered a friend by everybody, from high government officials to the people in the villages. They knew I could be trusted. I was not open to bribery and was impartial to the arguments over land and property that I had to make judgements about. Even during the period which led up to independence those contacts were never lost.

This story was told to me some years ago by a man of obvious integrity. He was working within a system and therefore within a limit, but within that limit he was capable of conducting his responsibilities with intelligence and reason, of adhering to the highest principles.

He was blessed with a wife who made his job all the easier. She had the power to communicate with anybody, a woman who had the greatest generosity of heart, flexibility of mind and ability to see things from another's point of view. She had her principles too, but like him was blessedly free from the rigidities of mind which do nothing but create division. As such she didn't keep herself separate, but regardless of the situation she was in and the people she met, she was able to create contact, and from that contact there naturally arose understanding. Needless to say both husband

and wife had in themselves an ultimately unifying principle to which they continually referred. They didn't speak about it very much. After all they were British, but it was evident in all they did. It was their faith.

They may be considered as figures from a past era, but regardless of what era we may live in the divine principles are always available. It's our task to discover that as a fact.

It is so important to step out and make contact, if for no other reason than it's impossible to live a happy life in isolation. It's entirely just that the people in the story were highly regarded as well as happy. From a unity within themselves they stepped beyond divisions and boundaries to create unity around them. We may learn much from people like this. If ever we feel separate ourselves, or meet those who themselves live in separation, our immediate task must be to make the first step.

**PRACTICE**

If true contentment is your aim
never work in isolation.

## Beyond the Limit

We all work within limits. How could it be otherwise? We all have our limitations. Those limitations are also evident in all those we meet, but the truth of the matter is that the more we are capable of connecting with the limitless within ourselves, the more it is possible to go beyond limits of any sort, either inflicted or self-imposed. As was discovered by my friends in Africa, there is the possibility of dissolving limitation, of creating something entirely new and unexpected, but this is done from a still mind, free from agitation, entirely open to possibility.

> I am training in dance. I see a difference between learning to dance and just dancing. As soon as I start thinking I lose connection. When I just dance there is silence in myself.

The most effective limits we work within are self-imposed. These self-imposed limits are supported by the constant conversations we have with ourselves about every aspect of 'me and mine', all those things which we have taken to ourselves, claimed and somehow made our own. All of this can create within us a considerable mental quarrel and in our actions a general sense of agitation. What this observation about dance is talking about is an experience of going beyond those limits, and of discovering in the midst of physical movement *silence in myself.*

All forms of self-consideration agitate the mind. The mirror of the mind, instead of retaining its still, reflective surface, splinters the conscious light, scatters it. Self-consideration attempts to reassemble these fragments according to personal interest, preconceptions and habits of mind. Out of this fragmented picture, the individual seeks to form an identity. That is unless he is overcome by inertia, and then the fragments cloud over and may even fail to come together in any coherent way. At its worst, the sense of self-knowledge may begin to be lost entirely.

Notice that in the observation there is just the dance and nothing but the dance. This dance is accompanied not by a perpetual commentary on how well or how badly she is doing. Although I'm sure that there is a multitude of minor adjustments going on, these are done so swiftly and so economically that the *silence in myself* is not disturbed in any way. Nor is there in this any sense of self-criticism, for the simple reason that ME as a limited individual doesn't exist under these circumstances.

The dancer is left with nothing but stillness in movement. This is the joy of performance. Under these circumstances there is a heightened awareness and freedom from the usual constraints that contain our experience of life. Our task is to develop the way of thinking and feeling which allows us to experience heightened awareness, not only in exceptional circumstances, but in the seemingly mundane and everyday. We can do this by constantly returning to the *still and reflective.*

**PRACTICE**

When the limits draw in ever tighter
abandon 'me and mine'.
Become reflective instead.

## Rise to the Occasion

When the circumstances are exceptional most of us are able to rise to the occasion. The fact that the majority of us dismiss most of our lives as unexceptional has the inevitable effect of making them unexceptional. The proximity of death awakens people to this fact, and they begin to treasure what they had previously neglected.

People are deeply concerned about neglect, but the most common form of neglect is self-neglect. The kind I have in mind is not so much letting things run down physically, although this has its part to play, rather it's to do with neglecting the ultimate gift of life. Rather than doing this, become a gourmet of life, a real connoisseur. Look upon every occasion as an occasion to be risen to regardless of whether it's exceptional or mundane. The very fact that we dismiss things as mundane makes them mundane. The truth is that every moment is exceptional. There is no one moment like another, and in every moment there is a need to be met, even if it is apparently a matter of not doing, of no effort, of coming to stillness and opening ourselves to infinite possibility.

Listen to Cézanne, not only a great painter but also a carrot revolutionary:

> Right now a moment of time is fleeting by! Capture its reality in paint! To do this we must put all else out of our minds. We must become that moment, make ourselves a sensitive recording plate.
>
> Surely a single bunch of carrots painted naively just as we personally see it is worth all the endless banalities of the schools of painting.
>
> The day is coming when a single carrot freshly observed will set off a revolution.[1]

Rise to the occasion. Rise to the moment. Open your eyes and see, allowing your dimension to follow your vision. Then rather than being satisfied with a moment's perception, look again and continue to look. Return to this present moment, prepared always to meet whatever the moment is asking of you, and if the moment offers nothing seemingly great and glorious be happy with carrots. Recognise that every mundane thing has its own greatness, but only when *freshly observed*. We can only see afresh at the point of all freshness. Rise to the occasion at the time the occasion rises, now.

**PRACTICE**

Rise to the occasion at the time the occasion rises.
Don't dismiss anything as mundane.

## When?

Are we to wait for the great and glorious
or will the everyday do just as well?

There is no prize in answering this question correctly. But a few comments might be called for.

There can only be one 'when'. Cézanne states: *Right now a moment of time is fleeting by!*

From the perspective of passing time this is true. Thinking like this stresses the importance of valuing the moment, of not treating it carelessly, as if of no importance.

When, however, the moment is seen not as a moment of fleeting time but as an eternal moment, and as such beyond time altogether, then this moment is invested with all the glories of the eternal. This is unlimited in every way. The divine qualities are not only unconnected to time and therefore eternal, they are also unconnected to space and therefore spatially limitless. The great philosophies of the world have constantly restated that we carry these divine imprints within us and are therefore not bound by time and space. Looking out into the vastness of space gives us a sense of what this limitlessness is like. Looking into the infinity of the infinitely small also provides us with another indication. We can so easily live our lives as a form amidst forms and by so doing omit the infinity that exists infinitely, infinite but utterly centred in the here and now.

When the mind changes, and we begin to see things beyond what we have learned to expect, everything changes. The way we think radically affects our experience of life. Instead of seeing everything as so much division, the underlying unity within which all this division finds its final significance, is also known. When this happens we don't have to wait for the great and glorious. We may come to recognise that the everyday is itself great and glorious, that under the movement of matter, under the laws that govern that movement, even beneath the great and glorious, unity resides.

That unity is not to be discovered in the duality of past and future. It is to be known at only one time, no matter how mundane the present may appear, and to break the limits within which we operate, it's to this moment we must constantly return.

**PRACTICE**

Discover unity at no other time but now.

## True Benefit

There is that in us which is always trying to seize something for ourselves. It's almost as if we can't help it. There is a well-known feature of human psychology which has been called 'the territorial imperative'. It's about claiming land, having an almost involuntary desire to possess and protect our plot. This of course has been a motivating force throughout history and has been a major cause of almost unimaginable death and destruction. What happens on a vast scale can also have its smaller, more domestic manifestation.

> We live in a large house which has been divided into flats. Rather than dividing up the grounds, they are held in common. When

> any of the flats are sold this feature is made very clear to those moving in. Neighbours become friends and, with a degree of sensitivity, the system works well. There are some, however, who, although willing to accept the idea as an idea, when it actually comes to it are unwilling to share the gardens with others. Unreasonable as it may seem, in the minds of these people the property is really theirs; all the other people are in some way intruders.
>
> One poor woman was so afflicted by this she forced her husband, rather against his will, to move. They went from one extreme to another, buying an isolated farmhouse with its own moat. Unfortunately she became desperately lonely, and ended up having a nervous breakdown.

Working within a small circle and being unable to think outside that circle forces a constraint upon the individual. He separates himself off and the natural connection that exists amongst those who live a full and nourishing life is lost.

For example, there was a lovely moment on the final day of an England versus India cricket match. England were on top. They just had to dismiss the tail-enders. The recognised batsmen had gone, and the seventeen-year-old wicketkeeper, Parthiv Patel, came in. What hope had he got? He seemed hardly taller than the wicket, and this was only his ninth first-class match. But try as they might, the English bowlers couldn't get him out. You can imagine how frustrating this was for both the English players and the English supporters. By this player's efforts the game was drawn. When it all ended it wasn't just the Indians in the crowd who stood to applaud him off the field. As the players walked to the pavilion the English captain put his arm round him by way of congratulations. The match may have had no clear winner, but the real winner was the spirit of the game, and everybody recognised that.

This spirit is the common ground, the unifying factor that is the essence of sportsmanship. When that goes it's no longer a game. The real purpose and pleasure of it has been lost. It may take a little while for this to sink in, but when the hard tacklers and the drug takers take over, everybody leaves the stadium with a bitter taste in their mouths.

Parthive Patel's innings benefited his team. It also benefited those with a love for the game. The report in the paper not only talked about his excellent technique but also his coolness and courage. The reporter didn't say anything about the response of the English team. That was taken for granted. It's within this atmosphere that the game is played, most of the time.

Think about the benefit of your actions. By stepping out of the small circle come to recognise the nature of benefit.

**PRACTICE**

Recognise in experience that that which is of true personal benefit must be of benefit to all.

## Cultivate Wonder

There's a quote from Einstein: *A scientist without a sense of wonder is worse than a snuffed out candle.*

What is this wonder that he is talking about? Is it human curiosity, that drive which impels us to inquire into all that comes our way? This is certainly a mark of human intelligence, something that a scientist must have by necessity. The human mind is forever ferreting into things, desperate to discover how things work, exploring the essential nature of things, the laws. The human mind digs and delves, formulates and postulates, draws conclusions. What is a scientist without this curiosity? In what he said Einstein must certainly have meant all of this.

But wonder can also refer to that very special kind of emotion that is aroused when what we encounter surpasses our expectation and experience. It goes beyond the known. Our minds cannot grasp after it, much as we would like to pin it down. In some mysterious way, we know there is a vastness somewhere that is quite beyond our understanding.

*The more we know the more we come to realise how little we do know.* This or something like it has been said over and over again.

Nearing death, Newton made the comment that he had spent his life like a small boy playing in the rock pools whilst the vast ocean lay before him undiscovered. The vast ocean he referred to is the ocean of the unknown.

You could imagine that a realisation of this nature would inevitably lead a scientist to ponder the futility of his task, or at least to experience a certain sense of inadequacy. Maybe, but it certainly hasn't prevented great minds from exploring the unknown. Rather, the very sense of the unknown has always led great minds to press on with their explorations. This is the human spark we all possess.

It has always been the role of educators to encourage that spark in every possible way, to cultivate a sense of wonder. You remember the sense of wonder that the fourteen-year-old experienced in Florence. The education we offer must be full of moments like this. You can tell people about those things that appear in the text books, but you can't tell them about this. You can't tell them, but you can help them come to experience it, and when this happens it's wonderful to see.

In any event you can encourage the sense of wonder in yourself by not being frightened of the unfamiliar, the unknown. This is a wonderful world. Whilst we might hope for miracles, we fail to recognise that we are living in the midst of one, and we are part of that miracle. By looking beyond familiar limits, we cannot help but open ourselves to the wonder in everything.

**PRACTICE**

Don't dismiss the familiar.
Think again.
Look beyond the limits.

STAGE SEVEN

# The Beauty of It All

IF WE WERE EVER TO SET out to discover beauty, we wouldn't have far to go. The great thing about nature is that it is, by nature, beautiful – everything about it – and nature surrounds us everywhere.

The only thing that stands in the way of a total recognition of this obvious fact is what we put up to prevent it.

But just in the same way that, by simply giving our attention to listening and looking, hearing can be sharpened and sight made more acute, so insight can be developed to make us aware of the presence of beauty everywhere.

What must be understood is that the outer beauty of the world could not be recognised if we didn't have beauty within. One rises to meet the other, but only if what stands in between, our habits of mind, are removed. This is how insight is developed.

The reflections in this stage encourage a rise in consciousness, give us a sense of our own inner beauty and grant us the open heart which allows us to recognise and employ the creative flow of life.

## Peculiar Charm

Take time to look again. It's so easy to dismiss or take for granted. We have a way of passing through life totally unaware of the beauty of things. Think how much more perceptive you are when visiting somewhere new. You are much more alert to the peculiar charm that everything about these places possess. It's the newness of our impressions that allows us to see this.

> I remember the first time I went to New York. I really enjoyed being a naive boy from the sticks. Everything was a source of curiosity and intense pleasure. I arrived late in the evening. The whole place was humming with vitality. The buildings, the bridges, even the potholes in the road were a subject of interest. The man who was driving me stopped at Central Station, allowing me to go in one entrance and come out another. Just to walk across that wide concourse with all the people hurrying to and fro was wonderful. Everything had such vibrancy. Was London like this and I hadn't noticed? Probably not, but when I returned I checked to see. It wasn't the same, but it had its own magical qualities, which I had previously ignored.

Or what about this observation?

> I went back to Dublin the other week. I hadn't been there for five years or more. I was amazed. All you have to do is lift your eyes about five degrees, just above the shop fronts and you realise that you're living in a beautiful Georgian city. How had I lived there all that time and not noticed?

There is a saying: familiarity breeds contempt. It's not really contempt, more ignorance. We're on automatic pilot most of the time, and the obvious becomes the unnoticed. We're part of the toiling masses, head down, oblivious. Not quite oblivious. We look up occasionally to take into account a few salient details, and between these moments we feel our way about, living inside our heads, reconstructing the past or imagining the future, lost to the beauty that lies before us in the present.

> I had this idea for a project for my design students. It was related to recycling. I asked them to abandon any preconception they

> might have and put on the rubber gloves I'd supplied. I then tipped in front of them the contents of two bags of rubbish which I'd picked up in Soho the night before. 'Can you find the beauty in that?' I challenged.

It seems a strange place to begin, but remember the task wasn't to revel in rubbish but to abandon preconception and find elements of beauty in unlikely places.

And the context for this exercise? A project on recycling, a concept which of itself has its own beauty, being all about valuing rather than discarding. One very effective way of recycling our experience of life is to learn to value the peculiar charm inherent in everything rather than reserving our sense of beauty for only special and rarefied circumstances.

More precisely, what is really needed are for those habits of mind, which encourage us to ignore the inherent beauty in things, to be removed so that the golden mind sees gold in everything. This is the task, and you can start by holding the idea of beauty before the mind. Open your eyes. Look up now and consciously recognise its presence.

**PRACTICE**

Lock off past and future.
Lock onto the present.
Lock off circling thoughts.
Lock onto immediate beauty.

## Awareness of Beauty/Serenity of Mind

You may choose which comes first. You can use the practice of *Self Remembering* to cleanse the agitations of heart and mind and become open to the possibility of beauty. Alternatively you can use the awareness of beauty to bring heart and mind to a more contemplative condition. One is a natural counterpart of the other.

The serene state of mind is a golden state. The alchemists were not only intent on chemistry, turning base metal into gold, they were also intent on psychological transformation, purifying the mind, ridding it of all the dross that clings to it, allowing the divine essence to be exposed. And it's certainly true to say that when we come to see true beauty our mind is both nourished and purified.

Remember the observation of the man crossing the bridge into Victoria Station when things had literally turned to gold?

> It was a dull overcast day. I sat on the train lost in thought. Suddenly something made me look up. I was crossing the river. My view suddenly opened up. The sky was black towards the east, but the low sun was shining brilliantly, turning all the buildings gold... It was stunningly beautiful.

What do you think had happened to this man's mind under these circumstances? Notice how he perceived the day? For him the day was dull. If what is seen reflects the state of mind, what state was his mind in? His state was made more evident when he describes where his mind was: *lost in thought.* Then what happened? *My view suddenly opened up.* Immediately there is transformation. It's like a door opening or curtains being drawn back. Space is discovered, and light floods in. He sees: *brilliance, gold* and *profound beauty,* all in the only time this can be appreciated: *this present moment.* Out of this arises a new understanding about the nature of true enjoyment.

In this whole process of transformation there is another factor which he doesn't mention but which must have been there – serenity. Under these circumstances, the mind falls still. All that has been occupying him no longer exists. The dullness drops away, or it might have been the agitation, both lead to much the same thing, lack of perception. Then the reception clears.

Speaking of alchemy, these are four lines from Sonnet 33 by Shakespeare:

> *Full many a glorious morning have I seen*
> *Flatter the mountain-tops with sovereign eye,*
> *Kissing with golden face the meadow green,*
> *Gilding pale streams with heavenly alchemy.*

What effect have they? These lines are undoubtedly beautiful? But what is this beauty? From where does it come? What is the inner beauty that rises in recognition of the outer expression of beauty? What effect does beauty have? And where does it lead the mind?

**PRACTICE**

What is this beauty? From where does it come?
What is the inner beauty that rises in recognition of the outer?
What effect does beauty have? And where does it lead the mind?
Pose these questions and, having posed them once,
return to them again and again.

## Come Back to Stillness

There is at the heart of things an inner stillness and peace. It is there, as Yeats says 'at the deep heart's core', and may be found even in the midst of the city. It may exist as a dim nostalgic memory or it may be a living reality, ready to be called upon regardless of the situation. In dealing with the problems of life, stillness of mind is essential. *In peace there nothing so becomes a man as modest stillness and humility.* Then when the need arises fair nature may be disguised by hard favoured rage. What these lines from Shakespeare's *Henry V* clearly indicate is that, regardless of what the situation is demanding of us, fair nature is the essential thing, and everything else is added to it. We may *lend the eye a terrible aspect* but what lies at the heart of things remains fair, that is balanced and harmonious. To achieve balance and harmony and then to work from that is essential regardless of what life is demanding.

The prayer for peace, one of the most beautiful parts of the prayer book, has these words of wisdom contained within it: *O God, who art the author of peace and lover of concord... whose service is perfect freedom. Defend us thy humble servants in all the assaults of our enemies.* The principles of peace, of concord and freedom are inherent in us all but are only discovered when the agitations of the mind are stilled. These are *the assaults of our enemies*. When this happens, life's inherent beauty is revealed, and to act beautifully is to act in a way that is perfectly measured to the demands of the situation.

> We were in Wales with a party of schoolboys on an outdoor pursuits course. As part of the course they were set problem-solving tasks. The centre catered not only for schoolboys but also for senior managers. To see the eleven-year-olds find solutions to problems that had defeated adults was beautiful. It was beautiful because of the intelligence they showed. It was beautiful because, despite all their rumbustiousness, at moments like this they were able to fall still and fully connect with what was being demanded of them.

Stillness of mind can be discovered through beauty and vice versa. Beauty is more readily discovered by a still mind than one fraught by agitation. In addition, a mind that is capable of coming to stillness is also one that is capable of finding balance and harmony. Balance and harmony are vital, particularly amidst the 'din of the crowded streets'. This is where most of us live for most of the time, for we carry that noise and agitation into our workplaces and our homes. No wonder conflict is not unfamiliar to most of us. This is why it's so important to return to stillness of mind, to remember balance and harmony, and to look for the beauty in everything we meet. You can't always do this by fleeing the city. If you recall what Marcus Aurelius said:

> Nowhere can a man find a quieter or more untroubled retreat than in his own soul... Avail yourself often then, of this retirement, and so continually renew yourself.

He had the right idea.

### PRACTICE

Find beauty, balance and harmony by constantly returning to inner stillness.
Find inner stillness by constantly recognising the beauty that surrounds you everywhere.

## Beauty Heals

In Plato's *Symposium*, the physician philosopher, Eryximachos, says:

> Medicine must indeed be able to make the most hostile elements in the body loving and friendly towards one another. It was by means of knowing how to introduce 'Eros' and harmony in these that, as the poets say, and I also believe, our forefather Asclepios established this art of ours.[1]

This was why in the ancient Greek health resorts exposure to beauty was an essential part of the treatment. From the text above you can see why. It's a matter of using beauty to bring the mind and body back into harmony. It wasn't for nothing that before Asclepios, Apollo, the leader of the muses, was also the god of healing.

These myths have within them the understanding that harmony of body follows harmony of mind, and harmony of mind is encouraged by the appreciation of beauty. That beauty may manifest in many different ways, and people will inevitably possess their own appreciation, but without that sense of aesthetic pleasure being consciously developed in some way, both with what we see with our eyes and work upon with our minds and hands, the nourishing power of beauty will not have its effect.

> We stayed for ten days in a town in southern Spain called Carmona. This is an old Moorish walled town. It felt as if it had deep roots. There were mosques that had centuries before been converted into churches and many churches that had been built thereafter. They were all beautiful. My impression now is of them being a dark and cool refuge from the fierce sun outside. The light of the sun pierced through the stained glass, creating pools of coloured light in the gloom. The town was of course steeped in history and tradition. Many saints' days were celebrated. Part of the people's devotions was involved in preparing

> for these. This was done by thoroughly cleaning their churches, by polishing all the silver, dressing up and taking part in services and processions. In addition to the religious significance of this, the striking thing about it was people's personal involvement in the beauty of it all. This had to be nourishing for heart and mind.

This observation is most revealing in a number of ways. It's about the traditions and rituals that bind a society together, and give it its *deep roots*. These roots are not just to do with history, about your family being associated with a certain place for many generations, for these roots run right down into the subsurface of society, the inner substance. As such, they are inevitably related to the spiritual life of the community, and it is this spiritual life that gives rise to things of beauty in the first place. This spiritual life manifests itself in an ongoing celebration, celebration that not only marks the passage of the church year, but also the important moments in a person's life. In this people are continually engaged.

To 'celebrate' means to 'perform publicly in due form, to solemnize, to honour and extol'. All this has the effect of making known the inner qualities, their goodness and their beauty. If the spiritual life is strong, the beauty that is found in the spiritual realm forces its way to the surface and finds expression. When this happens it not only nourishes those immediately involved in its first creation, but it continues to nourish people for centuries after. They become part of its ongoing expression.

Plato's *Symposium* is a record of a conversation about the nature of beauty and love. It is one of the most famous of all philosophical works. It's famous because it continues to be just as valid today as it was when it was written. When we open ourselves to beauty and love we cannot help but be nourished, harmonised and healed. Just like a community, an individual who is without these features has lost something essential about himself. That has its inevitable effect. Things become soulless and disjointed. This is why it's so vital to be aware of beauty and carry things of beauty with you as a reminder. This is particularly important when you are feeling disconnected and discordant.

**PRACTICE**

Bring body and mind back into harmony
by consciously seeking beauty and harmony around you.
Carry something of beauty with you as a constant reminder.

## The Wonder of Things

> I realise that I am often far from the present and miss the beauty that is there. I don't even know where I've been when I do come into the present. I constantly have to bring myself back.

This is a familiar and oft repeated observation, describing a state which we are all familiar with. It's about living a dream whilst life slips by. There are things, however, about this observation which offer great encouragement: *I constantly have to bring myself back.* In this there is indicated an acknowledgement of the situation. Not only that, there is also a willingness to do something about it. The speaker isn't saying, 'I make the effort once in a while.' Quite the opposite. This is a continuous effort that is being made. This is how the work has to be. Another entirely encouraging element is his sure knowledge that beauty is to be found in the present alone. People speak like this because of their experience. They are not speaking theoretically.

These are the words of Monet, talking of his endeavour to paint this moment:

> Wherever I go I try to grasp the fleeting, to understand the inexpressible mystery of things, and to savour the endlessly changing spectacle of life with heightened awareness. Life takes place in the setting of a miracle, and man can derive endless joy from contemplating it.[2]

In the *endlessly changing spectacle of life* there is, according to Monet, not only the possibility of *heightened awareness*, there is joy. What he discovered was that heightened awareness and joy go together. It's impossible to experience the one without the other.

What he also discovered was that in moments like this we appreciate the miraculous nature of things. When this is discovered beauty must be there also. How else could he have painted such wonderful pictures? Wonder, beauty, miraculous nature and heightened awareness, all of these are intimately linked.

As has already been mentioned, Max Planck, one of the world's greatest scientists, has some interesting things to say about the nature of beauty and of mystery. He speaks of how science can never hope to solve the *ultimate mystery of nature*, but he did believe that science was capable of bringing us into harmony. In his estimation the more we progress with both science and art the more we are brought into harmony with nature. This is the great service that they both perform. In an interview the following was put to him:

> Goethe once said that the highest achievement to which the human mind can attain is an attitude of wonder before the elemental phenomena of nature.

And this was his remarkable reply, all the more remarkable from a man with a rational mind of immense brilliance:

> Yes, we are always being brought face to face with the irrational. Else we couldn't have faith. And if we didn't have faith but could solve every puzzle in life with an application of human reason, what an unbearable burden life would be. We should have no art and no music and no wonderment.[3]

Monet, Goethe and Planck are no materialists. They, in their different ways, have come into the immediate present and even though they claim no final understanding, they have, through their work, expressed something of the magic and the mystery and the beauty that's discovered on entering the place where wonder is known.

Our task is to do the same. By thinking materially it's so easy to see things in a material way, and by so doing we become isolated from their inherent beauty. We may glimpse some surface impression, but this isn't the same thing as the deep wonder in things that these men are speaking of.

**PRACTICE**

Find the deep wonder in things
by not dismissing the world
as something merely material.

## Beauty Without/Beauty Within

> We had a family holiday in Nice. One day it rained heavily all day. We spent the afternoon going round the shops. There was one road filled with very expensive jewellers, each one more extravagant than the last. We scurried along under the shop awnings, the adults looking through the windows in a desultory way. My two and half year old grandson, showed little interest in all this until we got to this particular shop. 'Look!' he cried. 'Isn't it beautiful.' We looked through the window, wondering what had caught his eye.
>
> 'What?'
>
> 'The fly.'

What is this sense of beauty that seems to be there from the beginning? The child's sense of beauty may not be aroused by the same thing as an adult's sense is aroused by. Some may claim that his aesthetic sense is undeveloped, but who's to say that it hasn't its validity? Some have claimed that a sense of wonder and beauty is with us from the very beginning. We've already had two observations of a child's wide-eyed wonder, and I'm sure that anybody reading this book could add many more from their own experience.

So what is this sense of beauty that we are born with, which rises within us when sensory beauty is discovered? Does beauty actually exist without the conscious acknowledgement of it from within? Can beauty ever stand by itself? What is this principle of beauty which seems to be inherent in us all, and where does it come from?

These are questions that are often asked, and rightly so, because a sense of beauty seems to be closely linked to a more profound experience of life, and it's certainly true to say that when we are more acutely aware, it's automatic that our sense of beauty is equally aroused.

> I had a climbing accident in Spain. I slipped and fell. The rope came to an end just before I hit a jutting ledge, which certainly would have killed me. I was left dangling, badly injured, waiting to be rescued. After some initial fear I experienced a great sense of calm and of beauty and the awareness that I was something far more than this body.

In life and death situations there is often a heightened sense of awareness. We are able to cut through the clouds that usually cover life as we experience it and instead discover a more vivid reality. With this inevitably comes an increased awareness of beauty.

But is beauty just to do with the sensory world?

Planck wasn't the only scientist who believed that the sense of wonder and of beauty is not experienced just by the artist. In a paper 'Science and the Beautiful' written by Planck's fellow physicist, Werner Heisenberg, an observation is given about the nature of beauty.

> The significance of the beautiful for the discovery of the true has at all times been recognised and emphasized. The Latin motto: *Simplex sigillum veri* – 'The simple is the seal of the true' – is inscribed in large letters in the physics auditorium of the University of Göttingen as an admonition to those who discover what is new; another Latin motto: *Pulchritudo splendor viritas* – 'Beauty is the splendour of truth' – can also be interpreted to mean that the researcher first recognises truth by the splendour, by the way it shines forth.[4]

There is an opinion that physicists are interested only in the physical world. This has never been true of the great physicists. It wasn't true of Planck. It certainly wasn't true of Heisenberg. In this paper he talks not so much about sensory beauty, but about the splendour that *shines forth* from true ideas. As one of the founding fathers of quantum mechanics, Heisenberg was granted insights of the greatest importance. He believed that a central part of the process of discovery was to do with a recognition that these ideas had their own inherent beauty. More than that, he recognised that we have within us an aesthetic appreciation which allows us to recognise that beauty. *Things look beautiful because the mind is beautiful.*

The fact that Heisenberg is quoting Latin mottoes to support this thought indicates that this is not a new understanding. Simplicity and beauty are at the heart of the way things are, and we are able to appreciate this because we also possess simplicity and beauty.

In the same paper he refers to a philosopher older than the Roman thinkers just quoted. He refers to ideas found in Plato's dialogue, *Phaedrus:*

> The apprehension of Ideas by the human mind is more an artistic intuiting, a half-conscious intimation, than a knowledge conveyed by the understanding. It is reminiscence of forms that were already implanted in the soul before its existence on earth. The central idea is of the Beautiful and the Good, in which the divine becomes visible and at sight of which the wings of the soul begin to grow. A passage in the *Phaedrus* expresses the following thought: the soul is awe-stricken and shudders at the sight of the beautiful, for it feels that something is evoked in it which was not imparted to it from without by the senses but has always been already laid down there in a deeply unconscious region.[5]

In this extract he refers to the idea that we bring with us the principles of truth and beauty when we enter the world. This is not so surprising, because inherent in the laws which govern this world, people time and time again have discovered the same principles. It has become a recognised way of discerning what is valid and what isn't. In this recognition there is no division of subject and object. The qualities inherent in those physical laws which science seeks to discover are the same qualities that the mind, making that discovery, possesses. At this point what are apparently two unify.

In this process we experience something else which is found in the company of Truth and Beauty and that is Unity. We feel at one in moments of heightened awareness. This is why it is possible when dangling off the end of a climbing rope to not only see beauty but also experience peace. This is the beauty of it all. By opening your mind to the possibility of beauty you allow the beauty that surrounds you to unite with the beauty within and this must bring with it a deep abiding sense of peace.

**PRACTICE**

When you see something beautiful acknowledge the beauty within and the simplicity and the truth.

Consciously serve these divine principles.

## Life Beauty

And what of the beauty that's to be discovered in the nature of people's lives? There are those who have something about them. They have a generosity of spirit, an understanding, an ability to cope with life compassionately and dispassionately. These are the wise, and they undoubtedly have their beauty.

> My grandmother laughs at how she's lost her looks and lost her figure, lost everything that makes life worth living. She can laugh because the truth is that she hasn't lost the essential thing, the thing that makes her beautiful. She hasn't lost her spirit, and it is this that makes everybody love her. You can see this spirit in what she says, more importantly in what she does, how she is.

There are the wise and then there are the rest of us. We may not be wise all of the time, but all of us do have our opportunities. We can at least be aware of the possibility. We can also recognise wisdom in others. They don't have to show it all the time or even much of the time, but when 'fair action', as Plato calls it, is shown, then it should be consciously recognised and where appropriate celebrated.

> Recently I attended a memorial service for a good friend. It was full of tremendous sadness of course, but the sadness was relieved by the way her qualities were so vividly evident. There were many there to show their respect, and all agreed that what was said about her was beautiful. It was beautiful because she was beautiful. We could feel her presence. It was tangible. Those qualities she possessed, do they die when the person dies? She was very particular, utterly herself, but when she was spoken of it became evident that she, in her own way, demonstrated qualities which we could recognise and rejoice in because we knew about them ourselves. They lived on in us.

What is evident in this observation is that when we celebrate an individual we are also celebrating the universal qualities that they possess. When this happens, those qualities cannot help but be magnified in our own lives.

At the end of the term in the school where I work we said goodbye to some of our colleagues. One was leaving to have a baby, two were retiring and one was moving on to teach in a university. It was an unusual event for us. The school was founded some years ago, and all of us have devoted considerable time and effort to realising the ideals upon which the school was founded. Because of our dedication to those ideals the turnover of staff is low. The farewell party and the giving of gifts not only gave us the opportunity of expressing our gratitude, it also gave us the opportunity of describing the qualities of the people involved. This was done with considerable humour – everybody laughed a lot – and it was of course done with great affection. We know each other well.

All of the people leaving had made their contribution and, although they were going, their legacy will live on in the work they have done in the development of the school. Some of this is evident in the form of textbooks and courses. Some of it is to do more with their contribution to the school ethos, the intangible part, which in its way is the most important part. In talking about these people it gave us an opportunity of not only assessing the quality of their contribution, it also seemed to mark a defining moment in the development of the school. We were able to stand back and experience what had been created, a thing hard to do when one is involved in all the day-to-day demands.

It was also an expression of the unity of the school. The event took place on a beautiful summer's afternoon. The school's setting, on the banks of the Thames, is also beautiful, but the real beauty was to be found expressed in this sense of unity.

It's important that there are these occasions, but what's even more important is that we recognise the good in people's lives, their own particular beauty, for in doing that we are acknowledging the same qualities in ourselves. We wouldn't recognise them if we didn't possess them. It would be quite wrong to lay any kind of personal claim, but it's utterly necessary to celebrate these qualities in others and indeed in everything.

**PRACTICE**

Go out of your way to recognise the divine qualities in people. Look out for them and, where possible, in a way that's appropriate, celebrate them.

## The Spirit of Beauty

'Ethos' is an interesting word. The dictionary states that it is 'the prevalent tone or sentiment of a people or community, the genius of an institution or system'. It might also be described as the spirit permeating it all. When a particular ethos is tuned into the divine qualities of beauty and harmony then those qualities will fill the place.

There is no doubt that places do have their atmosphere, and when warmth and affection are the presiding qualities experienced by people who live there then the place takes on that imprint.

> I remember house-hunting. We visited this old house previously owned by a couple who had recently died. It was amazing. There had been no attempt to modernise the place at all. Everything about it was old, and yet it was beautifully maintained, and the atmosphere was remarkable. It felt so clean and bright. The whole house was pervaded with peace.

It can be, however, that, because of people's conduct, qualities of an altogether different kind are encouraged.

> Friends had recently taken over a large Georgian mansion which they were going to run as an hotel. The house was beautiful and so were the grounds, but the atmosphere of the place was awful. It had previously been run as a country club, and there were all kinds of rumours as to what had been going on. There was no doubt that one of the rooms had been used for cockfighting. The evidence was still there.
>
> Our friends were working on the house with a will. This for the most part involved getting rid of all evidence of the previous owners, ripping out the nasty fireplaces and the bar furniture that had been put in, stripping off wallpaper and ripping up carpets. Above all it involved cleaning the place. Everything was being scrubbed and scrubbed again.
>
> The difference in those parts of the house that had been worked on and those in which work was still to be done was remarkable. I remember walking into a room from which everything had been stripped, thoroughly cleaned and painted white. The shutters had been partially closed. A shaft of sunlight fell across the room. It was so beautiful. It was as if the true spirit of the house was reinstating itself.

This observation begs certain questions. Is there a fundamental spirit that pervades everything? Is there something underlying the physical forms that make up the recognisable fabric of life? Can we, in what we do and what we are, magnify the fundamental thing, allow it to shine through? Can we live a life which avoids obscuring life's fundamental beauty? May we in all we do make the sense of unity and the beauty that flows from it the guiding principle of life?

The answer that this book is suggesting to all these questions is yes. And it's not just in this book that this answer is to be found. This has been the prevailing message that has been stated and restated time and again. Here is one such statement made by Sir Arthur Eddington, another scientist of the first rank:

> Our deeper feelings are not of ourselves alone, but are glimpses of a reality transcending the narrow limits of our particular consciousness – that the harmony and beauty of the face of Nature is at root, one with the gladness that transfigures the face of man.[6]

For him it is evident that harmony, beauty and joy form the fundamental substance of life.

**PRACTICE**

Don't be content with the surface impression.
Go on to find the fundamental thing.
Serve that even when it's hard to recognise.

## With Eyes Wide Open

Let us return to where we started in this stage of the book, with eyes wide open, being aware of the beauty that surrounds us everywhere.

Our task is to open ourselves to that beauty – however it might manifest – to sensory beauty of all kind: the beauty of sight, of light, form and colour; the beauty of sound, not only the harmonies of music but also the harmonies of natural sound, of wind, of rain, of the sound of running water.

> It was night by the time we got to the Lake District. As we walked to the hotel we fell silent. All we could hear was the gurgling sound of running water, everywhere. It was beautiful.

Then there is the beauty of taste. It's important to really taste our food, to develop our taste for the freshest food beautifully cooked. Take time to taste. What is true of sight, sound and taste is also true of smell and touch. Our task is to freshen up our sensory awareness in order to be really in touch with whatever the senses offer and to be prepared to give it time.

Strangely enough this is achieved not by greedily grasping after ever more sensory enjoyment, but by being measured with our senses. Have you ever been round a gallery and discovered the senses can only take so much? This is usually because we are trying to collect impressions. By so doing we often end up seeing very little. In developing our sensory awareness we must use another mode of the mind. Be still and reflective.

With stillness comes connection. We must train the mind to be in touch with the senses, in touch with the here and now, alert to the present. It's here we may discover and appreciate not only the beauty of the physical world but also the beauty of conduct, of great ideas, and through and beyond all of this, gain some insight into the nature of beauty itself. This is how in the *Symposium* Plato describes such an intuition:

> Nor will his vision of the beautiful take the form of a face, or of hands, or of anything of the flesh... but subsisting of itself and by itself in an eternal oneness, while every lovely thing partakes of it in such sort that, however much the parts may wax and wane, it will be neither more nor less, but still the same inviolable whole.[7]

I will leave you to interpret the exact meaning of this statement. It's worthy of quiet reflection. One thing's certain, this text, forming the climax of one of the most famous of all philosophical works, has provided a source of inspiration for centuries. Another thing that's certain is that it speaks of the oneness of beauty from which all beautiful things derive their quality.

By opening our eyes to the constantly changing manifestations of beauty we open our minds to the constant nature of beauty that is never subject to change. In doing this we open ourselves to the constant within, the ultimate beauty that through all the play of life ever remains unified and whole.

All we need to know in life is that *truth is beauty and beauty is truth*. That was the belief of Keats. In attempting to reappraise and renew your life by discovering something of the truth about yourself you couldn't find a better place to begin than by opening the senses, the mind and the heart to the possibility of beauty. Pass it by with a cursory glance of recognition and you pass yourself by. What you also pass by is the vitality of life as it expresses itself in all its freshness.

## PRACTICE

Recognise the beauty of life; recognise its inherent vitality.
By so doing recognise your own vitality and inherent beauty.
Greet life with eyes wide open.
Don't pass life by with only a cursory glance.

## STAGE EIGHT

# The Gift of Yourself

WHAT DOES 'the gift of yourself' really mean? Is it true that in giving we receive?

There is this impression that we are isolated beings each with our separate consciousness, that we possess life for a short time, and at the end of our time we lose this consciousness and leave this life.

As isolated creatures we are left to fend for ourselves. We acquire. We protect. We fear to lose. All this is believable but only from a separate point of view. There is, however, a problem with this way of thinking.

Experience tells us that there is no satisfaction to be had out of life when it is lived in isolation. What must be discovered is that, without making a continual offering, the happiness we seek in acquiring and possessing is an impossibility. It is only in giving that we receive anything of lasting worth.

With every gift given, no matter how small, there must be a step out of isolation towards the unity that binds us all. And the principle of love insists that a deeper connection with another involves a deeper connection with ourselves. It's only in our own depths that we discover the source of real satisfaction and lasting happiness.

Use the reflections found in this chapter to dispossess yourself of the separate state of mind. Use them to discover another way of looking at life and, by seeing differently, be different. Become who you really are, and in the process give of yourself for the benefit of all.

## What's on Offer

Rather than thinking of what benefit you can get out of a situation that is presenting itself, consider instead what you might offer. This is such a simple idea, but turning from taking to offering is a simple movement which makes all the difference to our experience of life. Taking is about duality. Offering is about unity. When we desire to take there must be me on one side and the object of my desire on the other, and it must be about getting something for myself. Compare this with offering. Inherent in any offering is a movement out from me to you. At moments like this we are joining in rather than separating out.

Here is a verse from an Emily Dickinson poem which expresses just this. It speaks of her attitude to all she meets:

*Of visitors – the fairest –*
*For occupation – This –*
*The spreading wide my narrow Hands*
*To gather paradise.*[1]

This is the open-handed approach and open-eyed, and minded, and hearted. The poem is called *I Dwell in Possibility*, appropriately enough, for all kinds of possibilities open up under these circumstances.

Here is a recognisable example of just this:

> I made a resolution to give myself to the moment and seek life in ordinary things. I tried it for the first time whilst preparing for a dinner party. The first thing I did was to turn off the radio, which I habitually turn on before doing anything in the kitchen. What I then did was to give myself to the whole process of preparing the meal. What I discovered by doing this was the vitality of colour; all the food looked beautiful, and it smelt wonderful and

> there were all these textures that I'd never noticed before. What I realised was that cooking was an art rather than a chore.

This is a perfect example of abandoning the habitual, connecting mind with the senses and entering the present. In doing this we discover a life which is vital once more and beautiful. Food cooked in this way must taste better. The next wonderful way of making the offering is caring for your guests.

There is another kind offering you can make, the offering of yourself to yourself. To do this you must *live heliotropically*. Turn ever to the inner sun of your own being. Make that the essential reference point of your thoughts and deeds. In doing this you are turning away from all the pushes and pulls of life and turning to something far simpler, far more unified. By doing this you are giving up all the plots and manipulations that are involved in creating and protecting a separate existence. All that complication is cast aside. The inward turn must by necessity make us all more intelligent, more humane and more feeling.

> The soul is like the eye: when resting upon that on which truth and being shine, the soul perceives and understands and is radiant with intelligence.

This is what Plato had to say about the matter in the *Republic*. What do you think it will rest upon when the soul perceives, understands and is radiant with intelligence? Consider the question for a moment.

In the *Phaedo* he says this:

> The soul should collect and concentrate itself in itself.[2]

What exactly do you think is involved in the collection and concentration to which he refers? This is another question worthy of thought.

Both these injunctions involve us in turning away from all those influences in our lives that pull us hither and thither, in order to return to the principle of unity in ourselves. This principle of unity is also the light of our own consciousness. Elsewhere it's called the 'Light of Wisdom' or the 'Light of Reason'. In offering ourselves to the Helios of our own soul, the subtle knots and contortions that can create such physical and emotional tensions are dissolved.

In offering yourself to that, you are giving yourself permission to shine, and when that light is given simply and cleanly to anything to which you turn your attention, what then arises must by necessity be invested with the gift of yourself.

**PRACTICE**

Allow your consciousness to rest fully and naturally
on all the situations you meet,
not half attending, but fully.
That's all.

## Count your Blessings

*Counting your blessings* has long been recommended to those *bewailing their lot*. It is also a useful task for all of us at all times. We have so much to be thankful for in so many different ways. In the act of being thankful we cannot possibly take things for granted. By taking anything for granted we ignore the value of our own experience and life's inherent beauty. To pass through life oblivious of its force and immediacy is an oversight with major consequences. To meet death with only a vague idea of what life was all about is a state verging on madness. To avoid this requires a decision to be made now. As has already been stressed, later never comes.

*As a man is so he sees.* We live in a time in which the material has been concentrated on. This forces us to see in a particular kind of way. A subtle world of ideas has been created for us in order to encourage us to think materialistically. To see outside this established framework requires a radical change of mind, to think and see quite differently.

Goethe wrote these simple and entirely logical lines:

*Were the eye not of the sun,*
*How could we behold the light?*
*If God's might and ours were not as one,*
*How could His work enchant our sight?* [3]

He believed that just as eyesight developed in response to sunlight so we have within us the power to develop insight, but only if we acknowledge the presence of our own inner light. When this develops, the inner powers – such as the power of beauty – which hide behind the surface will become just as much a reality as their outer manifestation.

Earlier in the week I had a meeting with a colleague. We meet fairly regularly and these meetings always work out in a predictable sort of way, and I always end up with this sense of irritation, which I'm sure he shares. Of late I've been trying to train my mind to be alert to beauty.

Just before the meeting was about to begin I happened to glance out of my office window. There it was, this stunning sunset. There was beauty presenting itself in a most obvious way. You'd have had to be blind not to notice. As he came in I drew his attention to it.

That short time we stood looking at the sunset made all the difference to the way that meeting went.

To live life in a far more significant way we must meet it moment by moment, recognising the possibility that life is a sacred state and all that is offered by life is a blessing. Even considering a concept of this nature theoretically, gives some idea of the difference it would make. You might begin to respect the world around you. You might be intrigued by all the wonderful intricacies of life. Wonder would not be far from you, and beauty would be close at hand.

And yet to think about it is one thing, but to practise it is another. This book is designed for practical use. Why not, therefore, count your blessings? Why not look on life as a gift? Remember and practise. And having remembered and practised continue remembering and practising.

**PRACTICE**

Look beyond the dismissive attitude to life.
See life instead as a blessing full of beauty and grace.

## Food for Thought

We all need to be nourished, and there are so many ways that this is done. Firstly we think of physical nourishment: good food, fresh and well prepared. If we had any sense we would refuse anything else. We would certainly want to serve food of this kind. When food like this is served it's not just our stomach that is filled. This food is nourishing in many ways. One way is emotionally. When we take care about the way we prepare and serve our food then this becomes obvious.

The heart of the family is at the meal table. Remember the observation about preparing food no longer being a chore when it is done with care and attention? When this is the case, something quite different happens. Food becomes invested with that care and attention. When we serve food like that we serve love. This is convenience food in the sense that through it things come together, convene and make whole. In serving our family and friends food of this kind how can we do anything but nourish? Food like this is not only convenient, it's also wholesome. It makes whole.

Inherent in this is another factor, for there is both the food itself and then there is the serving of that food. Service in itself is nourishing. Through service you honour your guests. You acknowledge their value. When value is not given or received, the individual shrivels. This is true for those who do the honouring just as much as for those who are honoured. In acknowledging another we acknowledge ourselves. This is why company is so important, good company in particular.

There is also this other word: *generously*. If we could simply make the offering in whatever way comes to us in a generous spirit; just give time, service, attention, care, willingness, love – this would be a gift indeed.

We started this consideration with food for the body, but as you can see it soon becomes evident that you can't prepare good food for the body without it also involving good food for the mind and good food for the heart. Food of this kind requires a sense of measure. Ingredients and measure are key factors in any recipe, and the quality of the ingredients and the precision of measure is essential in philosophical living just as much as in cooking.

*Measure in all things* is a philosophical maxim with a long pedigree. Measure of this kind can only be discovered in the present, and the more we are sensitive to the present need, the more exact is our sense of measure. We give only what the situation demands.

All this is food for thought, things to consider and act upon. Just as the body needs continual nourishment so does the mind. By seeking nourishment of this kind, the principles which quality nourishment constantly feeds are opened up within us. In this sense you are reading a cookbook, but cookbooks are one thing, good food is another. For the ideas found here to be kept alive they must be practised.

> I kept the ideas alive by keeping them with me. I'm on the phone a lot at the office. The reflections that seem particularly appropriate I write out on Post-it notes and attach them to the telephone. Every time the phone rings I return to the idea.

By adopting reminders like this the principles become so familiar that we are able to express them not in any self-conscious way but in a way that is utterly natural and appropriate. It has to be natural because these principles are natural to us. Food of this kind doesn't so much fill, as open up and reveal. It's about accessing the essential thing.

**PRACTICE**

Serve the best food.
Feed yourself on what is best by constantly accessing the essential thing.
And having found what is the best food for yourself, generously serve it to others.

## The Chance to Shine

All that we have been discussing in the previous reflection has everything to do with what is to be considered here. Good food for the soul nourishes by opening up the powers we all possess. That in turn allows the light of these powers to be reflected. The reflections in this book are designed to be tools to allow that to happen. They are keys which have the power to open up the energy within. This is a light derived from a still mind. This is why the fundamental practice that acts as a foundation for everything else, *Self Remembering*, is designed to bring an agitated mind, caught up in the imaginings of past and future, to rest. This is in order to achieve one thing, the return to where reality is to be found, the present.

I'm sitting besides Lake Ontario in a beautiful town called Niagra on the Lake. As the name suggests this town is built on the outfall of the River Niagra. And that's where I'm sitting, on a bench in a park looking out over the lake. It's early morning in September. The sky is clear and there is no wind. To the right of me the river is flowing. Ahead of me is a little fort which at this point marks the beginning of the United States. To the left of me is the lake. The current is gently ruffling the surface of the water. Apart from that, the water is still. The morning sun to my right is reflecting across the water brilliantly. In the quiet and stillness everything is bright. With no agitation of mind this is a most creative time. The very situation encourages the mind to fall still and be reflective. I've slipped away from the wonderful company I've been keeping over the last few days – more of this anon – just to have a little time for quiet consideration and to get on with the book. The company has been animated and most enjoyable. There's a pleasure in that, and there's a pleasure in this too.

Just as the sunlight reflects on the lake so the still mind reflects your own inner light of consciousness.

*The still mind finds happiness in everything.*
*This kingdom within is the reservoir of peace and bliss.*
*No violence can reach there.*
*Devotion is the gentle art of unity.*

SHANTANAND SARASWATI[4]

These words are true, but their truth can only be confirmed in experience, and it's experience I'm speaking of, and it can only happen now. In this I am giving myself the chance to shine. The circumstances that I find myself in beside the lake may appear to be particularly conducive, maybe they are, but regardless of our situation we must give ourselves the opportunity to spend a little time in our own company. In doing this we allow others to do the same.

There's a lovely verse from Dante's 'Paradiso'. It's about the way in all naturalness love flows into a pure soul.

*The love of God, unutterable and perfect,*
*flows into a pure soul the way that light*
*rushes into a transparent object.*
*The more love that it finds, the more it gives*
*itself; so that, as we grow clear and open,*
*The more complete the joy of loving is.*
*And the more souls who resonate together,*
*the greater the intensity of their love,*
*for, mirror-like, each soul reflects the other.*[5]

We all have pure souls. It's just a matter of slipping beneath the surface agitation to discover this fact. For this we must give ourselves time. I slip away to do just that. Although times of opportunity are not always in the most ideal of situations like the one I have written about, all times have their possibility. With affirmation of this knowledge opportunities will arise. All we need to do is respond freely. This is how light is received and given.

**PRACTICE**

Let the still mind reflect the light of consciousness,
and in stillness, act freely in this given moment.

## Expand Your Offering

> I'm happy to do something as far as other people are concerned, but only up to a point. Enough is enough, surely.

Indeed enough is enough. When true measure is discovered so is what is perfectly required. The excessive is avoided and so is too little. You can swamp people with too much love, smother your children with affection. You can smother people with too much information and become one of those people others rather regret having inquired anything of. You can even give too much attention. The truly attentive avoid cornering people with concern. People do all these things, but a little less than what's required is also much practised. It is, as ever, a matter of finding the measure, and measure is not only to do with amount but also with quality, the effectiveness, and effectiveness is to do with the source of action. To judge the effectiveness of action it's good to pose the following question: 'Is what I'm doing at present intended to open up or close down?' And whether it's one or the other is to do with the source of action, what traditional wisdom refers to as 'the emotional ground'.

In the emotional ground are to be found the primary qualities that rule our lives. This book is designed to purify the emotional ground. At the heart of this ground, layered over with all our emotional involvements, lies love. In the purifying of our emotions what happens by necessity is the revelation of love. When we inquire into the nature of the good that we do, immediately the principle of the good is brought into play.

When there is an expansion of the offering, then the motive changes and so does the direction of the intent. It's outward. With this expansion there must be contained at the heart of the action a sense of service, and with service comes a deeper penetration of the emotional ground, a stripping away of the distortions and the confines to reveal the purity of love. At one and the same time we not only serve the outer circumstances but also the inner principle. This has an effect on our whole experience of life.

The emotional ground, although found within us, is not confined to the personal. Contained in the emotional ground are the universal qualities. By stripping away the self-contained we are automatically making a move into the all embracing. This involves a turn from separation to integration. In offering the good we experience the good.

If we are uncertain as to how to expand our offering, constantly return to memory of the good in all, and if we find that too abstract a concept, remember the deeds of goodness, remember the good that's been done to you and follow the example that you've been given.

> I remember when I was a child I had this glove puppet. Its head was beautifully modelled in some kind of ceramic. I had it in my pocket, and whilst I was chasing around in the playground at school I fell over, and it smashed. I was heartbroken. There was this young teacher. I had never seen her before. She asked me what the trouble was. After I had shown her the puppet, she asked me if she could take it home with her to mend. A few days later she brought it back all glued together with bristly hair stuck on top. I'll never forget that act of kindness. I remember it vividly even though it occurred many years ago. It makes you think about your own actions, what trace they leave behind.

We must expand our offering, and we can only do that by a process of continual assessment. Consider the things you do, and what they are serving

**PRACTICE**

Constantly appeal to the good in all as a source of action.
Don't give up when what arises seems anything but good.
Instead continue to seek the good and serve the good.

## Start with the Nearest Thing to Hand

As soon as we begin to recognise the need, and as soon as we seek to serve that need, there is an immediate problem. The need is everywhere, the problems are insurmountable, so much so that it seems hardly worth making a start. In much the same vein it seems that confusion can so easily set in when the demands start to build up. When there are 101 things to do and no clear place to start, don't lose your awareness through the force of confusion and the enormity of the task. Begin instead with the nearest thing to hand. That task may not appear to be some ultimate service to humanity, but simply serving the situation presented has its effect. By doing it in the right spirit you must in your own way, in a way that you alone can do best, serve the general good.

The good as a universal power can be served in an infinite number of ways. Serving the immediate need in your own inimitable fashion may appear to be utterly personal, as indeed it is, but the action, by the nature of the dedication, becomes a genuine act of service that transcends any limited capability. By holding in mind the good of all, there will be a growing resonance. By such service is the manifestation of the Good made possible.

The great joy in this is that we don't have to wait until we imagine that we have attained, in some mysterious way, the strength or the qualification. We can begin straight away, right now, at the only time we can start anything.

The Good as an eternal principle can only exist at one time, the eternal present. By being alert to the present need and by serving that need, no matter how it might manifest, the seeming importance of the service is immaterial. The immediacy of that service and the spirit in which it is done is what's important. Putting off action until you feel more capable is not an option if action is to take place when reality occurs. There is only one time. Anything else is only an idea. You may be high-minded, noble in intent, but nothing is actually happening. Have your high aspirations, but don't use them as an excuse for not meeting the present.

Serving the present, no matter how mundane the present may appear, has a great advantage. Such service is at the right time and in the right spirit. It also has another advantage. By giving our full attention to anything, with mind connected to the senses, there is a rise in consciousness. We shake off the daze that can so easily sweep over us, obliterating the present and turning it into a waking dream, and with a rise in consciousness, comes a rise in opportunity. Our world automatically expands, and with that come benefits for all.

**PRACTICE**

Rather than serving some ultimate end,
allow the good in all to manifest
by giving yourself to the immediate thing to hand.

## Avoiding the Screen of Self-Concern

Another great thing about giving yourself to the situations you meet is that there is less time for self-concern. One of the major forms of stress is directly derived from a background of nagging anxiety about personal outcomes. When the need of the present becomes all important, stress, depression and all those other things that arise from personal concern must inevitably fade.

If we are to act effectively where must our attention rest? What happens if instead of creating a clean connection with the event before us we factor in all kinds of personal considerations, which must include a variety of emotional attitudes, often in contradiction to each other? As far as the event is concerned, have these any importance?

These are questions worth asking of yourself. They apply to individual, self-contained events, but as events are rarely self-contained, and instead tumble over each other, they may also apply to whole periods of our lives. Emotional attitudes once adopted can even become indelibly imprinted on our psyches and affect the whole life, for with emotional colouring of this sort everything becomes infected.

Needless to say none of this is of the present, and yet it may have a dramatic effect on all we touch.

> A day in the city has its effects, of that there is no doubt. This is my working environment. The job seems to demand a certain response. There's a charge in the system. Where I work it's fierce and competitive. What effect does this have on my home life? That's a question I'd rather not answer. In my quieter moments I can see what effect it's having, but whilst it's running I can't seem to see it at all.

This is the working out of stress. In this observation you can see that it's not just the individual who is affected. He talks firstly about the working environment, and then he goes on to talk about his home life. Once having embraced a particular mode of conduct he has no choice but to pass it on. Conduct like this is the product of self-concern. His working environment seems to be demanding it of him, but even if this is true, his home life certainly isn't. In quieter moments there is observation, *but whilst it's running I can't seem to see it at all.*

There are two major factors that help us play our parts beautifully. One factor relates to our skills and aptitudes but, directly affecting that are all the thoughts we entertain about ourselves: what we are, what we are not, what we like and dislike, how good we are or how inadequate we believe ourselves to be, what kind of person we think we are. These are all distractions that interfere with the simple act of giving our attention to what the present need is asking of us.

**PRACTICE**

When a screen of personal concern is obscuring the issue,
recognise it for what it is,
nothing that has anything to do with reality.

## The Creative Approach

By adopting a life-offering rather than a life-acquiring approach we must become more creative. When you look around at the creation, within the midst of which we live, you will notice certain key features. We have already considered its obvious beauty, but what about its harmony? Whenever nature's balance is disturbed there is that in it which constantly strives to re-establish harmony. Having considered that, then what about its effectiveness, its efficiency, the coexistence of all its variety, the total intelligence of it all? Above all, consider what would happen if life were to stop making its continual offering.

The suggestion in all this is that if we seek to be truly creative we must be utterly practical, utterly effective in the service of a clear purpose and, above all, generous. We are, each in our own way, part of the creative act. By consciously recognising this fact, by allowing there to be no division between ourselves and the flow of creation, there would be far more possibility of effectiveness, efficiency, co-operation and intelligence. Attempting to live in a way that is unnatural must also have its effect.

To be truly creative we must be aware of the true need, the practical purpose, the perfect fit. This applies at every level.

I was speaking to a friend who is a research fellow in design at the Royal College of Art. His particular focus is creativity and innovation. I asked him how he judged the quality of the students projects and the commercial work he supervises. This was his interesting response.

> There's no doubt that the work produced has to serve a clearly identifiable need and this isn't just physical. It must also have a cultural, emotional and spiritual purpose as well.

It's self-evident that a product without a practical purpose is of little value. This may be readily recognised, but he doesn't stop there. He encourages his students to consider the emotional, cultural and spiritual aspects of their designs. How do you begin to assess the merits of these? And what about works of art that seem to have no practical value whatsoever, what about what is known as 'fine art'? Not practical, this work only serves an emotional, cultural or spiritual purpose.

We may begin to judge these works by the fact that they seem to have a sense of vitality about them or a kind of resonance that gives them a directness that is hard to resist. What often makes the difference is the place from which the artist is coming.

It might even be that two pieces of work are almost identical, and yet there is a difference. Standing before one is not the same as standing in front of the other. Over and above any differences in form, the thing that makes all the difference is the intention behind the work. When the intention is true, the action arises not out of some narrow desire or self-regard but from a simple love of the thing being created. When self-regard is the key factor, our actions and the product of our actions cannot be free but must work within the confines of our self-imposed motives. The steps towards life renewal always involve breaking the boundaries of self-regard.

> Something that's done just for the love of it carries a wonderful quality. When you see this in a work of art it seems as if the artist has joined the joy of creation. The poet, Kathleen Raine, said that beauty is the real aspect of things when you see it truly with the eyes of love. Her words are an example of the very thing she is talking about. It is a beautiful expression of a beautiful understanding.[6]

A creative act that is utterly complete and open-hearted has the power to open the hearts of others, to enable them to discover in the process more about themselves and how to make their own contribution. This is true of painting and poetry. It is also true of industrial design, and it's true of things in general.

**PRACTICE**

To connect with the truly creative,
be sure, in any situation, to adopt
the life-offering
rather than the life-acquiring approach.

## The Grace of Life

Creativity is to do with the outward thrust of life. An idea arises out of 'thin air' and through the creative process it reaches its full manifestation.

What is interesting about this outward thrust is that the more potent that thrust, the more beautiful it is. The more beautiful it is, the more penetrating becomes our gaze. The more penetrating our outward gaze becomes, the deeper becomes the inward turn.

We have already looked at the creative process elsewhere, but I would like to consider it further in the context of the *gift of yourself*. Shakespeare is not careless with words. He does say what he means. When he talks about the creative act he calls it a *fine frenzy*, but what does he mean by the word frenzy? We know that frenzy is a kind of insanity, but the frenzy he is talking about is *fine frenzy*. The fine does not engross, quite the opposite. It raises the soul. This is a divine madness that he's speaking of. Socrates was quite clear when he stated that it was only the divinely inspired poets who were allowed to enter the temple. Those who relied on numbers alone were not let in. Grace is our topic, and inspiration of this kind is undoubtedly an act of grace, but you have to put yourself in the way of grace. In the same speech Shakespeare talks of correspondence, the relationship, in his terms of *heaven* and *earth*. Grace is also to do with that correspondence.

*Earth* is this world with all its forms, physical and subtle. *Heaven* is the *Intelligible Realm* as Platonists call it. It's the realm of the divine principles. But what are these divine principles? There are a number that Shakespeare refers to, but one more than any other – Love. In his terms love is not a casual and transient emotion. It is a divine power that is to be sought after in all circumstances. We must be ready to recognise its manifestation and honour its presence. By being ever alert to the way love shows itself, by constantly praising its presence, we cannot help but become lovers ourselves, open and unselfish, and as such we create the correspondence and our own contribution to the way that love shows this. This is an act of grace.

As we considered earlier, according to ancient wisdom, love lies at the heart of the emotional ground. Everything we express emotionally is either a manifestation of that love or a covering of it. But even so, the covering, whatever it might be, is still empowered by the essential thing. That's why every emotional response provides us all with the opportunity of tracing that movement back to its source, that place where there is no motion. Only the still depths of love.

> I remember a question I often asked myself about concerts I went to. 'What is the difference between a good performance and an inspired one?' Certainly the good created satisfaction at its level. The inspired one conducted me to a different place. What enabled that person to perform like that? What were they reaching within themselves that enabled them to touch us, the audience, so deeply? Was there some kind of generosity that communicated itself so readily? Certainly listening to music of that kind had the immediate effect of lifting the spirits, of enabling one to engage more completely with life.

When Cézanne says that *out there* as a constant backdrop to the landscape he is painting is the realm of *light and love*, this isn't something material he is witnessing. Even though he describes it in terms of the observer on one side and the object of observation on the other, *out there* is also within here. At moments like this there is no division, no separation.

We were discussing these matters recently when somebody in the group made this comment:

> My immediate experience is of a dissolving, as if all the forms, not just the people and things around me, but also the inner

> forms seem to dissolve, and although I'm here, seemingly separate, my immediate experience is one of unity.

When this happens the happiness it generates makes it seem very much like an act of grace. It is in fact a gift, the gift of ourselves to ourselves. In moments like this the gift is complete and nothing stands between us and ourselves, no petty consideration, no idle concern. There is only the luminous present and the luminous presence of our own self. This is the grace we all possess when we are prepared to make the offering.

This experience will become ever more possible when we become alive to life, life in all its beauty and striking vibrancy. The happiness that we all yearn for can only become a reality for us when we consciously turn our minds to life's intrinsic power, and this is *our* life and *our* power that is being spoken of.

Life is an elusive phenomenon. We can certainly identify its presence, but to come to a satisfactory definition of exactly what it is, that's another matter. Life is described as being sacred, meaning that for some life is more spiritual than material. To look upon all the physical manifestations of life as the expression of something sacred opens up the possibility of seeing beyond the immediate forms, connecting instead with the underlying light and love which Cézanne experienced, or *the sacredness of all living things* as Matisse described it.

This is the grace of beauty, love and joy. This is the grace of life itself. Regardless of what we might meet in life, it's undoubtedly true to say that grace is far more likely to visit us if we act out of the recognition of beauty, love and joy.

## PRACTICE

Think of life not so much as something material but as an act of grace.

## See Beauty. Give Love. Experience Joy.

The three Graces have often been used as a subject for art, so much so that no self-respecting artist would now dare touch such a threadbare theme. Even so the Graces still retain their power: three beautiful women dancing with utter composure, both inwardly absorbed and yet outwardly expressing what they symbolise to me: beauty love and joy. Although to me each of the Graces represents one of these in particular, the three naturally flow into one another. Look at Botticelli's famous representation of them in his *Primavera* and you' ll see what I mean. What is undoubtedly true is that when we experience the beauty, we can't help but experience love for the thing we found beautiful. This in itself generates its own immediate happiness. It was during the Renaissance that the Graces gave of themselves to the full. Then the artists understood their true meaning. Ficino, the great Florentine philosopher, has already been quoted in this book. Here he is speaking again:

> This divine power of beauty stirs desire for itself in all things: and that is love. The world that was originally drawn out of God is thus drawn back to God; there is a continual attraction between them – from God to the world, and from the world to God – moving as it were in a circle. This circle is said to display three qualities: beginning in God, it is beauty; passing into the world, it is love; and returning to unite the creation with the creator, it is bliss... God is the beauty that all things desire: by this their longing was kindled, and in their possession of it they will be content. Here the ardour of all lovers come to rest, not because it is spent, but because it is fulfilled.[7]

In simple terms, there is, in the present moment, the possibility of not only witnessing the outward thrust, the moment of manifestation, but also the return. This movement doesn't happen in sequence. It happens all at once. When beauty is witnessed, love is experienced. This happens because your own inherent beauty cannot help but rise in sympathy, and this of course is a great joy. The

Graces appear as separate experiences, but in truth for me they are three expressions of the one consciousness that links us all. By continually returning in the present to our own essential consciousness, we cannot help but experience beauty, love and joy. Likewise, when in thoughts and deeds we serve any of these graces, we cannot help but allow there to be a rise in consciousness. This isn't experienced in sequence, but all at once right now.

If none of these come readily within your experience, don't dismiss your life as nothing out of the ordinary. Look again. Force your way past all the obstacles of heart and mind that impede the gift of yourself to yourself at the only time that's possible, the only time that you exist: here, now, in the fullness of this moment.

**PRACTICE**

Constantly and consciously return to the present
and see beauty, give love and experience joy.

STAGE NINE

# Timeless Moments

It's so easy to live a boring, humdrum existence. It requires no special effort. All that it needs is for us to stick with the habitual, and make no attempt to open our minds to what lies beyond; certainly make no attempt to savour the joy of life, to appreciate its potent simplicity, its fullness and depth.

Such a way of living is easy but unsatisfying. What encourages dissatisfaction is the memory that we all carry of something beyond the usual experience, a place where we might get in touch with our true vitality and certain happiness.

In timeless moments we discover ourselves. These timeless moments speak of knowledge, consciousness and bliss, the eternal powers, and we, being born into the framework of time, can only come to experience them in timeless moments.

There's only one time to experience these timeless moments, full of the potency of these powers. Now. Don't give up on the present. Constantly go back to where you might meet what all truly desire. Use these reflections to strengthen that resolve.

## Every Moment is Special

Every moment is special because it has its own particular beauty. This is the message that has already been stated. What has also been said is that the only time to discover this fact is when the moment takes place. Likewise the only time to discover the moment's own special energy is at the time that energy manifests. For both these reasons we need to be alert.

> Men who are foolish and ignorant are careless and never watchful; the man who lives in watchfulness considers it his greatest joy.[1]

This is what the Buddha had to say about the matter. For watchfulness to take place we must work towards a continual return to the point of attention and, at this point, to have in mind not only the object of observation but also the *Silent Witness* who throws light onto every situation. When the Buddha talks about watchfulness he is talking about a continual act of *Self Remembering*.

The conscious core that illuminates all we experience is the essential thing. Everything else is passing and peripheral. For higher states of consciousness to be achieved, recourse to consciousness must be our continual practice. Without this we will be sucked into the experiences that rise before the mind, and constantly seek to identify with those experiences – not only self-identification but also satisfaction. Our habitual modes of thinking will inevitably take this present experience and relate it back to the time those habits of mind first arose, in the past. This is all automatic unless a conscious impulse is put in, followed by consistent practice. The practice is to continuously refer things not to some sense of personal identity derived from the past, but to the *Silent Witness*, which is ever watchful and utterly of the present. Things can never become mundane when this takes place, never routine, because they are consciously lit in the conscious present. Out of this arises an entirely different and revitalised experience of life. This is why the Buddha states that *the man who lives in watchfulness considers it his greatest joy*.

There is something more to be said about the word 'mundane'. It has come to mean 'dull and routine', but originally it meant 'of this world, worldly, earthbound'. A mundane experience of life has no spiritual dimension. It cannot break through into the brilliance of the present, into the timeless moment that is the present. By treating our experience as mundane that's what it must remain.

Yet still there is grace, and whatever the modes of thinking and feeling we have adopted, the present and all the eternal powers cannot help but on occasion make their presence felt, however our habits of thought might confine them. We would die of despair otherwise. Our task is to connect with these powers in order to open up new possibilities, live life afresh revitalised by the source of all vitality.

There are those who are satisfied with life. They justify to themselves habits of mind which allow them to dream their life away. There are those who are miserable with what life offers. For them, strangely enough, it can be easier, for the simple reason that their dissatisfaction gives them a greater desire to break the mould.

> I've long had this habit of daydreaming. I've justified it on the grounds that it is creative thinking, but over the last year there has been an ever growing sense of dissatisfaction. Now I am more observant about how my mind works. What I have come to realise is that when I indulge myself in this way, my mind doesn't become more creative but quite the opposite. Now I am certain that any connection with brightness and perception can only take place by abandoning what I previously encouraged. Now, not only am I more awake, I am more content.

**PRACTICE**

Bring a sense of connection to all you do.
Stand back and be watchful
not only of the things that are outside yourself,
but also be observant of patterns of thought and emotion.

## With the Limitless in Mind

> I arrived in Miami to visit my son who is at university there. I was really looking forward to spending some time with him, but he was waiting at the airport with the devastating news that my father had just died in his house in Tahiti. I was shattered. I was

> for a moment utterly incapable of anything. Then suddenly everything changed. I faced the situation directly and acted. In what seemed a very short time phone calls had been made, arrangements changed and we were on a connecting flight to Tahiti. Within hours I was in my father's room. He was still in the chair where he'd died. His house is up a mountain overlooking the sea. He'd left instructions to his servants that if they found him dead he was to be turned to the window that faced the sea. That's where we found him.
>
> Throughout all this there was utter clarity of mind. He loved the sea, and that great expanse of the sea was what was present in the room.
>
> The rest of the family arrived during the day. They live much closer, but as chance would have it my son and I arrived first.
>
> As is the local custom we sat with him throughout the night. I loved my father deeply, and of course there was sorrow, but I was also profoundly grateful that things worked out in the way they did.

The sense of vastness that is evident at birth and death is an indication of an altogether different dimension to life. The vastness intrudes, and by being unflinching in the face of that vastness, by refusing to turn away from what the present is offering, we come within the presence of something that far transcends the limits within which we normally operate. These are the timeless moments, and this is the time for understanding. Our task in the whole process of self-development is to face each moment as a timeless moment and play out our part in life in the memory of the vastness that lies beyond the limits of our usual perception. This vastness may appear to be far from comforting when it bursts through the comfortable parameters of life as we know it, but when we face it with courage we will discover that what appears to be an emptiness is in fact a fullness, a great sea of love and joy. By facing these exceptional moments we may arrive at a far deeper understanding of life. However by turning away into some sense of the past and future and all the associated emotions that are to be found there, we can never experience anything more than a dream of the event. This goes for the exceptional moments. It goes for every moment.

One thing you might derive from this story is the knowledge that when you face the present you do the right thing. The woman who told the story on hearing of her father's death was faced with a choice – go to pieces or face the situation and act decisively. She chose to do the latter. By doing that she counted herself lucky. We say that, but it isn't luck at all. It's the result of fully facing the present with presence of mind and acting decisively in a way that is entirely appropriate to the present need.

She went on to tell how in the time shortly before his death her father did a number of interesting things. He visited her in London in order to settle some outstanding issues that were disturbing the family. He then sorted out his financial affairs, flew back to Tahiti and then on to another island where he had his ocean-going yacht moored, sailed it for a few days, and after bringing it back into port he gave instructions for it to be sold. He then returned to Tahiti and died, and even in death he was utterly clear. Why else did he leave instructions that he should be turned to face the sea? All this speaks of perfect timing, of facing the moment unflinchingly. The fact that he asked to be left facing the vast ocean also speaks of how he met that moment. It's good to meet death with the limitless in mind.

**PRACTICE**

Meet the moment with the limitless in mind.

## How to Hide What You Really Know

The whole realm of preconception covers practically every aspect of our lives. We come to the present with our ideas intact. We believe this to be our knowledge. We have built it up over years and invested our own identity in it. Experience is a valuable thing, especially if we manage to learn something from that experience, but if we claim that knowledge and make it our own, then the protection we put around it makes it almost impossible to use freely and appropriately in meeting the present need. It may even have the effect of becoming false knowledge in that it completely covers the knowledge that really exists in the situation.

> I am responsible for an international committee. It is one of several dealing with different aspects of an overall issue. Although all the committees should be working towards a common end, they sometimes forget this and allow narrower interests to take over. Rivalries develop over specific issues and heated exchanges sometimes occur.
>
> In one such exchange I remembered to apply 'Not this. Not this'. This was the first time I had applied the technique and the result was unexpected and impressive. I was immediately able to step back and disengage from the argument. The heat was taken out of the situation, and I was able to be more objective and effective.

In situations like the one described, what is being said Not this to are the emotional involvements that he is about to be locked into. Notice what takes its place: *I was able to be more objective and effective.* This effective knowledge doesn't involve the abandoning of the work you have made in preparation for the meeting. It does enable you, however, to transcend the preconceived and personal. This involves looking afresh and connecting with the knowledge that actually exists in this utterly original situation, and this includes all the negative emotion that is flying around the table. This is pure pragmatism informed by perfect ideals, true knowledge in action.

Making up your mind before you begin obliterates all this. Even more effective in shutting a situation down are emotional attitudes, particularly those of a negative nature. Here's an example of just this.

> My husband has a front door key and yet every evening when he comes home he insists on ringing the bell. This always annoys

> me. I've got into the habit of meeting him with this minor irritation in mind. The other day when this happened as usual 'Not this' came to mind. I could feel this little knot dissolving. When I went to the door I just met him. It was quite different. We spent a lovely evening together.

This is a simple enough observation, but the effect of attitudes of mind like this cannot be underestimated. An attitude like this can drive a wedge between people, prevent there ever being a proper meeting. Marriage takes place in the present. We think that we know what marriage is, but marriage in the sense of people coming together and uniting is not what is often experienced. It's not experienced because we are not there to experience it, not in truth, for the whole thing is filtered through a veil of preconceived thought and emotion.

Negative emotion not only limits possibility, it also debilitates. The consciousness that is available under these circumstances is severely limited. To be open-minded and open-hearted one must come into the present. In this we have no choice. In the moment possibilities open up. The greatest possibility the present has to offer is the transcending of the limits we have placed upon ourselves through years of habit, and to meet ourselves beyond these limits. These are the timeless moments. In entering these moments we discover what we know in reality. This includes love, an eternal principle and a vital ingredient of marriage.

**PRACTICE**

Stop hiding what you really know
by observing the mechanism that makes you do this.

## What's Presently on Offer?

When we experience great moments in our lives we carry them with us. They become the essential part of our experience of life. We look upon them as the high points. These times might be times of intense happiness or of great understanding or of an overwhelming sense of unity and peace. There is no doubt that these times are of the greatest importance, as they offer an indication of what, with consistent effort, may be achieved, and show us why it is important not to encourage those habits of heart and mind that lead to an increasingly confined experience of life. They indicate what is to be discovered in timeless moments. They are certainly never experienced except in the present. There is a danger about these times, however. They can breed dissatisfaction. Nothing else matches up. We start to blame our circumstances for not providing us with what we once possessed. We become restless and are unable to settle, to properly meet those circumstances which are ours alone to meet, to properly discharge our responsibilities, or create true and lasting relationships. We are forever measuring what is presently on offer against what was once experienced, concerned by the fact that what's on offer now doesn't really compare with what was once known.

> I was walking down a street one evening when I heard this music coming from a Sikh temple. It had such a profound effect on me that I decided there and then to become a convert. Many years have passed and I have devoted myself assiduously to my religion, but nothing has matched what I knew then. I'm starting to wonder if I've been wasting my time, and the whole thing's been a big mistake.

It is a waste of time if we are forever dreaming about what once was. If the present and all its needs are our total concern then how can life be a waste?

Another great area of regret can often be created by our relationships. Under the force of love people are propelled with such force into the present that suddenly the world is experienced in an entirely new way. Popular music has taken this as a theme for centuries, from Ben Jonson's poem 'To Celia':

*Drink to me only with thine eyes;*
*And I will pledge with mine:*

*Or leave a kiss but in the cup*
*And I'll not look for wine.*
*The thirst that from the soul doth rise*
*Doth ask a drink divine;*
*But might I of Jove's nectar sup,*
*I would not change for thine.*[2]

to Lerner & Lowe's 'On the Street Where You Live' from *My Fair Lady*:

*... all at once am I several stories high*
*Knowing I'm on the street where you live.*[3]

And on and on...

We must be grateful for this, and we must be grateful that we can be part of it, that we're all open to love. What we mustn't do, however, is to compare what we are currently experiencing with what we once knew.

*... one phantom figure*
*Remains on that slope, as when that night*
*Saw us alight.*

*I look and see it there, shrinking, shrinking,*
*I look back at it amid the rain*
*For the very last time; for my sand is sinking,*
*And I shall traverse old love's domain*
*Never again.*

THOMAS HARDY, 'At Castle Boterel'[4]

It's impossible to grasp after past happiness, past knowledge, past joy. Our opportunity is presented in the present. To fulfil our duties and responsibilities, to really explore the role that we alone have the opportunity of playing to perfection we mustn't meet the moment with a sense of regret. Trying to relive the past is at best a bitter sweet experience, at worse something much worse. Bring the mind back constantly to what the moment is offering. Touch that; taste that; meet that with generosity of spirit. It's impossible to recreate past experience, but it is possible to enter the world that those great times allowed you to enter. Events change; time moves on, but the eternal principles remain constant, true and ever the same. By bringing the mind back to those principles at the time when they manifest, all kinds of possibilities open up.

> We managed to get out of Iran with something, not what we had but with something. What we didn't have were our family and friends, that whole network which gives significance to life was no longer available to us nor were all those things that had created life as we had known it. This was far more important than any of the money we might have got out. This was our life, and now it had gone. But it's no good living burdened by regret. We had seen others do that. You must work with what's on offer and work with that. That's what we've done and in the process achieved far more than we ever imagined when we first arrived.

**PRACTICE**

Trying to grasp after what's gone
is a sure way of missing out on what's currently on offer.
Accept the present and work with that, regardless.

## Beauty, Love and Joy

So what is it that is to be discovered here in the present? What is to be discovered in these timeless moments? What are these eternal principles that manifest at this time only?

They have gone by many names. In the Vedic tradition they are *sat*, *chit* and *ananda*: Being, Consciousness and Bliss. In the Platonic tradition they are called the Beautiful and the Good. All speak of the Truth. Truth manifests in many ways. Directly rising from Truth are the virtues: Faith, Hope, Charity, Justice, Prudence,

Temperance and Fortitude. The first three are the Christian virtues, the last four the Platonic. They all in the end return to the essence of Love. This was certainly the belief of St Paul:

> And now abideth faith, hope and charity, these three; but the greatest of these is charity.[5]

In Psalm 85 the meeting with the timeless is described in this way:

> Mercy and truth are met together; righteousness and peace have kissed each other.
>
> Truth shall spring out of the earth; and righteousness shall look down from heaven.[6]

The Buddha was quite certain that as a result of living in the presence of the eternal, life would be transformed:

> *O let us live in joy, in love amongst those who hate!*
> *Among men who hate, let us live in love.*
> *O let us live in health amongst those who are ill!*
> *Among men who are ill, let us live in health.*
> *O let us live in joy, in peace amongst those who struggle!*
> *Among men who struggle, let us live in peace.*[7]

This is not an idle wish on his part. He is describing what the eternal present is like.

In the Upanishads there is this prayer:

> *Lead me from the unreal to the Real*
> *Lead me from darkness to Light*
> *Lead me from death to Immortality.*[8]

These are all great statements of Truth. They describe the desire to make the move out of the shifting and partial experience of life into the vital present. They describe things as they are when all the confines that we have placed upon the mind have dropped away and reality is revealed. St Paul expresses it like this in Corinthians chapter 13 verse 1:

> For now we see through a glass, darkly; but then face to face: now I know in part; but then shall I know as also I am known.

We may live in a situation that is far from perfect. We may be facing turmoil in our lives. The happiness that we once knew may appear to be taken from us. But regardless of our situation, this is the present; this is our moment of truth. Our understanding may be partial, but the present is our only opportunity and to this moment we must constantly return rather than adopting those habits of heart and mind that can do nothing but separate us from the vital principles of beauty, love and joy, the eternal within us.

**PRACTICE**

The eternal is to be discovered now.
Constantly bring the mind back to the time
of Beauty, Love and Joy.

## Find Time

When we begin to submit to the universal powers within us, we cannot help but be empowered by their presence for the good of all. Find time to discover them. *Self Remembering* provides the means.

It may be worth reminding you once more of the practical nature of this book. It is designed as a reference tool. It is designed to both encourage and inspire.

To encourage you to do what? To inspire you to do what?

To practise.

Time can be whipped away from us and life pass in a dream. We can be so desperate to press on to the next deadline that when we look back we wonder where we have been. This is what happens when we are ruled by time rather than coming under the power of the present. For there to be a change of experience we must adopt a practical approach. We must use this book and all that it recommends. You could carry its little companion volume, *New Life*, with you as a reminder. Go back to it constantly. Hold the reflections in mind. Work with them. The practices that are to be found in this book are all designed to settle the mind and draw you back to the present.

Every time you find that you are wrestling with problems, wrestling with events, step back from the point of tension.

> I am an engineer, and I have a reputation for problem solving. I get those projects that others have wrestled with and failed to crack. It may take a week or two but finally I find my way round it, whatever the problem might be.
>
> I often work on the sofa. I start by letting all the tensions go, physical and subtle. I dismiss all past and future concerns. I just allow the mind to come to stillness, deep stillness so there's hardly a ripple. Then I hold the problem in mind. I patiently feel my way all round it and look at it from every angle. Doing it as a purely mental exercise is a good discipline. I can't allow my mind to drift. The only way it's possible is to be utterly attentive and utterly single-minded. I can't think about what I'm doing later or what I was doing earlier. I have to rest in the present. It wouldn't be like that if I had it up on the computer screen.
>
> Every time I find my mind beginning to wrestle, and elements of frustration entering the situation, I just let go. Wrestling and frustration have got everything to do with my desire to solve the problem and nothing to do with the problem itself. They have everything to do with the future and nothing to do with the present. When this happens all that it does is to create a screen of interference between the mind and the problem.

This is a story of somebody who finds time on a regular basis. People might imagine that he's taking time. In fact he's finding that time where the present exists. That's where he works. In his method of work he makes certain that it couldn't be otherwise. This is a very fine point in time, and it requires single-pointed attention to enter that precise place. When agitation of mind exists that point is constantly being disturbed by desire and frustration. It has everything to do with our success. When heaviness and lethargy rule, the mind is constantly being drawn back into a dream. It wanders from one idle thought to another, lacking the energy to break free, but regardless of what state we are in, the task is always the same, to return to the present.

I was talking recently to a film-maker, and he was telling me about a documentary he had made about a free climber, a mountaineer who uses no ropes.

> The BBC wanted something really macho, but when it came to it the film turned out quite differently and to my mind was far more interesting. Of course there was the climb itself. Getting the cameras in position proved to be something of a technical feat, but the real centre of the film was the philosophy of the climber, the way he prepares himself. He takes time and is utterly meticulous. He works very quietly and is completely attentive to every feature of the climb. 'When I climb there needs to be no separation between me and the rock. It has to be inside me.'
>
> I learnt so much just being there in his company.

What he learnt of course was that the same thing applies to free climbing that applies to free film-making. What we need to learn is that it also applies to all aspects of life.

If lethargy rules it may be necessary to break out through action, but action can only be refined through reflection, and that's what this book is designed to encourage. When the mind falls still in the present, the divine powers are reflected in the mind. These powers do not come to visit us. They arise from within us. In the practice of *Self Remembering* we are discovering about the essential part of ourselves, the home of these powers.

**PRACTICE**

Step free from lethargy.
Bring the agitated mind to stillness
and by reflection expose yourself
to your own divine powers.

## Look Out. Look In.

You'll notice that the two observations in the last reflection had much in common. Both men took their time to come to rest in the present. They also had another feature in common. They both gave their complete attention to the task in hand and took the problem within them. This of course is unavoidable, whatever the problem might be, but by breaking down the separation, they recognised this consciously. *I just allow the mind to come to stillness, deep stillness so there's hardly a ripple. Then I hold the problem in mind.* When the mind becomes really still not only is the object of attention known but also the *Silent Witness*. The *Silent Witness* and the light of consciousness are one and the same. By dropping identification with the objects of attention this sense of consciousness becomes an increasing presence. What also becomes an increasing presence is a sense of unity. *'When I climb there needs to be no separation between me and the rock. It has to be inside me.'*

Under these circumstances we no longer find ourselves separated out, with so-called subjective on one side and so-called objective on another. By coming to a deeper understanding of the objects of knowledge we gain a deeper appreciation of ourselves.

These are the words of Planck speaking in general terms but also clearly speaking of his own experience:

> Science enhances the moral values of life because it furthers a love of truth and reverence – love of truth displaying itself in the constant endeavour to arrive at a more exact knowledge of the world of mind and matter around us, and reverence, because every advance in knowledge brings us face to face with the mystery of our own being.[9]

Notice how he describes the manner in which he approaches scientific investigation. His research is informed by the *love of truth*. This in itself has not so much to do with a study of the physical world but more to do with what arises in response to the physical world. From this love arises the desire for *exact knowledge*. By his own free admission all his work is imbued with the divine qualities.

'Theory' is derived from the Greek *theoria* which means 'seeing in depth'. Goethe was utterly certain in his mind that the scientific approach, by failing to understand theory in the Greek sense of the word, would concern itself with only a surface understanding and fail to recognise the divine qualities that lay beneath the surface, and by so doing never attain *an attitude of wonder before the elemental phenomena of nature.* Planck, like so many of the leading physicists of the twentieth century, could never be accused of this. Judging by his statements, he certainly didn't see things in physical terms alone. He, like so many of the great minds who explored quantum physics, was as much philosopher as physicist.

Perhaps the most remarkable thing about what Planck has to say is his comment on the nature of the reverence he feels for what he calls *the mystery of our own being.* In the world of becoming everything is in constant movement. Unlike becoming, being is utterly still. It is the constant within which becoming constantly moves. By coming to a deeper understanding of the laws which govern the nature of movement, Planck is inevitably moving from the constant movement of surface activity towards a discovery of the underlying constants. In this process he is arriving at a deeper experience of the unity that encompasses it all. This is not out there somewhere lying on the surface of matter, but held deeply within everything including ourselves. He makes it quite clear that this *being* he is speaking of is *our own being.* By coming to *a more exact knowledge of mind and matter around us* we are by necessity also coming to an ever deeper awareness of ourselves. The reverence that is experienced arises because the sense of self is not a sense of some small personal self but a sense of the *Self* of all, and within this we are all one.

The same thing applies when we are not so much exploring some ultimate scientific truth as trying to come to an understanding of the small truths that are our daily concern, trying to address with clarity of mind the usual web of confusion. If we endeavour with sincerity to come to a deeper understanding of all we face, we must by necessity come to a deeper understanding of ourselves.

Turning this statement around we may also say that to address wisely the constant welter of events we must not only look out, but also look in. Depth of understanding arises from depth of self-knowledge, and self-knowledge can only occur in the present. It is only in the timeless present that we escape the constant movement of time.

**PRACTICE**

For depth of understanding or depth of insight to be achieved enter more deeply into the situation before you, and at the same time more deeply into your own depth and stillness.
Look out. Look in.

## Love Life at the Time Life Lives

As has already been said, one of the eternal principles to be discovered in the present is of course love. It's impossible to love at any other time. Shakespeare was utterly adamant about this. In his Sonnet 116 he states that *love's not time's fool*. Love is not the foolish servant of time. Something else may be, something that is affected by the movement of time, and this sometimes goes by the name of love, but it's not love: *Love is not love which alters when it alteration finds*. Love is unalterable and is born out *even to the edge of doom*. So certain is he of the truth of what he says that he finishes his sonnet with these words:

*If this be error and upon me proved*
*I never writ nor no man ever loved.*

According to his estimation, love is an eternal principle unaffected by time. For this reason there is only one time for love to manifest and that is the eternal present.

It's interesting to note that the motivating powers behind the work of Planck were *love and reverence*. If Shakespeare is right, and all those inspired minds who thought in the same way as he did are right, there is only one time for this to manifest. There's no such thing as an old love. Love is a pressing matter and it presses only at one time. We often think of love being a limited affair, centred on a small area of our experience. In truth love is not only eternal it's also unlimited.

Here's a statement about love. It's Einstein writing about Planck:

> The longing to behold harmony is the source of the inexhaustible patience and perseverance with which Planck devoted himself to the most general problems of our science, refusing to let himself get diverted to more grateful and more easily attained ends. I have often heard colleagues try to attribute this attitude of his to extraordinary willpower and discipline – wrongly, in my opinion. The state of mind which enables a man to do work of this kind is akin to that of the religious worshipper or the lover; the daily effort comes from no deliberate intention or programme, but straight from the heart.
>
> There he sits, our beloved Planck, and smiles inside himself at my childish playing about with the lantern of Diogenes. Our affection for him needs no threadbare explanation. May the love of science continue to illumine his path in the future and lead him to the solution of the most important problems in present-day physics, which he himself has posed and done so much to solve.[10]

You'll notice that love manifests here in at least two ways and there may be others that you can detect. Firstly there is the love that Einstein recognises in Planck's attitude to his work: *The state of mind which enables a man to do work of this kind is akin to that of the religious worshipper or the lover*. Then there is the obvious love Einstein feels for Planck: *There he sits, our beloved Planck*. He says that Planck's work comes straight from the heart. This I'm sure is true. What is undoubtedly true is that Einstein's appreciation of Planck comes from no other place.

These men are intellectuals of the first rank. They are also great lovers. In our divisive way of thinking there is the opinion that the heart and the head are separate and contradictory psychological centres. When we touch the great powers within us everything about us is enlivened and unified – heart, head, body – and this can be at no other time but the present. It's no good hanging onto the past. No matter how desperately we desire to cling nor how justified our desire may appear, the best way we can serve the things we love is by serving the principle of love in the present. It's only this that will tell us what is the right and proper thing to do under the circumstances. *Learn to love life at the time life lives.* Let this determine your thought and deeds.

> My husband died a year ago. How could I forget him? We spent our life together. There is a period of mourning, and that period is over. The mourning is over, but not the love. Love's not limited; it's to be found in everything. I know that I can best serve my husband's memory by remembering this fact.

**PRACTICE**

There's no such thing as an old flame.
There's only one time to love.
Learn to love life at the time life lives.

## The Good they See is the Good they Give

The thing I'm sure you've noticed about the people whose stories feature in this book is that they are not cynics. This is not so much that a deliberate policy of debarring cynics has been adopted, more that cynicism is a hard philosophy to follow for those who have a genuine taste for life. When you have no belief in the good, it won't be the good you'll experience. The debarring is not only automatic it's self-imposed. If you don't give the good, there is no hope that you'll find the good, in anything.

The last story is a perfect example of this. It was this woman's insight into the good and the true that enabled her to see that the best way she might serve her husband's memory was to give the love that she had discovered in his company.

She came to me at the end of a concert asking about one of the poems I'd read. She said it had gone straight to her heart. It was then she told her story. This is the poem. It's by that great Persian poet Jalal-Ud-Din Rumi:

*Happy is the moment when we sit together,*
*With two forms, two faces, yet one soul,*
*you and I.*

*The flowers will bloom forever,*
*The birds will sing their eternal song,*
*The moment we enter the garden,*
*you and I.*

*The stars of heaven will come to watch us.*
*And we will show them*
*the light of a full moon –*
*you and I.*

*No more thought of 'you' and 'I',*
*Just the bliss of union –*
*Joyous, alive, free of care, you and I.*

*All the bright-winged birds of heaven*
*Will swoop down to drink of our sweet water –*
*The tears of our laughter, you and I.*

*What a miracle of fate, us sitting here.*
*Even at the opposite ends of the earth*
*We would still be together, you and I.*

*We have one form in this world,*
*another in the next,*
*To us belong an eternal heaven,*
*the endless delight of you and I.*

Translated by JONATHAN STAR AND SHAHRAM SHIVA[11]

I'm sure you'll agree that this poem was written by a person with a love for life and a love for that which transcends both life and death. When you give love you experience union, and this is supreme love that is being described here.

*No more thought of 'you' and 'I'.*
*Just the bliss of union –*
*Joyous, alive, free of care, you and I.*

You've been encouraged to *give what you lack*. In *Hamlet* Shakespeare says much the same sort of thing: *Adopt a virtue if you possess it not*. When you genuinely adopt a virtue and give what you lack you are forced to come out of the confines of habitual thought which drives you from the present into dreams of past and future. If you are to align yourself with the great powers, this alignment can only be achieved at the time they live. It's here you discover life, joy and freedom from care. Life flows unimpeded, and so can joy and freedom of care. When you find something good it's only natural that you should want to pass it on. This is the good news which we must share if we are to discover new life.

When the good is allowed to flow it attracts the good. Plato proposed another principle: *Like attracts like*. You can see the relevance in this context. The good is a universal. It's not a token to be used in barter and exchange. You don't invest the good in the hope of a return. When the good is given, it's the good you experience. It cannot be otherwise. It's immediate. Although it may manifest in a multitude of ways, there is only one good. And there is only one love. It may appear like *You and I*, but when *You and I* is experienced in all its depth there is *only union*.

## PRACTICE

Like attracts like.
See the good by giving the good.

## The Beauty of All Living Things

The poet and painter William Blake had many interesting things to say. Here's one example:

> The tree which moves some to tears of joy is in the eyes of others only a green thing which stands in the way... As a man is so he sees.[12]

In like vein, this is a story told about the English landscape painter, John Constable.

> To a lady who, looking at an engraving of a house, called it an ugly thing, he said, 'No, madam, there is nothing ugly; I never saw an ugly thing in my life: for let the form of an object be what it may – light, shade and perspective will always make it beautiful.'[13]

In this stage of the book we have talked of knowledge, love, the good and the true, all eternal powers. It's only natural now that we are nearing its end that we should return to the nature and experience of beauty. In respect of beauty we have a choice. We can train our minds to recognise beauty or we can draw a veil over the whole thing and refuse to acknowledge any such possibility, and the best way to do this is simply not to bother. The veil that we have drawn is a veil of our own creation.

> It's so easy to live a boring, humdrum existence. It requires no special effort. All that it needs is for us to stick with the habitual, and make no attempt to open our minds to what lies beyond, certainly to make no attempt to savour the joy of life, to appreciate its potent simplicity, its fullness and depth.

We might also add to this its beauty. We may easily see life as something that fails to move us to tears of joy. We might even consider it as something that gets in the way, and even if this isn't our general experience, we can meet apparent obstacles at every turn.

What is also utterly certain is that those with a sense of beauty do have a way of creating beauty and those with a sense of joy do have a way of creating happiness.

> I didn't want to end up rushing so I set the alarm a little bit earlier. I decided it would be good if, before we left, we took a leisurely stroll to the park. My son and my dog were having so much fun I stayed just that little bit longer. After all, I had given us some extra time.
>
> On the way back I felt myself losing the sense of the freedom I had felt only minutes before. I walked a little faster and started telling my son to stop wasting time.
>
> When we got home he wanted to choose a toy to take with us. 'Hurry up. We'll be late.' I heard the same tone in my voice, the same tone I'd heard so many times before. This time I checked myself. He fetched his toy and returned with a smile on his face. My reward.
>
> We walked hand in hand to the bus stop. It was a beautiful morning to go for a walk with my son.

In every situation there is always a choice: the habitual or the vital. The habitual is so much easier, but it's only with the vital that beauty is found.

Such a way of living is easy but unsatisfying. What encourages dissatisfaction is the memory that we all carry of something beyond the usual experience, a place where we might get in touch with our true vitality and certain happiness.

In timeless moments we discover ourselves. These timeless moments speak of being, consciousness and bliss, the eternal powers, and we, being born into the framework of time, can only come to experience them in timeless moments.

There's only one time to experience these timeless moments, full of the potency of these powers. Now. Constantly go back to where you might meet what all truly desire. Use these reflections to strengthen that resolve.

**PRACTICE**

When the mind and heart draw you away,
go back to that time where you might meet what all desire,
true vitality and certain happiness.

## Your Connection with the Eternal

The ancient Athenians like most of the ancients were quite clear about their connection with the eternal. They just had to glance up to the Acropolis, and there, towering above them, was the home of the goddess which their city was named after: Pallas Athene, the goddess of wisdom, goddess of inner stability and the golden mean. The fact that some of the wisest men in the ancient world worked and practised in her shadow indicates the effectiveness of her presence. Although her huge image is no longer in existence, to this day millions make the pilgrimage to her home. The Parthenon is a perfect mix of pure simplicity and supreme sophistication, one of the most beautiful buildings in the world. The purpose of the building may have been long forgotten but it still has its effect.

One of the myths associated with Athene is her helmet of invisibility. When the visor of her helmet was put down she became invisible. It was only by their devotion to her and all she represented that she was prepared to raise her helmet and reveal her divine form to anyone. This suggests a certain determination and steadiness of purpose. It has been said that her true follower is *one for whom, in the end, eternity fashions change within himself or herself.*

For us to evolve as human beings our lives must consist of a continual renewal. We make new where things are new – in the present. In this evolutionary process we inevitably participate in the eternal powers, because this is where they live. The change which is fashioned in this process consists in coming ever closer to the central reality of our own being, the first manifestation of which are these universal powers. This is inevitable. We may think it through or come at it by pure instinct. It may be achieved through thought, action or love but this is where we arrive, when we give of ourselves with open heart and mind to the present need. At these times the eternal qualities press in upon us.

Describing the creative process the painter, Matisse, speaks of what joy it is to

> ... work with my model until I have it enough in me to be able to improvise, to let my hand run while respecting the grandeur and sacredness of all living things.

He isn't talking here about how he would like things to be. This is how things actually are. This is what he is experiencing. Elsewhere he talks about his *religion*.

> My only religion is that of love for the work to be created, love of creation, and of great sincerity...[14]

All this arises because of what exists in *timeless moments*. The eternal principles are not ideals that we, in our more idealistic moments, might aspire to and at some time in the future imagine achieving. These are pressing realities. They are contained in what presents itself at present. For all of us this is our connection with the eternal.

## PRACTICE

Put yourself in the way of the eternal moments
by constantly honouring the present,
the time when the eternal principles press in.
By constantly bringing the mind back
make them your source of inspiration.

STAGE TEN

# Lasting Relationships

IT CAN APPEAR THAT LITTLE remains constant in the passage of time. Change is inevitable. There are obvious stages in life. We grow and develop in all kinds of ways. Opportunities arise and must be seized. We may constantly move on in our desire to enrich our lives, to gain something greater. This is all understandable, especially when we look round and see that the one thing certain in life is that nothing remains the same.

Yet despite this constant change there is that in us that yearns for stability, continuity and something upon which we may rely. The great ideal of friendship is that you can always turn to a friend. The great ideal of family is that it's always there for you and has been for generations. At the heart of the family lies love, and similarly it's a strong affection that makes for true friendship.

In these relationships we give and we receive. Lasting relationships grow in depth because the continuing journey of discovery, embarked on by those involved in fruitful lives, is undertaken in the company of family and friends.

The most potent of all the powers we possess is the capacity to love. Without it, does life have any real purpose? And no one ever loved alone. Use the reflections in this chapter to help strengthen what you already have and to forge new and lasting relationships.

## Serve Love

Love is a universal principle. There is little that is more central to life than love. If love were to be removed from our lives, think of the inevitable consequence. Think of those we love. Think also of those things we hold dear, those things in which we find beauty, how they become for us a source of happiness.

This is why the service of love is crucial. If we fail to serve the principle of love in our thoughts and deeds the terrible outcome is that love departs. It packs up and moves out, leaving the house empty. This indicates that even if we are motivated by self-interest we must serve love in order to gain love, for in giving love we receive love, and the advent of love, however it might manifest, marks the end of selfishness.

This is not where the story ends, however. In the expression of love, regardless of the motive, you can't help but in some way experience the gift of yourself. It has to happen, for in the giving of yourself to another, there is the accessing of love within. One gift leads to another: turning outward and giving out has its effect. Love is a universal principle. We may think of our love as being something personal, but when we express the spirit of love in what we say, think or do, we cannot help but join the greater whole. The thing is done in the spirit of love. In that, not only do we welcome love into our individual set-up, but we also serve love and aid its expression. We talk about expressing our love, but it's not our love as a personal possession that's being expressed. It's the spirit of love that's finding a form. This may appear to be something fleeting, but in that moment of expression there is nothing other than the fullness of that moment, and if that fullness is fully appreciated by us being totally present, the gift of ourselves cannot help but have its power, the power not only to impact on the lives of others, but also to affect all aspects of our own life.

> A human being is part of the whole, called by us 'Universe', a part limited in time and space. He experiences himself, his thoughts and feelings as something separated from the rest – a kind of

> optical delusion of his consciousness. This delusion is a kind of prison for us, restricting us to our personal desires and to affection for a few persons nearest to us. Our task must be to free ourselves from this prison by widening our circle of compassion to embrace all living creatures and the whole of nature in its beauty.[1]

This is Albert Einstein speaking; he is expressing the universal spirit of love, and with it not only the power of love, but also the ever growing sense of its expansion, an expansion which, when love is served properly, may last a lifetime.

Lasting relationships are vehicles for love's service. If we have adopted the habit of holding back on our affections with those we have chosen to share our lives with, then we must give ourselves instead. This means at that very moment you detect the reservation, that is the very time when you must give, at that very moment. When it comes to the service of love, respond immediately to your inner promptings. Listen to that voice. This is how love expands. When you refuse to listen, the voice grows weaker and with it the experience of love grows weaker too. In the service of love our relationships are bound to deepen, and in this way we nourish our lives together, and build unity at every level.

**PRACTICE**

Let it be a constant motivation to seek to serve love
in a practical way, free from sentimentality.

## Give What You Lack

The practice of giving the very thing that you believe you lack in yourself is an excellent practice to adopt. What you are being told by this sense of lack is that a division has been created within you. You have been cut off from the essential spirit that animates your life. This separation is what is creating the pain. You may put this pain down to exterior circumstances, and this may have its validity. We undoubtedly do encounter suffering in life, but how we meet and deal with this suffering is another matter. We may bow before misfortune, or alternatively we may be strengthened by adversity. Those who do find strength have managed to take the source of sorrow back to the underlying substratum of love and found there not only the means of enduring, but also a far deeper understanding of what lies behind the movement of life.

> It was in the new year that I discovered the terrible news. Shortly after I had to go away and play a major part in a course. The others had little idea of what I was trying to cope with. I couldn't sleep and sat up all night first thinking and then later giving up thought. When the thoughts came I just let them go. I felt that I had no resource of my own to cope, so I eventually gave up and asked for help instead.
>
> I think it must have been towards dawn when it seemed that all the emotion that I had been burdened with gave way; and what I discovered was what I can only describe as an immense sea of gold. And this sea of gold was made of nothing but love. And the knowledge that I was granted at that time seemed to say that, if I were only to remember the love that I experienced then, all the suffering I was encountering or might encounter in the future would find its proper place.
>
> Although this was about what I was experiencing in my life, the knowledge that was granted was quite beyond what was contained by something limited like my life.

Those who find strength in the midst of their suffering have learnt to transcend the confines of their own heart and indeed the confines of their own life. The worst thing you can do in the face of adversity is to harden your heart. In this you deliberately cut yourself off from the source of your own compassion, and when you want compassion for yourself it's not available.

What is compassion after all but the power to give of yourself, to join the flow of life, to practise what we have been given to practise – being human, which means acting humanely in the fullest sense of the word.

There is the view that the heart is a confined thing. The heart, as a psychological principle which is named after a physical organ and is associated with it in experience, can easily be experienced in a limited way. This is particularly so when we look upon emotions as being things that are entirely personal; after all it is our own emotions that mean the most to us, both positively and negatively. All this is true, but what is also true is that love, the most profound of all emotions, although having a personal expression, is utterly universal. This is why, when we open up to what is most fundamental to us by giving what we lack, we also open up to the common bond, which is central to all of us – most central but also transcendent of this individual life.

> Lack of self-belief doesn't lead to great happiness. I have for the past twenty years been suffering from a feeling of inadequacy, of low self-esteem. Because I didn't love myself very much I found it difficult to give myself to others. This has prevented me from forming strong relationships. Since practising what I've heard here things are changing. It started with me being more generous, of not automatically dismissing myself as unworthy, but rather of learning to value my contribution. In that I'm giving myself the love that I long denied myself. This brings with it confidence. Since doing this I've found that I'm more at ease in company. My attention is no longer on myself. Strangely enough, now that I'm more generous with myself, I'm more generous with others, because my attention is not so much on my own apparent inadequacy. It's as if a whole burden which I've been carrying around with me for so long has been lifted.

As you might suspect all this has had a direct effect on this person's relationships. Being so much easier with herself, she is so much easier to be with. The first step is to give what you seem to lack in yourself. You can do this because in truth there is no lack at all. This is the story of one person who believed there was a lack and sustained that belief for twenty years to disastrous effect. It required a change of mind to disabuse her of this belief.

What this story also illustrates is that compassion for others must sometimes begin not with care for others but with oneself. In dismissing ourselves we dismiss our connection with life. When we are cut off in this way developing lasting relationships is a considerable problem.

**PRACTICE**
Give what you lack.

## In Praise

I can't think of a better time to be writing this. The reason I could write about Lake Ontario, as I did earlier, is because I was invited to a big fiftieth wedding anniversary party. The man who organised it was determined on one thing, to celebrate the important things in his life, primarily to celebrate fifty years of marriage to the woman he loves.

When you marry anything together, and humans are no exception, two discrete and separate things are forged into one, and by so doing they are no longer separate. They become part of the same thing. The central reference in any marriage is the principle of unity. When we marry, to a lesser or greater extent, our individual will serves the greater whole.

Something that was said in this celebration of marriage were these simple words:

> Individually, these are remarkable people. Together they are something far greater.

This was beautifully said because it happens to be true. It is particularly true of these two people whose long marriage we were celebrating, but it is also true of any successful marriage. When two people are in a lasting relationship, with all their different aspirations, different perceptions, and different qualities, and they combine their strengths, then they have the possibility of moderating each other's understanding, and gaining new perspectives into the challenges they meet together.

> There are times when my feelings get the better of me. I know that. I know also that even if I don't ask him, the knowledge that his stability is there is a source of strength.
>
> My wife has a slant on things that I simply don't possess. I sometimes wonder where she's coming from, but when you respect someone's judgement, you know that you would be stupid to ignore what they think.

Observations like this are examples of people blending their strengths. To talk about the strengths of your partner and hold them in mind is a marvellous way of praising the virtues that we all possess, and, by praising them, to realise them within ourselves. This is more than blending qualities. Before blending begins there must first be the realisation of these qualities. Marriage can be a marvellous mechanism for such realisation.

In the Renaissance there was an idea which has survived in a misunderstood way even to this day. It is known as platonic love. True marriage involves pleasure and companionship. These are of undoubted importance, but platonic love goes beyond this. It's about spiritual recognition.

This is how Ficino defined platonic love:

> The spiritual love for another human being that is but a disguised love of the soul for its own eternal being.[2]

In a full and true marriage are to be found all of these things: pleasure, companionship *and* spiritual recognition. What Ficino states is that through our devotions we find expression for the eternal truths which are sown in our own hearts from the very beginning and, as has been mentioned previously, nothing in this creation stands alone. By recognising and, as this reflection encourages, praising the good qualities in others, those same qualities that are held within us cannot help but rise in response.

At the climax of the anniversary celebrations there was a gala dinner. It was interesting to see how the couples who were in attendance responded when the devotion of the couple was praised. The spirit of devotion, of which the marriage of our hosts was an embodiment, could be seen reflected in all our own relationships. We sat closer.

By celebrating the good qualities of those you love you cannot help but encourage those qualities to manifest in yourself. This has the obvious effect of drawing people together and of uniting them.

**PRACTICE**

Find the opportunity to praise the good qualities of those you love. Do it appropriately, but don't hold back.

## Consuming Desire and Lasting Love

There is a difference. Consuming desire does what it suggests it does. It consumes. There's a line in *Romeo and Juliet* which expresses this perfectly:

*These violent delights have violent ends*
*And in their triumph die, like fire and powder,*
*Which when they kiss consume.*

In Shakespeare's comedies marriage marks the conclusion. After all the complications and inevitable conflict, marriage serves as a symbol of unity, unity in diversity, constancy in change.

*love is not love*
*Which alters when it alteration finds*
*Or bends with the remover to remove.*
*O, no, it is an ever fixed mark*
*That looks on tempests and is never shaken;*

These are those lines from Sonnet 116 by Shakespeare, one of the best-loved poems of all times. It expresses to perfection what he considers to be the true nature of love, *the marriage of true minds*. These are not minds caught up by any passing whim, consumed by any transient passion. Such emotions confine and consume. What they consume is the consciousness that animates our lives. If in doubt about this, give way to passion. I think that you'll find that when your consciousness is consumed not only are you left feeling exhausted, but your capacity to see things clearly, to play out your life under the steady and rational influence of true perception, is severely curtailed.

In *Romeo and Juliet* the grace of love becomes ruled by passion. There is a line that marks the transition from one state to the other. Juliet has just bid Romeo farewell with these words:

*Good night, good night! As sweet repose and rest*
*Come to thy heart as that within my breast.*

His reply is this:

*O, wilt thou leave me so unsatisfied?*

Although entirely understandable, sentiments of this kind, quite unlike the words of unity expressed by Juliet, are in the final analysis concerned with personal satisfaction, or what we believe provides personal satisfaction. Such desires may well have negative outcomes. In *Romeo and Juliet* as is well known it involved the deaths of both lovers. This play, being a tragedy, traces a decline in consciousness and that decline's inevitable outcome. By the decisions we make, consciousness becomes more or less a potent factor in our lives.

The evident potency of nature, bearing ever outward the force of consciousness, surrounds us everywhere. As conscious human beings we have the power to be something more than the recipients of this force, driven blindly onward by its energy. For Shakespeare, man's sovereign power is the light of reason, which for all intents and purposes is the same as the light of consciousness. When consciousness becomes the central reference in our lives, we come under the influence of our own essential nature, for what could be more central than the conscious energy that empowers us all. This is why self-discovery is so important to us. Rather than being driven by nature's driving energy, through the power of self-knowledge we are capable of resting in the stillness at nature's creative source. It's here that we discover what it means to be truly rational and loving. When our relationships have as their central reference this source, they cannot help but deepen. Paradoxically, it is by turning inwards that our relationships may expand, growing in understanding and compassion.

In Sonnet 116 Shakespeare talks about true love bearing out *even to the edge of doom*. This is not love lasting for 50 years or even a lifetime. This is love quite beyond the bounds of time. This is the eternal principle of love of which we may in our lives become an expression. It requires us to return to the centre, the source of self-knowledge.

**PRACTICE**

If our intention is to evolve –
become more expansive, however that might manifest –
choose lasting love and not consuming passion.

## What is the Atmoshere We Create?

This is a good question for all of us to keep in mind.

> I have a boss who is very difficult to work for. There is nothing about her which is straightforward. She is herself defensive, and this makes us all feel the same. We all continually guard our backs, not knowing what she might do in response to what she sees as a threat to her own position. Although she has responsibility for the whole office, she seems incapable of taking a wider view. This doesn't make for a happy working environment.

This is a very recognisable situation. What is described is easily seen in others, but is it so easy to recognise the same thing in ourselves? As we have already observed, there is always a justification. Even if you are unable to spot the fact that you're being trapped by your own complexities, making justifications is a sure sign that you have been entangled. As I'm sure you've realised, there's somebody at the heart of the manipulative approach, ME. It's ME who seeks to protect itself in every situation.

If you were to read that observation again you would see that all the difficulties encountered in that office are caused by one thing – fear. We all have our egos, because we all have our part to play in life. The problem is that the ego when centred only on itself can be very defensive. When, however, it is placed under the guiding influence of the universal powers that connect us all, it becomes an expression of those powers. The more this happens the more those powers are able to work through us in order to serve the need that the present moment presents. In times like this the complications disappear, and there is no need to manipulate according to some private agenda. Instead there is only the need and the need simply and directly met, whatever that need might be. With this simplicity there begins to arise ease and contentment.

Situations met in this way point to another simple fact. When your attention is on the need it is not on yourself. If this is true, what is equally true is that if your attention is on yourself, the way to meet the situation clearly and without complication is obscured. As the observation makes very clear, this doesn't lead to the effective running of an office.

If this is true in the office context, it is equally true in our personal relationships. The great thing about marriage is that the individual, through marriage, is married to a greater whole. When that unity is served, we are serving the same unity in ourselves. This unity is the source of harmony, and from that harmony arise ease and contentment. In this service we are stepping out of separation to join the great flow of creation. This flow, by the nature of its source, although brimming with vitality, flows unimpeded. When we are part of that, what we offer others is the same unimpeded flow, in no way confined by personal concern or in any way cramped by fear. It flows into all our relationships to create that lasting happiness we all long for. What a joy it is to enter the company of somebody who is at rest in themselves, who is contented.

What is the quality of their judgements? What is it they offer others, and what in turn are they given? What better basis could there be for lasting relationships than they be undertaken by people who, although not self-centred, are centred in themselves.

**PRACTICE**

When you find yourself making life complicated
and seeking justification for doing so,
drop the justification,
undo the complication.

## Unite in Love

The Greek god Apollo, much admired as a symbol of all that was truly Hellenic, the very light of reason, is a symbol of unity. As the personification of one, Apollo represents the unifying factor that holds all together and grants final coherence. Another term that was given to this principle was monad. By doubling the monad there arises the dyad, two. The dyad rules the world as we generally know it, the world of difference and of change. It is the world of duality: past, future; birth, death; subject, object; male, female; day, night; black, white and so on and so on. This world within which we live out our life can be experienced as a world of almost continuous conflict.

The dyad was unlimited: birth, growth, matter, nature, anguish. As these terms indicate, there is tremendous power in this world of continuous generation and movement. This is the force of nature. It is also the source of division, and the source of conflict and of inevitable anguish. Held implicit in the dyad there is, however, the third factor. Its name quite naturally is triad. It is by the third term, three, that the divisions are bridged. In the relationship formed by the triad, *harmonia* is formed. Through the power of three many qualities arise. The Pythagorean philosophers called the triad peace, perfection, friendship and marriage. From this it can be seen that the triad embodies many of the things that we have been considering. In three the division and possible conflict implicit in two turn back and are resolved into the original unity.

So what has such abstract thinking to do with human relationships? I asked the son of the couple whose long and successful marriage we had been celebrating why all this effort was necessary. He, more than anybody, had a lot to do with the time-consuming preparations for the celebration. The fact that everything went beautifully was a clear indication of the spirit in which he tackled the task. He said some interesting things:

> It is necessary for people to be provided with the right vehicle in order that important things are spoken about. It's important that people are given this opportunity. These things do need to be recognised and celebrated. My father and mother made their vows fifty years ago and they haven't broken them. We're here to celebrate the truth of people's word, and the strength that arises out of such vows. How else are we to ever recognise the presence of these principles if they are not witnessed by what we do in our lives?

These two people gave their word and in so doing acknowledged what existed between them. In this there is an expression of their own duality and, in the vow they made to each other, the third element, that which allows unity to be expressed – marriage. In the celebration of their marriage a more unified event would be hard to imagine. The whole thing was conducted to perfection. All the separate and diverse people who were gathered there were united in the spirit that flowed through everything that took place.

There is a choice all of us have to make. It's between giving and self-seeking. For the two whose marriage we were celebrating that choice took place fifty years before. It was marked by the exchanging of vows. This is a gift of the most precious kind. It is a promise that each of them made to the other, a promise to serve one another regardless of what might befall. Much has been written about the nature of the marriage vows. It's not my intent to explore them further, but let me say one thing: in making them you are evoking the power of love in the spirit of truth. Marriage provides a formal and steady context for further generation, a vehicle for the love which is an utterly central and necessary ingredient for the full flowering of family life. It also, through the principle of three, returns the isolated and separate back in the movement of their lives to the fundamental unity out of which everything arises and by which everything is sustained and to which everything finally returns. It acts as an outward manifestation of the spirit of life.

It's not for nothing that marriage vows are marked by the giving of rings, for rings are a link. They link two back into one. A marriage ring is a solid band of gold, one of the most precious metals. As a complete circle it will admit to no division. It is a complete unity. As a circle it also represents the circle of return, from multiplicity and division back to unity. This is the power the triad possesses, the power to harmonise and unify. This is the power of three and the power of marriage.

**PRACTICE**

There is a choice all of us have to make.
It's a choice between giving and self-seeking.
Be alert to the way that choice constantly manifests.

## The Eternal Principle of Love

In this chapter are already to be found quotes from *Romeo and Juliet*. I hope you don't mind if we return to the most famous of all love stories once more.

Before passion has consumed their reason, Juliet says this to Romeo:

*My bounty is as boundless as the sea,*
*My love as deep; the more I give to thee*
*The more I have, for both are infinite.*

This is a beautiful indication as to the nature of the love we are reflecting on here in this chapter. Her character in the play is a girl in love, and it is out of this love she speaks, and no doubt, given the clarity and beauty of the statement, Shakespeare is also speaking out of his own knowledge. This is something that appears in experience to arise and subside, but in truth it remains as a constant presence.

The trouble with Romeo and Juliet is that they allow this power which they have discovered through their love to be consumed in the heat of passion. This flares up in a moment and, shortly after, is utterly consumed in their own suicides. Juliet, before she submits to Romeo's entreaties, describes it perfectly as being:

> *... too rash, too unadvised, too sudden;*
> *Too like the lightning which doth cease to be*
> *Ere one can say it lightens.*

The eternal principle of love, however, lasts a little longer than a flash of passion, regardless of how powerful that passion is. By the power of true love we are capable, as we might suspect, of being dragged out of the passage of time and into the presence of the eternal. This seems to be Juliet's experience when she talks about her love being as boundless and deep as the sea.

When poetry is real poetry it speaks the truth. Shakespeare doesn't just write pretty words. These are the words of an inspired poet. They describe what is known when you arrive at the intersection between the passing and the eternal.

The German philosopher Hegel, in his Lectures on Aesthetics, writes that the poet is like a statue who rises out of the shadows to find his centre in brighter, loftier air.

This turning back to the centre involves turning back to the unified light of consciousness which unites us all. Hegel's words begin to explain the nature of that power and passion that seem to gather around great words. It's no wonder that Shakespeare was known as the divine Shakespeare, even in his own lifetime. People believed his words were divinely inspired. He was capable of connecting us with the world of the gods, who are but humanised forms of such powers as the Good and the Beautiful, and indeed of Love itself.

Juliet is rooted in the drama of life – what is she after all but a character in a play – but she is also the product of a divine imagination and as such she carries with her the light of the divine.

*But, soft! What light through yonder window breaks?*
*It is the east and Juliet is the sun!*

The play *Romeo and Juliet* has gone a long way to create the accepted idea of romantic love. These are fictional characters who have had much to do with an altogether different expectation as to the relationships between men and women. In their opening engagement what can also be recognised in their relationship is platonic love.

Romeo couldn't have recognised Juliet's spiritual power if it hadn't awakened that same power within himself. He describes Juliet as his *bright angel*:

*... As glorious to this night, being o'er my head,*
*As is the winged messenger of heaven*
*Unto the white upturned wond'ring eyes*
*Of mortals, that fall back to gaze on him*
*When he bestrides the lazy-pacing clouds*
*And sails upon the bosom of the air.*

This winged messenger he speaks of is Mercury – or to give him his Greek name, Hermes – the messenger of the gods. Myth tells us how Hermes draws the soul from the familiar patterns of thought and emotion into the realm of the divine powers.

Moments like this seem to be given by grace. Usually we live in another world altogether, and as for our relationships, calling them mundane might be considered a fair assessment. But don't forget that things are mundane because we make them mundane. We do that because we fail to visit that time when the divine powers live, the present. Don't lose what was once known through the force of familiarity, but instead honour those we love by constantly coming back and meeting them in the present. It is only in this way that we may embark on a truly lasting relationship.

**PRACTICE**

Serve the relationships you have.
They create the means of contacting the eternal.

## The Healing Element

Love is a higher emotion, and as such it is all inclusive, but love as it usually manifests is love within limits, and love *within limits* suggests that there are loves within the limits and something else outside. Love of this kind is very much linked to desire. Our attachments, powered by love, can create the most powerful bonds and sometimes the most terrible outcomes. The reason why love is considered by some to be such a powerful force is because in its purest form it is nothing but pure consciousness. When this force is fed into a limit, and when we as individuals strongly identify with that limit, then that power can create the most destructive tendencies. Everything that is found within a limit is related to the centre of that limit: me and everything I hold dear. Everything outside that limit is somehow alien to me and therefore a matter of indifference or, worse still, the source of potential danger.

We can live a life that encourages the expansion of that circle of compassion, or we can live a life of contraction. In extreme cases when a life of contraction is led we can end up with only ourselves within the circle and everything else alien to it. This, of course, is self-destructive. When we alienate ourselves from the principle of love we alienate ourselves from ourselves.

Our task is to connect with the power that heals division not only with those around us but also the division we find within ourselves, the division between who we believe ourselves to be and who we truly are.

> My father is a typical Italian. He is overprotective and very emotional. This clouds everything. Although I have left home and established my own life, to him I am still his little girl. You can imagine the conflict that this has led to. We all seem to get swept up in the emotions that are flying around. I have of late been attempting to work not from my separate point of view but from the undoubted love that links us.

What you'll notice from this observation is the love that exists between the two: *the undoubted love that links us*. What this woman is describing is the recognition of this and how this recognition allows there to be a new perspective. They both have their love, but both are antagonistic. The rational approach indicates that when there is division we should appeal to the next highest unity for a resolution of that division. This is exactly what she is doing. In it the universal principle of love can be established. She is looking out beyond her own perspective and moving into the common ground.

> I was writing a document at work and was very busy. Just at that moment my manager decided it would be good idea to indirectly pass on a client's complaint. I felt very angry. I could have killed him. Now I look back it was so stupid, but there was so much justification at the time.

There's always justification. Have you noticed how no matter what terrible things have been committed there's always someone there to justify them? Have you noticed how quickly the voice of self justification arises in your own mind? This person is speaking metaphorically, but she did feel it, and there was someone there to justify her feelings – at the time. It's only later that we can look back more rationally. Our task in living life anew is not to allow wisdom to arise later but to be wise at the time and that can only be achieved by holding the principles in mind, regardless of the situation.

> When my mother was dying, and I was doing my duty every week and my sister was in this emotional state and criticising me and never asking about my husband's brain tumour, I was in this negative state, and constantly justified my being there.

Little wonder. It's moments like this when we really need our friends, when we have almost all our strength stripped from us, when we feel so weak and like giving in, it's then we need the love of our friends, then more than any other time. She had the opportunity of saying what she had to say because she had someone to turn to, and the love she received helped to heal, and allowed her to love in turn. She was certainly surrounded by people who needed her love. Love given helps all to forgive and to serve.

When there is perceived wrong this move is more difficult than at any other time, for in it there is another universal principle at work which is almost as powerful as love: justice. We can only begin to mend perceived wrong when the two aspects of justice go together: justice and mercy. When mercy seasons justice there is the possibility of forgiveness. Forgiveness is impelled by love. Every possibility must be left open for love to enter, even in the most dire situation. This is crucial in the general run of things. When it comes to personal relationships it's essential. Our task is not to seek retribution but to love our enemies and to do everything that is possible to prevent making an enemy of our friend. This requires real strength of character and a determination to stay true to the spirit of compassion, the healing power of love.

**PRACTICE**

Retaliation isn't the only answer.
Resist the temptation.

## Pitfalls and Traps

If we surround ourselves with lines of defence we do have a way of hemming ourselves in, of living in isolation. If in any way at all we find ourselves doing something like this it's worth asking why? What do we hope to achieve? It's worth thinking about seriously. There's a whole frame of mind involved in this, and this frame of mind doesn't encourage trust, and it doesn't encourage lasting relationships. There is an alternative.

> I've recently had my brother living with me after a long separation. We are the best of friends and the worst of enemies. An issue came up and we had this row over the phone. It ended up with us both ranting and raving. By the time he came back I'd just about managed to calm down. But as soon as he came in he started the row again. With some effort I was able to let go, and he began to calm down himself. He had to leave shortly after, but we managed to have a two hour conversation before he left. We began to see the thing from each other's point of view. It was as if we had transcended 'the battle ground', the habitual way in which we meet each other. We began to relate to each other quite differently.

Little wonder they haven't seen much of each other. One can't help but think that after their conversation something will change, that the set attitudes which have typified their relationship will now transform into something more positive and productive.

This example shows very clearly the relationship between love and reason. In essence they are the same thing. Love which is unreasonable is not love at all. It's possession. Reason without love is nothing but cold analysis, logical, irrevocable and often unreasonable. The final relationship which makes sense of everything is missing, the relationship with unity. Our task is, as ever, to serve the unity, the unity of our community: family, friends, nation, mankind. We are human, and this is our role. To transcend the battle ground, we must appeal to the principle of unity, and this is done through love and reason.

There are of course those relationships which are not only totally unreasonable but also full of hate. The truth of the matter is that those relationships which are filled with hate are by necessity unreasonable. Hatred is not a reasonable emotion to cultivate. Hatred serves nobody, certainly not ourselves. To deliberately choose hate rather than love is a self-destructive choice. Hatred not only corrodes our relationships, it corrodes ourselves.

Reason will tell us that if we feel that our life's a battle, and that we're surrounded by pitfalls and traps it's worth asking who is creating them and why. Usually in any battle both sides lay mines. Because of the self-destructive nature of negative emotion, we will, in the minefield of life, be injured not so much by the mines our enemies lay but more by those that we lay ourselves. There's no such thing as friendly fire. Our best defence therefore is to destroy our lines of defence, even if our enemies insist on retaining theirs.

If insult is offered you don't have to accept it, and if you don't accept it, with whom must it remain? Although this may be true, there is a problem about this piece of logic. It misses out the unity. If we were to serve that unity, not only in the company of our friends but also in the company of our enemies we might discover that we have fewer enemies and more friends.

**PRACTICE**

If you seem to be surrounded by anti-personnel devices
make sure that you're not the one who is laying them.

## Be Constant

*The one remains; the many change and pass;*[3]

This line by Shelley states in essence what we have been discussing in this section of the book. Things are constantly changing. Our lives continually move on. As we are all subject to mortality, one day we will make the final move. But in the midst of all this movement is there something which remains as a constant, beyond life and beyond death? The poem from which the line is quoted is 'Adonais', an elegy on the death of his fellow poet and friend, John Keats. This is how the poem continues:

> *Heaven's light forever shines, earth's shadows fly;*
> *Life like a dome of many-coloured glass,*
> *Stains the white radiance of Eternity.*

The sense of the constant movement of experience that we, as individuals, experience and which we identify as our lives is available to us as experience because behind all our identifications lies something which remains as a constant presence. It has been there from the very beginning and is always present, the *Silent Witness* of our lives. It's impossible to experience the *Witness* because, in the final analysis, it's not possible to look at it without the *Witness* no longer being a witness but instead an object of observation. Because this final *Witness* has been there from the beginning we all have a sense of something remaining as a constant regardless of the changes that we experience in life. Looking back we have a sense of ourselves, unaltered, unaffected. When we consider all our memories, right back to the very earliest, there remains as a constant, unchanging factor, the light of our own consciousness, both observing and empowering.

Although this presence is the most intimate of presences – nothing could be closer – what is to be understood is that what is particular is also universal. It's easy to see that the gift of consciousness is not particular.

When the eminent physicist Erwin Schrödinger was coming to his revolutionary conclusions concerning quantum mechanics he was also considering other matters of universal consequence. Here is an extract from his book *My View of the World*.

> You can throw yourself flat on the ground, stretched out upon Mother Earth, with the certain conviction that you are one with her and she with you. You are as firmly established, as invulnerable as she, indeed a thousand times firmer and more invulnerable. As surely she will engulf you tomorrow, so surely she will bring you forth anew to a new striving and suffering. And not merely 'some day': now, today, everyday she is bringing you forth, not once but thousands upon thousands of times, just as everyday she engulfs you a thousand times over. For eternally and

> always there is only now, once and the same now; the present is the only thing that has no end.[4]

He was certain that: *No self stands alone*, and that *All consciousness is one*. Whenever there is a clarity of awareness, whenever there is a deeper sense of one's true nature, there is also a deeper sense of unity and love. Einstein was very much of the same mind as Schrödinger. Remember what he said: *A human being is part of the whole*, and that our task is to widen *our circle of compassion to embrace all living creatures and the whole of nature in its beauty*.

Love by its very nature conjoins. Therefore, when unity is experienced so is love. Our task is to express this unity and this love in all we do. To this we must remain constant. If we change with the changes we experience in life, forever shifting and inconstant, then we are one thing one moment and a moment later something else. Worse still we become fragmented in the face of the eternal present and our integrity is lost. Our task is always to return to that which is constant, and throughout the changing phases of life to allow that constancy to take us to an ever deeper relationship with everything we meet and at the same time an ever deeper understanding of ourselves.

> Lasting relationships grow in depth because the continuing journey of discovery embarked on by those involved in fruitful lives is undertaken in the company of family and friends.

We must find an ever deeper unity with those we love, always serving the principle of love, which is more deeply understood and experienced when we consciously act in its service. This is *widening our circle of compassion* through an ever growing understanding of the unity that links us all.

## PRACTICE

Be constant.
By being constant your relationships will deepen,
and your understanding.

STAGE ELEVEN

# From Strength to Strength

THERE ARE TIMES WHEN the normal confines we work within give way to something greater. It would appear that we have a power within us that is unlocked either by the demands of the moment or just by the joy of being alive. We possess a new-found vitality, a strength to take on things that were previously beyond us.

This is what we know before our habitual framework of thought closes in and the energy drains away and we go back to feeding on things which weaken rather than confirm our strength.

There is an answer to this: believe in what you experience in those times of power rather than in the opinion you have trained your mind to accept. Feed on things which encourage that strength to grow. Then go on to gather more by giving to others what you have gained for yourself. This is going from strength to strength, and it doesn't stop at personal empowerment, for by reclaiming your own strength you help others reclaim theirs.

Use the reflections in this stage of the book to connect with your own inner strength, and by recognising your own power, allow others to recognise theirs.

## Lean on Yourself

In moments of weakness there's always the desire to find something to lean on, something from which we may take strength, and we must be grateful if we have those to whom we can turn. What we must also be grateful for is inner strength. Inner strength is always with us and we must come to trust in that inner strength and power and then, rather than relying on things that might not always be there for us, we have something that is utterly dependable. Obvious questions arise however as to what it is that we might turn to and where we might find it. Is it amongst the stock of abilities upon which we normally depend or does it lie beyond?

> It was one of those times in life of considerable anguish, of almost despair. Suffering at times like this can be extreme, and none of the ways by which we deal with difficulties encountered in life seem enough. I had tried to cope by using all my rational powers, but in this case whatever I had to draw on from the usual collection of tools made no difference.
>
> The pain was such that I knew that there was no chance of thinking about things using the usual tools. I turned to prayer instead. When you have no resource of your own, there's no other option but to seek some alternative.
>
> I have no idea how long it took, but at some point the despair that seemed to have me totally in its grip simply dropped away. What it was replaced with was what I can only describe as a limitless sense of unity. What then arose was not some conclusion drawn from my observation, rather a direct message: 'Remember what you are experiencing now.' I had no doubt then, and I have no doubt now. By it I was given relief from my sorrow and a clear direction as to how to meet future events. But that, in a way, was not the most important thing. What was evident was that when the truth is spoken there is a lasting recognition. This is true when you hear the truth from someone else, even more so when it rises from within, not from your own stock of good sense, valid though that may be, but from a far deeper resource.

To know from experience that there are inner powers, far deeper than what appears to be of a personal nature, is knowledge worth having. This is self-reliance of a remarkable kind. This isn't fixed opinion or self-delusion; this is the knowledge in the experience that there is that upon which you may rely, something which transcends the usual experience of life, regardless of how all consuming this life may be.

It also begs another question. When it comes to an ultimate individual identity, what is essential and what is peripheral? One thing's certain: the presiding power of unity and love, which the insights of the wise have constantly referred to, exists as something utterly essential to our human experience and yet ultimately transcendent of this particular life. In order to gain strength – in whatever way that strength's required – it's worth remembering this.

**PRACTICE**

Constantly turn to your own inner strength.
Allow the problem, whatever it is,
to find a resolution in reference to that.

## The Need to Practise

There is information and there is experience. What this book is encouraging is experience. The information the book contains is there only to encourage practice. Consistent practice is required if the change of heart and mind that is being indicated here is to be found in life and not merely between the covers of this book. There is another good reason why practice is essential. There can never be confirmation of what is being explored here without putting it to the test in experience. The stories that are included in the book are stories of people who, by practising, are, each in their own way, bringing to their active lives an element of contemplation. In this they are gaining insight into the nature and purpose of their lives. They are discovering much about peace and happiness, about beauty and creativity. Above all they are discovering something of the truth about themselves. Read back over some of these stories and you will see that this is only too evident.

There is life lived on the surface of life, and whilst this happens, regardless of how successful you might be, the satisfaction of living life in depth is missing.

> There is always so much to do working as a graphic designer, there's always some deadline to meet, and constantly coming up in front of you are obstacles which seem to prevent you from getting where you want to be. All this can be terribly exhausting, and the more tired you get the more insurmountable the obstacles appear.
>
> I had so much to do today. The thought of sustaining any kind of practice was quite beyond me. The only thing that made a difference was when I phoned my wife and told her how I felt. She said that she thought I should come to the group. I knew she was right, and it was at that moment of decision that everything changed. During the course of the afternoon several situations resolved themselves. It seemed that she allowed me to stay true to the principles I'd been introduced to here, to return to the present and to meet things in an entirely different way.

Resolution is what this reflection is encouraging. The occasional flash is given in a flash and like a flash it's gone. Things that make a difference have to be sustained, and there is only one thing that will sustain efforts of this nature, the resolve to constantly remember who we are and what we are, to constantly return to the present where life lives, and free ourselves from the habitual modes which continually creep up and reinforce the limited view we have of ourselves. It is this limited view which will prevent us from living out this life without achieving any real understanding.

**PRACTICE**

Sustain resolution.
Constantly return to the practice of *Self Remembering.*
The occasional flash of understanding encourages,
but only your own resolve will lead to anything lasting.

## On What Do I Feed My Mind?

I have a friend who is a Vietnam veteran. He has an interesting tale to tell of how the war changed his attitude to life.

> During the first year I was in Vietnam I spent the whole time with one repeating thought in mind: 'Why me?' This was the last place in the world that I wanted to be. This was the last thing in the world that I wanted to do, and yet there I was separated from my wife and my young child, locked into a war of the most horrific kind.
>
> Suddenly one day everything changed. Instead of: 'Why me?' a new thought arose: 'Why not me?' I was there after all. I wasn't at home. Although I didn't like anything about it, this was life for me.

After this time there arose an entirely different attitude to what he was doing. As he had no desire to personally kill anybody, service in a way a soldier is normally asked to serve was a problem. He decided, therefore, that the best way that he could meet the situation was by serving the other men. One of the things that he took up as a discipline was to collect food. The soldiers were terribly wasteful so he quietly collected the food that was thrown away and kept it in his knapsack and distributed it when the need arose.

As a well-qualified engineer and a very practical and perceptive man, it was inevitable that he quickly rose through the ranks and was repeatedly asked to take a commission. This he refused to do for the simple reason that he didn't want to be forced into issuing orders which would involve the death of anybody. At last he was called back to headquarters in order to answer to his superiors. Whilst he was absent his platoon was ambushed and wiped out.

All this had its inevitable effect upon him. So much so that come the end of the war he couldn't bring himself to make decisions about his future career. What he did, therefore, was to follow the line that he had taken in Vietnam and open himself to the situation as it manifested in the present.

> I went back to my home town in Pennsylvania, gave up any idea of pursuing engineering, and became an odd-job man. One job I got was to repair the porch of a local church. I finished the job, but I thought it would look better if the porch had some ornamental brackets; so I carved the brackets and put them in. They were much appreciated by the congregation, and I was

> asked, therefore, a few months later, to redesign the church doors. This I did and whilst I was about it I put some relief carving into those doors. By this time the people were getting enthusiastic and collected money for me to carve a screen, and so it went on. I carved my way down the church until I ended by carving a crucifixion scene for the altar. By that time I knew how to carve wood.

This man went on to become one of America's finest wood carvers with work in the Smithsonian Institute and the White House. What the story describes is a journey from strength to strength, from a state of total dismay and despair to one that required him to meet the situation with fullness of spirit. When he did that the world, which before was a very hard, cruel and dark place, began to open up, and once he had entirely devoted himself to what the present was offering, it carried on opening up.

And it's all to do with what you are lending your mind to. There are repetitive thoughts that are utterly destructive. These enter ever more deeply into the heart and mind the more they are dwelt on, so much so that we are hardly aware of their presence. There are thoughts, however, that have the opposite effect. These are ever expansive. When you put your life in the way of the principles that these thoughts encourage, then weakness and general debilitation will not typify your experience of life, quite the opposite.

**PRACTICE**

Constantly return to that form of thinking
that will strengthen heart and mind.
Turn from that which will do nothing but debilitate.

## Strengthen Strength

Self-assessment is always a useful thing, self-criticism never is. One of the most destructive things that you can do is to spend your time feeling negative about yourself. Taking a quiet look at what works and what doesn't work is not the same thing. When the energy is flowing assess why. Don't do this in any self-congratulatory sort of way. Just consider what it is about the conduct of heart and mind that has removed the obstacles, remembering that self-congratulation, like self-criticism is one of these blocks. Open yourself to what is there to be known, both outwardly and inwardly. One of the things that might well be known, if only by its absence, is the block. Here's a rather telling observation. It's by an Italian chef.

> I've been trying to practise what you've been talking about, and it's made no difference to me whatsoever.
>
> And those you work with, how have they found you?
>
> Well it's funny that you should mention that. My boss was asking me what I was on because he noticed I was so much more calm.

Here's another observation from a computer engineer:

> I've had the most terrible four days. There was a most disastrous computer failure. We went through everything searching for the fault. We worked way into the night. I say it was terrible, but actually that's wrong. It should have been terrible, but every time I felt the usual set of emotions come crowding in I remembered what we've been practising and simply let them go. I remembered 'Not this, not this.' I wasn't all this anger and frustration. Remembering that brought me back to myself and allowed me to see the situation clearly and intelligently. It even gave me a sense of the whole task. When that was remembered then the time didn't matter, the whole thing simply had to unfold, but unfold under observation. This is something worth remembering.

It's worth remembering because without some degree of self-assessment, nothing is remembered, and the next wave of claims and involvement roll in and you're lost in the usual set of identifications that create the block to intelligence and creativity. The thing about this matrix is that it has a name written right through it: ME. It's ME that gets angry and frustrated. It's ME that is unable to see when new possibilities start to enter, and because they cannot be seen these possibilities slip away as quietly as they came. There is no chance of building on your insights when ME prevails. When there is even a little relief from ME, things begin to change.

Here's another observation. Whilst reading it it's useful to consider what happened before the habitual reaction would have normally slotted into place.

> Increasingly I find that I am being asked to speak publicly. I've always refused, saying that I couldn't do it. I am not a natural speaker. It would be a disaster etcetera. Then last week I was asked again. I paused before answering. On the instant I accepted the engagement and knew what I had to do.
>
> I contacted an actor friend of mine and asked her to train me. We made a date, but when the day arrived I found myself thinking up every excuse not to go. 'Haven't got the time. Won't enjoy it. She's too busy. It's beyond me ...'
>
> I paused and knew I had to go!
>
> It turned out to be great and has changed my whole outlook. I feel far more confident and actually look forward to being asked again.

In that moment of *pause*, there arises recognition, not recognition of all those adopted impediments which we mistakenly believe have something to do with ME, but a recognition of what is there essentially. This is the practice of *Self Remembering* which forms the key element to this book. When that is returned to, all kinds of possibilities open up to us. We access our strengths and by using them become confident about their validity and more confident in ourselves, our real selves. This is how to strengthen strength.

## PRACTICE

When everything seems to be working well,
when the power is there to accomplish what is being asked of you,
consider the factors that are at play.
Then strengthen your strength
by constantly returning to the source of strength.

## From Rest to Rest

When you're feeling exhausted it's usually because at the end of any action you have forgotten to return your energy to stillness.

The idea of returning energy to stillness is an interesting one, because there's an obvious implication in this advice. The implication is that the energy employed in the active living out of our lives has this source. It also suggests that movement arises out of stillness. This may be dismissed as an illogical assumption because it indicates that something can arise out of its seeming opposite.

But then again, this is not so unusual a concept. Where did this vast creation of which we are part arise from anyway? Many statements have been made about the nature of the creative act and what was there before it occurred. For most of us it forms one of the great imponderables. Andrei Linde, a proponent of the big bang theory, alludes to these imponderables when he talks about how the theory to which he subscribes – which claims that the universe appears out of nothing, expands and then contracts back into nothing – begs a question: what is this nothing from which our universe is born, and what is this nothing into which it disappears?

> ...This is the same question everyone asks about himself. 'What is this nothing I was born from, and what is this nothing to which I return?'

He might also have asked, 'What is this nothing which sustains it all?'

The anonymous English author of a fourteenth century manual of contemplation called *The Cloud of Unknowing* answers this question beautifully when he says:

> ...What is he that calls it nothing? Surely it is our outer man, and not our inner. Our inner man calls it All.[1]

He might have gone on to say:

> Out of this All all things come. In this All they are all sustained. Towards this All all things tend. And to this All they finally return.

Returning to stillness is a way of disengaging from those forms towards which our energy constantly runs and by which our energy is consumed. This energy appears to be a personal resource to be spent how we best decide, but in reality what appears as our own is only the manifestation of an energy that lies beyond any personal possession or personal decision as to how best it might be spent.

Energy lies around us everywhere. We may look at the world pulsating with life; we may look at our entirely natural engagement with that life, however it manifests, but the source of that life is something else. It is regular disengagement in order to return to the source that this book is encouraging, and it's to that source we should return when the action is over, not wasting it by running back over something which has already reached its full measure, or dashing into the next event without the previous one coming properly to rest. Coming to rest in this way is touching base in the most profound manner. It is a way of creating measure. It is also a way – as the name, *Self Remembering*, suggests – of returning to one's true self.

**PRACTICE**

To find true measure –
the perfect length, the perfect amount, the perfect timing,
move from rest to rest – rest in perfect stillness.

## Letting Go

One of the most obvious ways of preventing the growth of natural energy, and the movement from strength to strength, is by giving energy to the wrong things. The most destructive thing that we give ourselves to is negative emotion. This we have already discussed, but if we are thinking about the growth of strength then it would be useful to think of it again in this context.

People who give themselves to negative energy may, through that energy, appear strong, but if you consider the final result of all their fulmination, it is very little in terms of real understanding either of themselves or of the world in which they live. Real strength is a clear and rational thing, and if action is required it's done from reason with quiet decisiveness. These actions may have huge effects but the source of them is still and reflective.

> How is my soul's helmsman going about his task? For in that lies everything. All else, within my control or beyond it, is dead bones and vapour.[2]

Marcus Aurelius, who was a ruler of the Roman Empire, was quite clear as to what was important. He was determined on one thing only, to head home. This was his continual reference point. All else, including the control of his vast empire, was of secondary importance: *dead bones and vapour*. It's only when the orientation is right that the good and the useful can follow. Something which is dead bones and vapour has already passed the point of vitality, and yet this is what everybody takes notice of. Vital action takes place elsewhere, ruled by different principles. Manifestation may have the signs of vitality, may appear inspired, but only if the source of action is genuinely alive. When that source is true, actions can be seen for what they are, inspired by wisdom.

If individuality actually exists as something more than an imagined creation, it has one function and that is to steer this centre of consciousness away from all the petty involvements that consume us, back to the centre of our lives.

Of these consuming factors in our lives, involvement in negative emotion is the most consuming, the most destructive of conscious energy and the avowed enemy of measure.

> I was ill last week and not attending work. Normally I get very worried about not being there and constantly phone up to check what's going on. On this occasion I decided I wouldn't get involved. I think I recovered more quickly than I normally do. I

had changed something that I had done all my working life and felt much better for it.

On the face of things this observation seems unrelated to the subject in hand, but just consider the habit which is being broken – not engaging in negative emotion by worrying about things the invalid had no control over, and instead of expending his energy on that, devoting himself to getting well. This decision has much more of a sense of measure to it. He was ill for a week, got up and went back to work. He didn't try to struggle on and make the matter worse in the process. He didn't destroy the energy that his body needed to get well by useless worrying about things over which he had no control. He simply disengaged from his concerns and allowed the illness to create its own measure, a measure shortened by the conscious decision he took.

If letting go of mild worry can create strength, think how much more strength may be gained by giving up on some of those 'diseases' that can easily dominate a whole life: anger, frustration, jealousy and resentment. Think what might come in to take their place if they were no longer a feature of life. All that is natural to you would fill the space previously occupied by these usurpers. More precisely, what is natural would be expressed, because there wouldn't be anything there to prevent it.

**PRACTICE**

Gain strength by letting go of self-generated sources of debilitation.
Don't toy with them.
Immediately they're recognised, let them go.

## Punctuation

Life needs to be experienced, and then we grow in experience, and it is possible that through experience we may grow in wisdom. This is undoubtedly going from strength to strength. Alternatively we may go on making the same mistake over and over again, and so ingrained will become this habit, that it will seem the most obvious thing to do. The outcome of this is that we will pass through life learning little of significance, certainly finding little measure in our thoughts and actions and therefore little wisdom or peace.

The Stoic philosopher Epictitus had this to say on the matter:

> If you seek peace with groaning and sorrow outside yourself you will follow what is stronger than you, and never be at peace, for you seek it where it is not, and refuse to seek where it is.[3]

And how many of us seek our satisfactions, including our peace, outside ourselves and in the process chase from one frustration to the next, turning what could be a measured and rational life into one long jumble, into nothing but a dream of achievement. It must be a dream because it isn't present. By doing this we learn nothing, because the simple truth of the matter is that we are not there. We are in hot pursuit of our dreams, harried by our fears. This is what we all experience unless something comes to create an alternative. Listen to this young woman's observation. Like most of the stories in this book it describes a familiar situation.

> I've had a stressful week. The landlord was due to arrive this morning about the flat. I am involved in politics and had to organise a gig.
>
> Yesterday I went out to lunch and just sat down and ate a salad. The taste was incredible! All I had to do was taste. The sense of taste got me there. Previously through all the stress I kept trying to get there myself. I tried to think reflectively. Nothing worked, but then it just happened. I had no regrets about what went before, but then I knew everything would be achieved. Even now I can see the orange cloth, the trees outside the window – all so clear and detailed.

There is one obvious thing derived from that moment of connection, strength in the form of confidence and conviction. *I knew everything would be achieved.* It also speaks of a sudden absence of fear. All the concerns she previously felt disappeared and what she was left with was a vivid impression of the present: *the trees outside the window – all so clear and detailed.* Think how many times you have spent lunch worrying over some problem, totally oblivious to anything but your concerns, certainly not aware of the incredible taste of a simple salad.

Notice also that previously she had tried to free herself from the stress she was experiencing, *to get there,* but all to no avail. Yet her efforts, although yielding, apparently, no immediate result, allowed for a touch of bliss to enter the situation, and the grace to bring her back to the present, to free her from fear. It also allowed her the awareness to experience the beauty of life with new-found intensity. This is the product of reflective living. This is why it is so important to punctuate life by constantly coming to rest, by reconnecting with the here and now, and appreciating the vastness that underlies all the concerns that captivate our minds, and, even if apparently it has no immediate effect, by persevering with determination. The truth is that no effort in this work is ever wasted. The touches of bliss may come uninvited, but very rarely. For real insight and inspiration practice is crucial.

**PRACTICE**

Regardless of what you imagine to be success or failure,
keep practising.
No effort in this work is ever wasted.

## The Natural Measure

In the *Meditations* of Marcus Aurelius he makes this beautiful statement:

> The soul attains her perfectly rounded form when she is neither straining out after something nor shrinking back; neither disseminating herself piecemeal nor yet sinking down in collapse but is bathed in a radiance which reveals to her the world and herself in their true colours.[4]

Think of this statement in the light of the young woman's observation made in the previous reflection. What was happening when she was experiencing stress? She was, in the terms that Marcus Aurelius was using, *straining out and shrinking back*. What are we doing when we experience stress? Much the same thing.

What happens when contact is made? The world is revealed in its true colours. How do you think that Cézanne could paint landscape with the quiet intensity that made him so valued as an artist if something of this truth had not revealed itself to him? So much so in fact that, if you recall, this, as he claims, was the real reason for painting. Painting was a tool by which to make that contact.

But Marcus Aurelius doesn't stop there. He is not just talking about the true colours of the outer world. He is also talking about the truth of our inner world, a world which he claims is bathed in a radiance which reveals true colour.

We may consider what he says in a number of ways. There is undoubtedly that within us which appreciates the beauty of colour and form. It has already been claimed earlier in the book that we wouldn't be able to appreciate outer beauty if the inner wasn't already in place ready to rise in response. We may also say that this outer world in all its vastness is being perceived from within through this instrument of mind. It is by this miraculous mechanism we have been given that we appreciate the wonder of the world. It appears out there, but in truth all of it is being seen within. These are the words of the physicist, Sir Arthur Eddington. He is speaking of our appreciation of the physical world:

> Some influence from it [the physical world] plays on the extremity of the nerve, starting a series of physical and chemical changes which are propagated along the nerve to a brain-cell; there the mystery happens, and an image or sensation arises in the mind which cannot purport to resemble the stimulus which excites it. Everything known about the material world must in one way or another have been inferred from these stimuli transmitted along the nerves. It is an astonishing feat of deciphering that we should have been able to infer an orderly scheme of natural knowledge from such indirect communication.[5]

He goes on to make the observation, which although obvious, is often overlooked:

> The mind is the first and most direct thing in our experience; all else is remote inference.

The mind, through some continuous miracle, is not only capable of witnessing the outside world but is also able to appreciate its beauty, its harmony, its perfect precision. The mind is capable of recognising all these eternal qualities because it is also part of the natural world, a natural world in which these qualities find a central place. Some claim that these powers are the source of the natural world.

This may be true, but experience can often indicate something quite different. Marcus Aurelius again points out the reason why. The soul is often in a state of distortion, reaching out or sinking back. Reaching out involves that striving to which we are often prone, driven by a state of continual agitation which allows for no rest but instead a cycle of desire and disappointment, elation and depression. And when the disappointment and depression arise what do we experience but a sinking back.

All of this has a profound effect on how we view the world. The radiance is blocked or coloured. The mirror of the mind loses its inherent radiance. It no longer reflects cleanly and purely the light of consciousness which allows us to see and appreciate with clarity and intelligence. Only when the soul takes on its natural shape do things begin to be known in their true light. For this reason we must continually work for equanimity. The perfect circle is only achieved from a state of equality: neither reaching out nor sinking back. Arising from equanimity is measured action, action which starts from a point of rest and, having met the need that calls it forth, returns to rest. Equanimity and equality are both to do with the return to evenness and balance, which is the power of unity being expressed in a world that seems to be full of division and diversity.

The figure of justice is often represented as blindfolded, indicating that she is blind to partiality. In her hand she holds a balance, and in the scales of that balance the evidence is impartially weighed. The process of justice involves an intelligent appraisal of all the factors. An objective view is made in which any sense of personal involvement is not allowed to effect the outcome.

If this is true of justice in general it must also be true for us personally. How else might we deal justly and wisely with our own situation? Is it possible to deal justly and wisely when our mind is unsettled? Is it not much more likely that this will happen when the mind is still and clear and lit? When we return ourselves back to ourselves and enter into a state of self-knowledge then equanimity is achieved.

**PRACTICE**

Return to the practice of *Self Remembering* whenever you remember. If you habitually fail to remember, leave prompts to remind yourself. Do this until it is inconceivable to do anything other than work from *Self Remembering*.

## Exuberance from Stillness

But does all this that we have been discussing mean the end of life that is full of vibrancy and vitality? Does it mean that the brilliance of life is to be turned into a rather dull affair, a vacancy even? Some philosophies have tried to assert that the final reality that lies behind life is a void but, regardless of this view, life has a wonderful way of asserting itself, making itself known. There is a delightful statement by Proclus, the Platonic philosopher, about the nature of the gods:

> The laughter of the gods must be defined to be their exuberant energy in the universe, and the gladness of all mundane creatures.[6]

Life has this sense of undeniability. It forces itself upon us. Find yourself in a room of five-year-olds and you will know all about exuberance. This is the will to live expressing itself at full power. We might ask ourselves what it takes to live with all the exuberance of the gods. This isn't such a far-fetched question. Think about the times when you feel really alive. What are the qualities associated with those times? What do you experience?

> Beauty is the real aspect of things when seen aright and with the eyes of love.[7]

Above are the words of the poet Kathleen Raine, and the following was said by the painter Samuel Palmer of his friend, the poet William Blake:

> To walk with Blake in the country is to perceive the soul of beauty through the forms of matter.[8]

This is beauty being known by those awake to the power of the present. All three of the people I have just mentioned are known for their power to connect fully with life. There is no doubt that with a rise in consciousness we rise out of the normal experience of life to become part of an entirely new expression of life – new because it's living now – and the nature of this life is beauty and love.

But this can only be discovered through the process of continual renewal, by returning to stillness and space.

This involves us stepping out of the play into the light that illuminates that play, the still light of consciousness. A description of such a step was formulated thousands of years ago in Kashmir. It provides advice on the art of 'centring'.

> Enter space, supportless, eternal, still.[9]

The fully perfected circle can only be achieved by constantly holding in mind the circle's still centre. This is true of any circle. It is certainly true of the soul's perfected circle.

**PRACTICE**

Find the stillness and space
from which arises action which is
clear, articulate and beautifully measured to the need.

## When the Time for Action is Over

And when the time for action is over leave it. Return to your source of strength. According to the Vedic system there are three primary states of mind: the active, the inactive and the reflective. In the natural run of things we tend to veer between the highly active and the inactive: forever pursuing our objectives in life: *getting and spending* as Wordsworth describes it, and in this, according to him, *we lay waste our power*. We lay waste our power because the third element, the reflective, is not a feature of our lives. Instead we veer from wilful self-determination to an exhausted state where it seems there is little energy for anything. But having said this we all have within us the source of renewal. To go from strength to strength we need to continually revisit this source. We need to adopt, as a conscious practice, reflection.

When the action is over leave it. Let it go. *Not this, not this.* Instead return to stillness and space, not as a means of escape but as a means of renewal, as a means of revitalisation, as a means of self-discovery.

In addition we need to develop mind practices which allow us to constantly return to where the energy is to be found. Going back over things undoubtedly wastes energy. How many times have you caught yourself in the 'if only' state of mind? 'If only I had said this.' 'If only I'd done that.' Rearranging events so as to provide what you imagine to be a better outcome – for you personally – is inevitably an act of the imagination and has nothing whatsoever to do with the present need, which has an altogether different kind of imperative. It's different because it's now and not then. It's different because it has its own reality, not a reality which you have provided out of some sense of self-regard. Energy comes when serving the present need. Energy is depleted when serving a self-created image of yourself. Try it and see.

Serving the immediate need requires a movement into reality and a movement into the present. Serving a sense of self-regard requires a movement away from reality and away from the present. In our doing this the magic of life is lost. What is also lost is a genuine sense of self-identity. Think about it. By creating for yourself an imaginary identity, you are in fact making it impossible to find what you know in moments of insight: the truth about yourself. You are cutting yourself off from yourself. By so doing you are removing yourself from the beauty of life and the genuine source of happiness. Reality lies elsewhere. It is our purpose to discover that reality. Emerson assures us of its presence:

> For you there is a reality... Place yourself in the middle of the stream of power and wisdom which animates all whom it floats, and you are without effort impelled to truth, to right, and perfect contentment.[10]

**PRACTICE**

Cool analysis is one thing, action replay another.
Assess certainly, draw wise conclusions,
but don't try to relive.
Instead, return to life.
Go back to the stream of power.

## Determined Action – Greater Strength

> There's a whole world of difference between vague inspiration and determined action. One never leads to much except a vague sense of ineffectuality. Through the other there is the chance of finding one's true purpose and that must lead to satisfaction. One saps strength. The other provides it.

As we have already stated, a comment like this is true just so long as the little me is not ruled by limited preconception.

What is undoubtedly true is that determination is required when it comes to developing a deeper understanding of life. There is always a tendency to let things run down. But the enquiring mind, the truly alive mind, is never really satisfied with small, inconsequential matters. It deals, quite necessarily, with a welter of these, but it does it with effectiveness and good humour. It does it in this way because it does it whilst keeping in mind the larger context.

> It was not for small things but for great that God created humanity, who, knowing the great, is not satisfied with small things. Indeed, it was for the limitless alone that he created men and women, who are the only beings on earth to have rediscovered their infinite nature and who are not fully satisfied with anything limited, however great that thing may be.[11]

This quotation from Marsilio Ficino indicates that as far as he is concerned, regardless of whoever we are, we are never truly satisfied until we start moving back the barriers, expanding our horizons, until we start addressing the largest issues of all. It's not for small things that God created man.

The very idea of seeking greatness has about it a certain nobility, a sense of human possibility. Fame was something that men pursued, not so much so that they could claim some vast merit for themselves but more so that virtue could be known. Our understanding of this concept has declined so much that fame and infamy are considered as being not so much opposites but as much the same sort of thing. You can now become famous for your misdeeds. You even become famous for promoting the most destructive forms of thought.

In reality the only true reason why fame might be considered important is that in being famous someone becomes a vehicle for the expression of the divine qualities. In the *Symposium* Socrates repeats the words of his teacher, Diotima. This is what she says about the purpose of the artists and the poets:

> Wisdom and all her sister virtues; it is the office of every poet to beget them, and of every artist whom we may call creative.[12]

The human race is supremely creative. It is one of our great strengths, and being creative is not just the prerogative of poets and artists. We are all creative. Diotima's words apply to us all.

To pursue fame for its own sake is, however, fraught with danger. It could mean that somebody could come along who lays personal claim to all that comes with fame. In this way their actions, by the nature of their motivation, would no longer be those associated with fame in the true sense of the word. This is why all the great traditions warn against pride. Self-abnegation has long been practised and maybe justifiably so. To try and contain qualities which have no limit into the very narrow confines of the ego is utterly destructive of those qualities.

Having said this, we, as has been mentioned many times in this book, are all perfect vehicles for the universal powers. Consider those who are truly famous, and this will become only too evident, as indeed it is when you consider those whose name has only travelled as far as a narrow circle of family and friends. What qualities do they possess? What qualities do they offer as an example to others?

Having clarified that the reason for determined action is not so much to gain any kind of personal glory, or personal power, or personal name, let us return to the reason for determination. There can only be one true and lasting reason for determination. So that what is true and lasting may be known in the transient play of things. So that the truly great things may, by living through us, find their time and place. As Ficino says, it's not for the petty, meaningless things that we were created, nor was it, in the final analysis, for the great things. It was, in his thinking, for that which has no limit, and the limitless is clearly quite beyond the bounds of any limited objective, no matter how great or pressing that objective may be.

The other thing that must be considered is the time for determined action of this sort. Limited objectives must happen in time and place, and the determination that is required lasts only as long as it takes to achieve them. We easily see our determination in those terms only. It is certainly true that when we are setting out to achieve our objectives, strength is derived from steady determination. It is also equally true that nothing is ever achieved from vague aspiration. That gives us no strength but only a kind of weakness that debilitates us rather than offering what we seek.

There is, however, another kind of determination that is not about limited objectives, but a determination to rejoice in the present for the simple reason that you cannot bring the past to life, nor forge the future to suit personal desire. Above all, reality lives only in the present. The strength of life is realised now. The great powers that are eternally present live at no other time than the eternal present. Our real determination must be, therefore, to connect with those powers as they manifest. Our real determination must be to transcend the desires that draw us away into the imaginary half-life of things yearned for, of regret for things lost never to be regained. Real strength is discovered here and now.

There is only one question that is really important when dealing with all the problems that beset us, when dealing with all the decisions that we inevitably face. It's what Marcus Aurelius speaks of when he asks, *How is my soul's helmsman going about his task?* The ultimate purpose in life is not the successful achievement of some limited objective, but the determination to make ever deeper contact with that within us which has no limit.

Learning to work from the limitless is what, in the final analysis, provides *purpose and true satisfaction*. The great philosophers assure us that in so doing we are granted the capability of living, regardless of what we might face, truly in touch with our humanity. Making conscious recourse to the limitless, a central feature of our lives allows us to go from strength to strength for the simple reason that we have taught the mind to constantly return to the final source of strength.

## PRACTICE

Return to the unlimited.
Gain strength from the final source of strength.
Use it to empower your role in life,
to make of your life something noble.

STAGE TWELVE

# Life Achievement

WE HAVE BEEN BORN as human beings with all the powers humans possess. This is an achievement in itself. It may not appear to be anything to do with any personal effort we may have made. To us has been freely given the gift of life. When we consider all the things we would like to achieve we must hold in mind what we were given at the beginning: that thing without which nothing could be done. To remain true to that must involve us in making good use of this miraculous tool of mind and body. It would be absurd to think that we were given them merely to squander.

The desire to give of ourselves in the same measure as it has been given would provide a firm basis for life's true achievement.

Use what is to be found in this stage of the book to make creative use of the gifts you have been given; in the process discover your unique purpose, that which is yours alone to fulfil.

## What's at The Beginning will be at The End

Whatever there is at the beginning of an action is bound to have a decided effect on everything that follows thereafter. It colours it all. When events meet you, you alone are the vehicle for action, whatever that action might be. Out of the realm of infinite possibility arises a response. How perfectly measured that response is to the purpose intended is for you alone to discover at that time. What is evident in the meeting of any need is that the attention can rest on nothing other than what there is when that need becomes known. If self-consideration becomes the predominant factor the focus must be lost and with it the energy.

> There is a vitality, a life force, an energy, a quickening, that is translated through you into action, and because there is only one of you in all time, this expression is unique. And if you block it, it will never exist through any other medium and will be lost.[1]

These are the words of Martha Graham the renowned choreographer. Blocking what is yours alone to do may very well arise out of the simple desire to ignore what the situation is demanding of you, to not do it, or to do it with all kinds of personal considerations affecting the result. Here Martha Graham is talking about the creative act. Our creative acts may not be something placed under a spotlight in a public theatre, but we do create. We cannot help it. We are creating all the time, for good or ill.

If your motive for acting is nothing whatsoever to do with meeting a genuine need, but is rather to do with the expression of some entirely self-motivated desire, then the whole thing is going to be coloured by a narrow determination, and imported into it will be all kinds of excitement and frustration. What is produced out of this can never be clear-cut and simple, quite the opposite. It's bound to be complicated, full of an emotional pressure that has to have its effect on outcomes. Again it is one of those paradoxes that in order to produce something that is utterly our own – in the sense that Martha Graham speaks of it – we have to learn to remove from our actions things that complicate and confuse. Personal desire often does just that. Dedicating our actions to the greater good is a practice of long pedigree designed to create something that goes beyond any self-imposed limit.

Here, for instance, is the way Saint Augustine formulates it and his approach is radical: *Love and do what thou wilt.* Needless to say he is not talking about a love which is bound up in self-seeking but one that is boundless and free. To have love at the start of any action, will allow love to be a central quality of whatever results.

There is another approach, Martha Graham again:

> Each day of rehearsal for a new ballet I arrive a little before two in the afternoon and sit in my studio to have a moment of stillness before the dancers enter. I tease myself and say I am cultivating my Buddha nature; but it is really just such a comforting place for me to be – secure, clear and with large mirrors so that I can be completely within myself.

To arrive early and to come to stillness is very much in accord with *Self Remembering*. What is she doing in this but coming to herself? It's here, if anywhere, that we may find comfort and security. Quietly reflecting in this grounded place is a marvellous preparation for the creativity that comes afterwards. But why the mirror?… *and with large mirrors so that I can be completely within myself.*

I don't know the answer. Only she could say why. One thing comes to mind however. There are mirrors in any dance studio, and maybe for her these mirrors not only reflect the dancers' bodies in movement, but they also reflect, in the quiet moments that she describes, the inner mirror, the mirror of the mind. This mirror, as you will remember, reflects both the forms that come before the mind and the consciousness which allows those forms to be illuminated. In the *Philokalia*, The Love of Spiritual Beauty – that great work of spirituality from the Russian Orthodox Church – there is a practice of reflection which involves, at the moment attention is aroused, the returning to the memory of the light of consciousness rather than being sucked into the physical and mental forms, which can so easily possess the mind. Returning to the memory of the light rather than being possessed by the forms is a marvellous starting point for any action. It also goes a long way to explain why some of the results of human creativity have this luminous quality, a quality that has the power to remind us of our own true nature, the light of consciousness which empowers it all.

**PRACTICE**

Make sure you start any action from the right place:
stillness not agitation, harmony not discord.

## Coming into Harmony

It's so easy to treat this wonderful instrument we have been given with indifference, disdain even, and yet what a miracle it is. Science can make some rudimentary interventions into this world, but of its vast subtlety we can only stand in awe. Consider what it consists of: a few elementary chemicals, which if they were broken down into their constituent elements could be purchased for next to nothing, and yet what miracles arise from the combination of these elements. We believe we have intelligence, but just consider the intelligence that goes into the making and sustaining of this body of ours. Lying behind our personal intelligence there seems to be an intelligence of an altogether different order, which we might in our foolishness impede but not control.

Think for a moment about this body which we believe is stable and recognisably our own:

- 98% of the body's atoms were not there a year ago.
- The skeleton that we now possess was not there three months ago, for, although bone cells remain constant, atoms pass freely backwards and forwards.
- The skin is completely renewed over the course of a month.
- The stomach lining is renewed over the course of four days, the liver over a period of six months.
- Even though the brain cells are not renewed once they die, the content of carbon, oxygen, hydrogen, nitrogen and other gases is totally different today from what it was a year ago.
- In addition there is a free flow of carbon, oxygen, hydrogen and nitrogen in those things we use up the fastest: earth in the form of food; water; fire in the form of sunlight, and air.

If this isn't an exquisite tool working with infinite subtlety, ruled by an intelligence with which we intervene at our peril, what is it? Our task must be to adopt a lifestyle which allows this brilliant thing we call 'my body' to operate according to its own beautiful measures.

The practices and ways of thinking that are encouraged throughout this book will bring harmony to both mind and body. This will enable us to achieve things in life that can never be achieved when mind and body are racked by tension, and the measure is lost.

**PRACTICE**

Avoid maltreating what has been freely given.
Work in accord with nature, not against it.
In respecting the mind and body, allow them to work freely.
Resolve tension.
Come back to balance and harmony.

## Seizing the Opportunities

When we have a clear sense of measure we know when it's time to act and when it's time to cease from action. One of the great arts of life is knowing when to stop. But we also need to know when to start. To avoid acting when action is necessary is the best way to destroy the opportunity to develop and achieve. Developing the habit of putting things off involves turning away from the energy given. By turning away from the energy given, less and less energy becomes available. Without that energy nothing can be done.

*By accident most strange bountiful Fortune,*
*Now my dear lady, hath mine enemies*
*Brought to this shore; and by my prescience*
*I find my zenith doth depend upon*
*A most auspicious star, whose influence*
*If now I court not, but omit, my fortunes*
*Will ever after droop.*

In these lines from Shakespeare's *The Tempest* the magician, Prospero, recognises that his time for action has arrived. He recognises this because of his knowledge of the stars. Through the position of these he acknowledges that his fortune will fade, not just temporarily, but for evermore, unless he takes clear and firm action now, in this present moment. Fortune in his terms is not financial reward, but a goddess. Her name is Fortuna, and she is the principle of chance. The wheel of fortune rises and falls. In this time of action, Prospero recognises that for him the wheel of fortune is rising and the planets are aligned in sympathy with his objectives.

Fortuna is associated with the planets of Jupiter and Venus, and though he talks about his enemies, it is the spirit of these two gods that rules Prospero's actions. Jupiter is the god of light and of the day as well as of thunder and lightning. He rules over the councils of the gods. He is the final dispenser of justice and therefore he thunders. He takes the prime site in our solar system and as such he is also associated with that other quality of justice – balance – and it is the balanced view that prevails in Prospero's dispensation of justice. He tempers justice with mercy and performs not an act of cruel revenge upon his 'enemies' but a judgement which brings about rightful law under the rule of love, and in this Venus plays her inevitable part.

Our actions may not have the consequence of Prospero's actions, which is the realignment of his dukedom in accordance with divine principles, but this doesn't mean that the spirit in which he acts cannot be the same spirit in which we act, vitally alive to the present need, acting when action is possible in the spirit of reason, justice and love.

If we are ruled by the power of inertia, all this is impossible. We put off the moment for action and the energy is lost. Alternatively we may not so much act as react, and when our reactions are ill-conceived, driven by no other motive than a personal one, the results must carry with them all the qualities of their inception. But there is a third alternative. In rather stark terms all three are described in that source of great wisdom, the *Bhagavad-gita*:

> Purity brings happiness. Passion commotion, and Ignorance, which obscures wisdom, leads to a life of failure.
>
> When Purity is in the ascendant, the man evolves; when Passion, he neither evolves or degenerates; when Ignorance, he is lost.[2]

The indication given by these verses is that to achieve something of lasting consequence in life we must do all that we can to encourage that power which is here described as Purity. Elsewhere this same power is associated with clarity, stillness and lucidity. These are the qualities associated with the mind when the light of reason rules.

Later in *The Tempest* Prospero says this:

> *Though with their high wrongs I am struck to th' quick*
> *Yet with my nobler reason 'gainst my fury*
> *Do I take part; the rarer action is*
> *In virtue than in vengeance.*

Rarer in this context doesn't only mean unusual but also finer and nobler and more wise. It's by these qualities that our actions must be ruled.

**PRACTICE**

Act when action is required at the only time action is possible, the present, the moment when the eternal qualities live.

## Using Your Own Particular Gifts

It is undoubtedly true that we will never discover our true destiny without making clear and conscious efforts to explore what has been given to us to do personally, to realise our own individual talents. These won't be discovered unless our energy is wisely invested. They certainly won't be discovered by using energy mindlessly to chase after first one thing and then another. Likewise our talents certainly won't be discovered if we insist on burying them in the ground. Real discovery requires action when action is possible.

> I habitually avoid the issue. I don't face the challenges. Better the devil you know. I look through the job columns in the paper, and though I'm certain I could do most of those things that catch my attention, I convince myself that I can't because it would involve hard work and facing certain aspects of myself which I would rather leave unexplored.

We cannot do that. Action is required, continuously, and this requires perseverance and determination, even when inertia seems to be in the ascendant; indeed particularly when inertia seems to be in the ascendant.

There are those times when negative emotion seems to rule out any possibility of discovering what it is that is given for us to do. Here are some examples of just this:

> I have this very basic sense of failure. When I hand in anything at work there is this profound belief in my own failure.

> You can so easily get attracted to the trivial. It has the sense of self-indulgence. I've seen myself in these situations when it feels completely justified to sulk and indulge in it!

Then there is distraction, or in this case, not so much distraction more obsession:

> I am looking for a place to live, a flat to buy. I have this idea of living just where I am now, a spacious leafy street in a London suburb. In fact I've made an offer on one just down the road. I'm so excited that I can't sleep. It seems all my future happiness depends on it. I seem incapable of thinking about anything else.

A common experience? From our own experience, what effect does this kind of thinking have? Does it not inevitably fill the mind with an agitation which removes us from the present.

Here's another story of a different kind:

> Of late I have found that I am much more able to look at my role in life and not get so confused. Last week there was good reason to practise *Self Remembering*. At work I am the chairman of the

> union branch, and have to represent members of staff. I often feel myself getting annoyed with certain individuals on the management team. Some of their ideas are so short-sighted. One can allow these attitudes to cloud the issue and then react and get angry. I remembered what was said about giving to the situation rather taking from it. This allowed me to let it all go, to step back and observe the whole in an uninvolved way. It seemed so important to have recourse to this so as not to add fire to fire.
>
> When this happens the conversation takes place on a different level. All that is left is a cool analysis of the facts.

Under these circumstances do you think this individual is more effective as a negotiator or less? Indeed, do you think that by being ruled by reason he has developed a talent for it? A talent like this naturally arises because of clear connection and cool observation.

**PRACTICE**

Give expression to your true talents
by clear connection and cool observation.
This is the best way to measure out perfectly
the power you possess.

## Seek the Creative Solution

There can often be a tendency to reject any novel or creative approach to life and instead be driven to respond in the same old way; in the way that has been tried so many times in the past – so many times indeed that it has become almost inconceivable that there could be an alternative. There is nothing in the situation to suggest anything different. It doesn't suggest itself because we allow no space for anything other than what has always been practised, the regular response. The buttons have been pressed and everything automatically unfolds. What is very evident about this entirely automatic approach is that there is something at the heart of the whole thing, a set of cherished ideas and long-adopted attributes that goes by the name of ME. And because these attributes are what we think *we* are they are particularly potent. We have a personal interest in sustaining them.

As individuals we have an entirely understandable desire to protect this individual life. It seems a central motive. Consider how tenaciously we cling to life. Yet despite this, life is forever placing this apparent individual into something far larger. No man is an island. He is cast into a context which goes beyond his separate self. In fact he is born into such a context. It's called the family. From the beginning his very life is dependent on others, utterly dependent. He is born out of another, the product of another's creative act.

And it is in the spirit of true creativity, which involves stepping beyond himself, that he should act. Lying beyond all his personal identifications is a far wider place, a far deeper place, a far more significant place. Paradoxically enough, although not entirely familiar, it is in fact a place which is far closer to a sense of his own true self than the personal world he normally inhabits. Being wider, deeper and more significant, it is also more creative. Many have considered this place to be the very source of creativity. The Platonists called it the Intelligible World, the world of the eternal truths.

This way of thinking lies at the heart of the very meaning of the word 'imagination'. This is part of the definition given by the *Oxford English Dictionary*: 'the power to give consistency of reality to ideal forms'.

Coleridge, the poet and philosopher, a man of great creative powers, says this of the creative imagination:

> The poet diffuses a tone and spirit of unity by sympathetic and magical power to which we have exclusively appropriated the name of imagination...[3]

He goes on to talk about how this imagination has the power to reconcile opposites including reconciling the idea with the image. The image is drawn from the 'passing reality' of this material world, and the idea belongs to the realm of the ideal, of 'eternal reality'. And to connect the two requires sympathetic and magical powers.

What this indicates is that by being creative, or even just by being part of the creative act merely as an onlooker, we go beyond the cramped quarters of personal existence to discover something far more profound.

I remember the midwife who delivered two of my children saying, 'Each one's a miracle. It's always a wonder.' And she had been delivering children for forty years. She had a talent for it and a love. Although a spinster herself, her family was vast, and the world in which she lived was just as big.

When, through experience, the joy of living in the larger world becomes familiar to us, it's so much easier to step over the impediments of personal identification. To step over one has also to step back, step back from all the identifications into unidentified observation. To do this one must constantly practise *Self Remembering*. The world which *Self Remembering* leads us to, rather than being a passionless void as some people fear, allows us to see everything in its beauty and wonder. Out of it comes the creative solution, the one that perfectly meets the need.

**PRACTICE**

Make it a requirement of life
to seek in any situation the larger world.
Look there for the creative solution.

## See Things as if for the First Time

Have you noticed that the experience of life can consist of so many labels, of colour-coded files? How easy it is to keep on doing exactly the same thing in life. In this way we have no need to think. All our impressions slot into a well-organised and consistently maintained set of preconceptions but, like colour-coded files on a computer, this is all done mechanically.

> Standing at the end of a moving train, I had a clear view through to the far end of the carriage. I could see most of the passengers. Having used the Underground for many years this scene was not new to me.

My usual experience of tube travel is one of unease and discomfort. The desire to be elsewhere usually prevails. This time was no different, but something caused me to stop. I observed something else. I became aware that we were all one thing. We were all moving together. Then came an awareness of unity. The passengers and the space became one. The view had changed, and I was aware that I was looking at something wondrous.

I believe that the ideas that I have been considering of late have enabled the shift from a feeling of discomfort to something very different.

This, on the face of things, might seem unrelated to what we are considering here, but that's not the case at all. In living an open life, rather than one closed in by the usual confines, possibilities start to arise, insights and creative impulses.

In Plato's dialogue *Phaedrus* this question is raised:

> Am I a monster with more heads than Typhon, more full of fire and fury? Or am I a simpler and calmer being, sharing in some divine and favourable destiny, partaking in a quiet understanding?[4]

In discovering this simplicity and calm, Plato suggests we find a divine destiny. In doing this we must come out of all the confines that either deaden or agitate and enter the clear simplicity of the present, and there discover something that's very different from our so-called 'normal' experience of life. This simplicity and calm is not bland. What is to be discovered here is full of intelligent detail and true vitality.

Here's an insight which is also very illuminating providing, as it does, a way in which we may stand free and connect with that which manifests now, to be able to rest with nothing other than the simple act of observation.

A couple of days ago I was riding home on the bus when I practised *Self Remembering*. I noticed myself watching how people were walking outside on the street. I found myself being

> fascinated by their movements. Although I was fascinated, there didn't seem to be any sense of involvement, but remarkably enough, despite this seeming lack of involvement, or perhaps because of it, I seemed to be granted some kind of insight into their natures. What I also noticed was that at the same time there seemed to be a freedom from my usual sense of myself, which surprisingly gave me an awareness that was really acute.

Here is another example of the simple power of observation, in this case without involvement or comment. It's from a dancer:

> When I dance there is this wisdom in my body. Dancing is playful and in the NOW. There is contact without words or judgement.

To enter the NOW is not just the dancer's task, this is the same task for us all. Avoid clouding the mind with all the usual ideas rooted in personal identification but, instead, enter the here and now, simply and directly and with total commitment.

**PRACTICE**

When you find that you are looking through eyes that seem old
and tired,
find something of your true destiny
by stepping back into the realm of quiet understanding.

## Persistence and Method

It's not the sudden insight or unexpected life-enhancing moments that change a life. These undoubtedly point towards a direction, but for any of us to naturalise what is natural to us we must adopt a way of thinking that neutralises those thoughts and feelings that tend to negate the strengths we have.

What is being encouraged here is that which will allow our selves to connect with the depths of our own potential as human beings. In the whole process of self-discovery there is the undisguised intention to live a fulfilled life for the benefit of all. To achieve this we must continually return to source, go back to the central nature of things, that which allows us to be the fully conscious human beings that we have every capability of being. It's only by doing this that we may separate out what is useful to us and what isn't. It also provides the strength to deal with self-inflicted debilitation, the confines and constraints and general tensions we place ourselves under.

To continue growing and expanding and achieving all that we are destined to achieve, steady persistence is required. We must constantly return to our source of strength rather than our source of weakness.

Much scientific research has been carried out over recent years to explore both the physical and psychological effects of adopting a more reflective lifestyle. Here are some of the benefits:

## Physiological Benefits

- Reduction in blood pressure and heart rate
- Marked increase in oxygen consumption, metabolic rate, respiratory rate and minute ventilation
- Reduction of serum cholesterol, increase in skin resistance [low skin resistance is a marker of stress responses], decrease in blood lactates
- Changes in EEG patterns including an increase in alpha and theta waves
- Reduction of epileptic seizure frequency
- Reduced TSH and T3 levels [thyroid hormones]
- Improved immune function through reversal of the immunosuppressive effects of stress

And if the physiological effects are clearly evident, the psychological effects are even more so.

## Psychological Effects

- Decreased anxiety
- Better pain control

- More optimism, less depression as indicted by elevation of serotonin
- Greater self-awareness and self-actualisation
- Improved coping capabilities
- Reduced reliance on drugs, prescribed or non-prescribed, or on alcohol
- Improved sleep
- Reduced aggression and criminal tendency
- Greater efficiency and output and reduced stress at work
- Improved sensory perceptiveness
- Improved concentration and memory

*New Frontiers in Medicine*, Dr Craig Hassed

Although our life has already been achieved for us, working on ourselves in a reflective fashion does enable us to both prolong life and, even more importantly, make of life, regardless of its length, something entirely productive. By possessing a fit body we have the strength to achieve what is ours to achieve, and by having a fit heart and mind we have the will, the intelligence and the creative energy to be of genuine service to life. What the Buddha said is utterly true: *Our life is shaped by our minds.* The intent of this book is to encourage the shaping of our life into something that is natural to life, rather than it being deformed by something that isn't.

There is however a problem in following this instruction. If what is utterly unnatural has become second nature, how can we differentiate between the natural and the unnatural? Here's a story which goes some way to answering this question.

> I have suffered from headaches every day for the past fifteen years. After countless doctor's visits, EEGs and brain scans nothing appeared to be out of the ordinary. Miraculously after a year of putting what I have heard here into practice they have disappeared.
>
> There were several steps involved in this process. The first step came with the realisation of just how much activity was going on in my mind. It was overwhelming; I found myself thinking of

> three or four things at once while trying to perform any given action. The next step involved listening to the mind chatter, which I discovered was predominantly concerned with making judgements. Virtually every action, no matter how simple, was judged, and for the most part these judgements were negative. They would be played over and over again in my mind.
>
> After noticing the judgements, I tried to understand their purpose. What came about was a realisation that I had created an internal reward system that I was completely unaware of. I discovered that every desire had to be earned, and only after the desire had been earned would I be rewarded. These desires were common needs such as having a drink or using the bathroom. For example I would mentally make a list of things to do before I was allowed a drink of water, like tidying up the dishes, putting shoes away, etc. Only after these actions had been performed would I permit myself to have a drink. Furthermore, whilst I was performing each action it would be judged.
>
> At this acknowledgement, I consciously stopped the reward system and tried to detach myself from the judgements, and the headaches, as well as the judgements, began to subside.

This woman's headaches finally came to an end with the realisation that as a child she had inherited this whole thing from her mother, who conducted her life in the same fashion.

With this discovery came the opportunity of being of assistance, rather than handing her condition on to her own children just as it had been handed on to her. And in addition, she could bring the insight that she had gained to the aid of others who might be suffering from the detrimental effects of ingrained habits of thought.

The other thing that is worth observing about this story is how the truth of her situation was revealed by the practice of *Self Remembering*. What *Self Remembering* also provided was a means to prevent her from returning to this state of affliction. It helped her overcome a destructive habit of mind. Let us not forget, however, what this whole reflection is about: persistence and method.

She was allowed an insight into her predicament by the power of the reflective exercise she had been introduced to, and it is the persistent return to this practice which will allow her, and indeed all of us, to step free from those impediments of mind which in extreme circumstances can blight an entire life.

**PRACTICE**

For the new to replace the old it is essential to continually practise. Continually practise.

## In What do You Place Your Belief?

It's very easy to adopt a negative attitude to life by placing your belief in those things that arise in heart and mind and proclaim themselves as being utterly true because they appear to be born out in experience.

> This is how I feel. This is what I think. You may tell me something different, and it may be true for you, but I know from experience what's true for me.

The woman with her constant headaches is an example. That's a physiological result of a pattern of thought. Such patterns could be even more common than we think. This story was told to me recently by a medical student facing an impediment which was in his own words like a brick wall.

> I did all that I could to get into medical school. Having achieved my ambition, I set out on the course with a will. Now I'm into my fourth year, and I feel I've hit a wall. I went back to medical school in September only to find that two of my close friends had dropped out. They could no longer take the pressure. I then went on a hospital placement and was put in a children's ward. I was horrified to find a considerable degree of cynicism amongst the doctors. Maybe I'm too young and idealistic, but to be faced with this kind of attitude was something I found hard to take.
>
> The whole thing got so bad that I seriously contemplated

> dropping out myself. I spoke to the college authorities and they suggested that I took a year out. I was frightened that if I did that I would never return. They had already offered antidepressants. When I refused they claimed that half the students on my course were on them. This made me even more depressed.
>
> In the end I decided to come home for a couple of weeks just to think things over. It was my parents who suggested I attended the class. Up till now all my energy has done nothing but feed this depression that had taken over my life. Everything I had went into that, and the more I fed it the more 'real' it became until it was hard to think that there could be any alternative.

The truth of the matter is that when you're in the grip of something like this there is no alternative. The chemical construction of your body, triggered by negative thinking, is creating a reality for you which seems utterly credible and inescapable. This is why people are advised to turn to chemical intervention – antidepressant drugs. These don't so much return you to the understanding you once had as cover over the manifestation of your disease. Only a change of mind can effect a proper cure. In his account the medical student made an interesting comment:

> Since attending the class, in just two weeks the whole thing has lifted.

In traditional pantomime the central and always the most expensive scene is the 'transformation scene'. I remember vividly as a child going to pantomimes at Christmas, and for me the most memorable of these scenes was in *Aladdin*. In it Aladdin goes down into the cave to discover the wonderful lamp. To do this he comes to a rock face, finds the stone which hides the mouth of the cave and rolls it back. At this point in the action the lights come up behind the gauze curtain on which the rock face is painted, and what is to the audience's eye a solid wall becomes transparent, revealing the cave's magical interior.

This was always a source of wonder to us children. Reality had changed. The curtain had lifted to reveal an inner world. And for this medical student the curtain of his depression had lifted to reveal what had been there all along but entirely obscured by his emotional state. Through a timely reminder, the lights came up behind the wall of his depression, and he saw it for what it was – something in which he had placed his belief, something which he was empowering with the same energy he discovered in far greater abundance behind the veil.

By seeing what lay behind this wall of negativity he was able to return to medical school with his enthusiasm renewed. He withdrew his belief from what had previously seemed so real.

To sustain that enthusiasm his practice will have to be maintained. Environmental pressures and habits of mind combine to create an impression of life with which we totally identify. Our task is to go beyond that, to discover what lies at the heart of the cave. *Aladdin*, like most traditional stories, does have its inner meaning, and, if you remember, the genie doesn't come out of the magic lamp without a little rubbing.

**PRACTICE**

Withdraw your belief from the world your mind seems to be creating for you, especially if that world is full of negative influence. Who would place their trust in something that denies and debilitates?

## True Desires

> It is better to turn to true desires rather than those that are destructive. But who is to say what are true desires?
>
> What is right for somebody else may not be right for me, and what was right for me once may not be right any longer.

What is true has to be assessed in the light of a whole set of shifting identities, passing passions, habits of heart and mind. May we ever discover established truth, the truth that is always true when what we have available to make such a discovery is so partial and shifting?

It would appear unlikely. It is for this reason that we must do all that we can to step free from the toils of the mind.

These are the words of the Buddhist philosophers:

> To aim at lasting achievements whilst still exposed to this world's distractions – that prolongs the bondage.
>
> To try and understand one's inner mind still chained to hopes and fears – that prolongs the bondage.[5]

These are words from one of the most respected of texts. They clearly state the view the Buddhists hold – that to escape the toils of this world one has step free of personal desire. The question has often been put: 'Does this mean desires of every kind?'

In one sense, yes, it does mean the hopes and fears of this little self in its attempt to grasp after that which is important to its own sense of self-identity. Desires of this nature can do nothing but reinforce that sense of identity. Buddhists believe that serving this identity sustains separation. Nirvana, the goal of the Buddhist aspirant, involves a blowing away of all this tightness and confinement, and when this gives way there comes the realisation that everything that appears to be concerned with personal attainment is in fact to do with nothing but personal containment. These are the walls which we build out of the fabric of our hopes and fears.

In another sense the answer to the same question is 'no'. The Buddhists are not so much concerned with doctrine as with the right way to live, and for them the right way to live is to fill this life with compassion and care. Spiritual truths are not to be gained as some kind of personal attainment. That would be entirely against the true spirit of things. True desires can never be personal in the sense of gaining something which is of personal benefit. We must instead look beyond the personal.

Here again is Einstein's beautiful statement concerning the personal and the universal:

> A human being is part of the whole, called by us 'Universe', a part limited in time and space. He experiences himself, his thoughts

> and feelings, as something separated from the rest – a kind of optical delusion of his consciousness. This delusion is a kind of prison for us, restricting us to our personal desires and to affection for a few persons nearest to us. Our task must be to free ourselves from this prison by widening our circle of compassion to embrace all living creatures and the whole of nature in its beauty.[6]

This is a perfect example of somebody identifying true desires and working throughout life for their achievement. And who can say his achievements were not great?

The persistence and determination he gave to the proving of the theorems which he will ever be famous for arose out of strength and enthusiasm, or as he describes it: love. Without determination and persistence there can be no growth of strength and enthusiasm, there can be no self-discovery or the ever expanding realisation of love.

**PRACTICE**

Find your desires, the unconfined ones, ever expansive,
and in serving them discover the strength to serve.

## Of the Greater Good there is No Limit

> Is it not true that the really fundamental desires are not personal but serve something much bigger than myself?

Most people would claim that their fundamental desire is to achieve lasting happiness and fulfilment in their lives. People attempt to do this in many different ways and with differing levels of success. As life is in a constant state of flux, and eventually, regardless of what success may be achieved in this life, all of it is taken from us, achievement, however great, is bound to be transitory: but this is only true from a personal point of view.

When we in some way serve something larger than this, then such limitations disappear. Me and mine, or rather what we have come to believe to be me and mine, cease to be of ultimate importance. What may well be discovered in adopting such an approach is something of far greater validity, and this, by its very nature, goes far beyond the enforced limits of personal claim.

We, as creatures with the power of reason and imagination, must create. In this we have no choice. Bound by personal desire, we can easily consider our creation to be some kind of personal achievement for our personal benefit, but the truth of the matter is that there cannot be beneficial achievement unless that achievement is gained in the service of the greater good. We are in a sense all individual, but it doesn't take much to realise that we are in no way separate. We are part of the greater whole and by serving the greater whole we are not left out of the good we do. If, however, we achieve things by harming the greater good, we must inevitably in the course of time be harmed ourselves. If this doesn't seem obvious at the time, it will become obvious.

The other reason for serving the greater good is that it takes our actions beyond the limited. It places them within a wider context, and the philosophers tell us it's only when we look beyond the personal, that we may tap into the universal forces which allow us to fulfil our true purpose. This was the thinking in ancient Greece. It was thinking in the last great Renaissance. It was the great poets' thought, and it was true of great scientists like Newton and Einstein. By serving the greater good some would say we are serving the widest context of all, because to the greater good there is no limit.

There may, however, arise from this another question: *How can I with my limited knowledge and capabilities hope to achieve something of genuine and lasting value?*

We are born into life empowered by the universe, the elements of which are running through us both physically and subtly as a constant fact. Our agitations of mind may bind us to this individual identity that we devote so much time and effort to sustaining, but in truth we are something quite different. Our true identity lies beyond the purely personal. Sometimes by chance we may glimpse that fact. It comes unbidden, seemingly like an act of grace. Sometimes the exceptional nature of the circumstances we meet seems to arouse a knowledge which has, in the movement and concern of life, remained hidden. Then we have knowledge which by its nature quite transcends the limited view that creates our usual understanding.

These are the thoughts of Edgar J. Mitchell who was an astronaut on Apollo 14:

> We can see the earth set against the background of billions of stars and galaxies and clusters of galaxies. I had the experience of recognising that it's all connected – that it is not, as we in science had tended to believe, a cosmic accident; it's all not that way at all – that the molecules of my body and the molecules of the spacecraft were manufactured in the furnaces of ancient stars billions of years ago. Everything was part of this process that created us, and that there is a connection between all of it; and that it's an intelligent universe, not just a piece of inanimate matter floating around.[7]

It's understanding of this nature that grants true happiness, that allows us to fulfil our fundamental desires. It does this because, as Edgar J. Mitchell understood in a moment of blinding insight, in truth what we are transcending is our inclination to think of ourselves as separate, and by serving the greater whole we serve our ultimate and unlimited selves.

**PRACTICE**

Give up serving the limited self.
Serve your unlimited Self instead.
By doing that discover your life and being.

## Adopt Measure

It's highly appropriate that the insights of Edgar Mitchell happened on board a spacecraft called Apollo. As we have heard, Apollo is the spirit of light and harmony. Every civilisation creates myths in order to express understanding of this kind. Apollo was the god that the ancient Greeks most fully embraced and endeavoured to realise in their lives. Through the inspiration of Apollo they sought the ideals of harmony and proportion, and health of heart and mind. Above all they saw in Apollo the light of wisdom, the still light of consciousness, and it was this which gave measure to their great works of art and architecture. If this sense of measure lay at the heart of their art, it was because it lay at the heart of their philosophy. It was the Greeks who gave us the word 'philosophy'. It means 'the love of wisdom'. When we return to the light of wisdom as a constant and central resource in our lives then we may discover a measure and beauty in all that we do, and thus live philosophically.

Remember what the Romans took from the Greeks, thinking like this: *Beauty is splendour of truth. The simple is the seal of the true.*

These mottoes link truth not only with beauty but also with simplicity. The simple, the beautiful and the true: these are the indications of wisdom. They are also the indications of true measure.

Measure occurs in our response to life when we unravel the complications that our personal desires can easily create, and simply serve the need that the moment is presenting. It's at these times that we return to the simplicity and directness that conscious recourse to this wisdom grants. This is the spirit of Apollo working through us. In addition, our conscious core is also our creative centre. What we must remember of Apollo is that he is also the leader of the nine Muses, the power behind all creative activity.

*Be thou the tenth Muse, ten times more in worth*
*Than those old nine that rhymers invocate:*
*And he that calls on thee, let him bring forth*
*Eternal numbers to outlive long date.*

SHAKESPEARE, Sonnet 38

The mark of the really creative solution, regardless of what field one is working in, is that nothing can be added or taken from it but for the worse. It has its own perfection. What this reflection is encouraging us to do is to find our own perfection by interacting with life simply, directly and beautifully, and that can only be achieved by constant recourse to the light of Apollo, which illuminates all that we do.

**PRACTICE**

Stand back from all those personal involvements
that have such a binding effect upon us.
Step back into the light.

## Living for the Love of It

The universal principles are with us always. Inevitably our life is experienced according to the level of consciousness available. This varies radically at different times, even, it would seem, from moment to moment, and those differences are entirely dependent on our state of mind, and our state of mind is entirely dependent upon our involvements. This is what the Buddha says:

> Our life is shaped by our mind; we become what we think. Suffering follows an evil thought as the wheels of a cart follow the oxen that draw it.
>
> Our life is shaped by our mind; we become what we think. Joy follows a pure thought like a shadow that never leaves.[8]

Everything found in this book has encouraged a reassessment of how we use our minds. And indeed how we use our hearts. It has been encouraging a reassessment of the nature and purpose of our lives, of what we dedicate our lives to, and when we actually attempt to live. It has opened up the question of self-knowledge, and of how, with a greater understanding of ourselves, there naturally arises a greater understanding of those around us, a greater understanding and a greater sympathy. This book has explored how we can live in unity and not division, and how, with a greater understanding of the unity, there arises quite naturally a greater energy to deal with all the demands of life, and a greater creativity to help us perfectly meet those demands with a response that is utterly measured to the need. So many of the stories in this book have described just this.

All of this will naturally occur for the simple reason that, with a rise in consciousness, there arises a movement out of a life circumscribed by habit into an awareness of how the universal powers of beauty, love and joy inform everything. In discovering more about all this, we are learning to love life, living for the love of it. When we give of ourselves to life, however it may manifest, out of a sheer love of life, then we learn to live in the spirit in which life is offered to us. By so doing we discover something of the spiritual principles which are utterly transcendent of the limitations that this particular life we call mine seems to lay upon us. We become alive to life in its greater totality, meeting it when it arises, in the eternal present.

It is only in this moment that it is possible to connect the outer surface of life to life's eternal core. Here things never grow old but are forever fresh and new. Impressions are no longer cold and hard, but instead vital and alive. It is here that true wealth is discovered. It is here that life is achieved, and it is only by returning to this place, over and over again, in fact drawing our minds back from the past and future to dwell in the living presence of this life, that we may, at the seeming end of life, realise that the passage of our days has been lived in the presence of the eternal. This is living life in the spirit of love, and by achieving this we discover something that is truly lasting, something that is both with us in every moment of our lives, but, at the same time, utterly unbound by time.

**PRACTICE**

Learn to be alive to life
by consciously living for the love of it.

# *Final Thought*

Vital in the outward thrust of life, calm within,
all desire to possess these wonderful gifts,
for they change everything.

The use of these reflections leads you on a path of self-knowledge, understanding and certainty, all of which enable you to meet the demands of life with a new source of creative energy.

Return to what is to be found in this book over and over again. Put these reflections to the test in all the situations you meet.

What is wisdom after all but discovery in experience?

What is the only change worth making but for the better?

Be reflective. Use Reason. Live consciously.

By doing this you may discover how the love of wisdom works.

# References

**Stage One**
1 Robert Frost, *Collected Poems of Robert Frost*, (Henry Holt & Co, 1969)
2 Plotinius, *Enneads*, trans. Elmer O'Brien (Mentor Books, 1964)

**Stage Two**
1 Plato, *Dialogues of Plato*, trans. Benjamin Jowett (Oxford University Press, 1871)
2 Plato, *Phaedrus*, trans. Benjamin Jowett (Oxford University Press, 1871)
3 Plotinius, *Enneads*, trans. Elmer O'Brien (Mentor Books, 1964)

**Stage Three**
1 P'ang Yun, poem taken from *The Enlightened Heart: An Anthology of Sacred Poetry*, ed. Stephen Mitchell (Harper and Row, 1989)
2 P'ei Ti, *Poems of Solitude*, trans. Jerome Ch'in and Michael Bullock (Abelard Schuman, 1960)
3 W.B. Yeats, 'Lake Isle of Innisfree' *Selected Poems* (Macmillan, 1962)
4 Marcus Aurelius, *Meditations*, trans. Matthew Staniforth (Penguin Classics,1964)
5 William Wordsworth, 'Ode ('Intimations of Immortality') *Selected Poetry* (Penguin, 1992)
6 Purohit Swami and W.B. Yeats eds., *The Ten Principal Upanishads*, (Faber and Faber, 1937)

**Stage Four**
1 William Blake, *The Complete Poems* (Penguin English Classics, 1974)
2 Purohit Swami and W.B. Yeats eds., *The Ten Principal Upanishads*, (Faber and Faber, 1937)

**Stage Five**
1 Thomas Traherne, *Centuries*, Edited and Published Bertram Dobell, 1908
2 Pablo Casals from programme notes of Bach Cantata Pilgrimage, 2001
3 Paul Klee, *On Modern Art*, trans. Paul Findlay (Faber and Faber 1966)
4 Federico Garcia Lorca, *Lorca* trans. J.L. Gill (Penguin Poets, 1960)

**Stage Six**
1 Rainer Maria Rilke, *Letters on Cézanne*, ed. Clara Rilke, trans. Joel Agee (Fromm International, 1992)

**Stage Seven**
1 Plato, *Symposium*, trans. Benjamin Jowett (Oxford University Press, 1871)
2 Bernard Denvir ed., *The Impressionists at First Hand* (Thames and Hudson, 1987)
3 Max Planck Interview quoted in *Where is Science Going?* (Norton 1932)
4 Werner Heisenberg, *Scientific and Religious Truths* trans. as *Across the Frontiers* (Harper and Row, 1974)
5 Plato, *Phaedrus*, trans. Benjamin Jowett (Oxford University Press, 1871)
6 Sir Arthur Eddington, *The Nature of the Physical World* (Cambridge University Press, 1929)
7 Plato, *Symposium*, trans. Benjamin Jowett (Oxford University Press, 1871)

**Stage Eight**
1 Emily Dickinson, *The Selected Poems of Emily Dickinson* (Wordsworth Poetry Library, 1994)
2 Plato, *Phaedo*, trans. Benjamin Jowett (Oxford University Press, 1871)
3 J.W. Goethe, *Collected Works in English*, ed. trans. Douglas Miller (Princetown University Reissue Edition, 1987)
4 Sri Shantanand Saraswati, unpublished conversations. Additional material to be found in *The Man Who Wanted to Meet God* (Element Press, 1996)
5 Dante, 'Paradiso', taken from *The Enlightened Heart: An Anthology of Sacred Poetry*, trans. Stephen Mitchell (Harper and Row, 1989)
6 Michael Mayne, *This Sunrise of Wonder: A Quest for God in Art and Nature* (Fount,1995)
7 *The Letters of Marsilio Ficino* Vol. 1 (Shepheard Walwyn, 1975)

**Stage Nine**

1 Buddha, *The Dhammapada*, trans. Juan Mascaro (Penguin, 1973)
2 Ben Jonson, 'To Celia', 1616
3 'The Street Where You Live' from *My Fair Lady*, Lerner and Lowe (Hal Leonard Publishing Corporation, 1981)
4 Thomas Hardy, 'Castle Boterel' from *Selected Poems of Thomas Hardy* (Penguin Classics, 1993)
5 I Corinthians, verse 1
6 Book of Psalms
7 Buddha, *The Dhammapada*, trans. Juan Mascaro (Penguin, 1973)
8 Purohit Swami and W.B. Yeats eds., *The Ten Principal Upanishads*, (Faber and Faber, 1937)
9 Max Planck, *Where is Science Going?* (Norton, 1932)
10 Ken Wilber, *Quantum Questions* (Shambhala, 1985)
11 Rumi, *The Arms of the Beloved* trans. by Jonathan Star and Shahram Shiva (Penguin Putnam, 1997)
12 William Blake, *The Complete Poems* (Penguin English Classics, 1974)
13 painterskeys.com
14 Alfred H. Barr, *Henri Matisse* (Museum of Modern Art, 1951)

**Stage Ten**

1 Albert Einstein, *The World As I See It* (Citadel Press Reissue edition, 1993)
2 Marsilio Ficino, *Commentary on Plato's Symposium*, trans. Jayne Sears (Spring Publications, 1985)
3 Percy Bysshe Shelley, 'Adonais', 1821
4 Schrödinger, *My View of the World*, (Cambridge University Press, 1964)

**Stage Eleven**

1 Anon, *Cloud of Unknowing* (Penguin Classics Reissue, 2002)
2 Marcus Aurelius, *Meditations*, trans. Matthew Staniforth (Penguin Classics, 1964)
3 Epictitus, *Enchiridon*, trans. George Long (Prometheus Books Reprint edition, 1955)
4 Marcus Aurelius, *Meditations*, trans. Matthew Staniforth (Penguin Classics, 1964)
5 Sir Arthur Eddington, *The Nature of the Physical World* (Cambridge University Press, 1929)
6 *Proclus' Mystical Hymns of Orpheus*, trans. Thomas Taylor, (Prometheus Trust Originally published in 1824)
7 Kathleen Raine, 'A Sense of Beauty', article from *Resurgence*, 114, January 1986
8 Samuel Palmer, *The Parting Light: Selected Writings of Samuel Palmer*, ed. Mark Abley (Carcanet, 1985)
9 *Zen Flesh Zen Bones*, trans. Nyogen Senzaki, ed. Paul Reps (Doubleday Anchor, 1976)
10 Ralph Waldo Emerson, *The Essential Writings of Ralph Waldo Emerson* (Modern Library Paperback Classics, 2000)
11 Marsilio Ficino, *The Letters of Marsilio Ficino* Vol 1. (Shepherd Walwyn, 1975)
12 Plato, *Symposium*, trans. Benjamin Jowett (Oxford University Press, 1871)

**Stage Twelve**

1 Martha Graham, *Martha Graham An Autobiography: Blood Memory* (Washington Square Press, 1991)
2 *Bhagavad-gita*, trans. Sri Purohit Swami (Faber and Faber, 1935)
3 Samuel Coleridge, *Biographia Literaria* (1817)
4 Plato, *Phaedrus*, trans. Benjamin Jowett (Oxford University Press, 1871)
5 Buddha, *The Living Thoughts of Gotama the Buddha*, trans. Ananda K. Coomaraswamy and I.B. Horner (Cassell & Company, 1948)
6 Albert Einstein, *The World As I See It* (Citadel Press Reissue, 1993)
7 From a broadcast by Edgar Mitchell
8 Buddha, *The Living Thoughts of Gotama the Buddha*, trans. Ananda K. Coomaraswamy and I.B. Horner (Cassell & Company, 1948)